THE TRUTH

Judy Wade

JOHN BLAKE

Published by John Blake Publishing Ltd,
3 Bramber Court, 2 Bramber Road, London W14 9PB, England

ISBN 1 903402 14 X

All rights reserved. No part of this publication may be
reproduced, stored in a retrieval system, or in any form or
by any means, without the prior permission in writing of the
publisher, nor be otherwise circulated in any form of binding
or cover other than that in which it is published and without
a similar condition including this condition being imposed
on the subsequent purchaser.

British Library Cataloguing-in-Publication Data:
A catalogue record for this book is available from
the British Library.

Typeset by Jon Davies

Printed in England by CPD, Wales

1 3 5 7 9 10 8 6 4 2

© Text copyright Judy Wade

Pictures reproduced by kind permission of Alpha
and Jayne Fincher (Photographers International).

Papers used by John Blake Publishing Ltd are natural,
recyclable products made from wood grown in sustainable forests.
The manufacturing processes conform to the
environmental regulations of the country of origin.

For Lucy

PROLOGUE

On an early summer Saturday in 1997, the rumble of traffic along Kensington High Street was just a distant drone in the quiet, gravelled courtyard. Most of the occupants of the vast complex of buildings, designed by Sir Christopher Wren for King William III in 1689, had left London for the weekend and an uncommon calm had descended on Kensington Palace. But inside the imposing portico of Apartments 8 and 9, the home of Diana, Princess of Wales, the black front door stood half open. Stuck on it was a note bearing the words 'Come on up'.

Natalie Symons, the Princess's 27-year-old hairstylist, hesitated before walking in and closing the door. Normally, when she arrived punctually on weekday mornings at 9.00am to style Diana's hair, the butler Paul Burrell would greet her. Natalie would then walk into the luxury kitchen and wait, chatting to the staff, until the Princess buzzed down, the signal for Natalie to go upstairs. After her separation from the Prince of Wales, Diana no longer spent weekends in the country, and had decided she needed to have her hair styled six days a week.

On this particular Saturday, no one was in the kitchen and the entire building seemed to have been abandoned. Warily, the hairstylist walked slowly up the main staircase, calling out, 'Hello! Where are you?' There was no reply, so she continued on up until she reached the top of the stairs and turned left into the master bedroom suite. Suddenly, she heard a voice floating out of the Princess's bathroom.

'I'm in here!'

Peering through the doorway, Natalie was astonished to see Diana down on her knees vigorously scrubbing the bathtub. Turning to wave her yellow gloved hands, she explained, 'Well, there's no one here today to clean up, so I have to do it all myself.'

Natalie could not help laughing. 'Those Marigolds really suit you!' she teased.

After three years of styling the hair of the world's favourite Princess, Natalie should not have been so surprised. She had learned that, inside the privacy of Kensington Palace, Diana was totally different from her public image as the world's most dazzling fashion icon.

Despite wardrobes bulging with designer clothes, at home she chose to wear ordinary, chain store bargains available in every high street throughout Britain. In winter, Natalie would arrive to find her fresh from the shower wearing only a white or pale blue towelling robe. She also owned one with a large 'S' embroidered on the front. She explained it came from the Savoy. In summer, Diana covered up in cool sun dresses. A favourite was a floaty, sleeveless white Laura Ashley one with cerise flowers splashed across it.

Another hairstylist, Tess Rock, who also styled Diana's hair on alternate months, turned up one morning in a black dress which the Princess admired, so she told her it came from Marks and Spencer. Royal dresser Angela Benjamin, who had just walked in, said, 'My outfit's from M&S, too!' Then Diana laughed and pointed to her pale blue sleeveless frock. 'Guess what. So is mine!'

The woman who wore expensive Jimmy Choo stilettos on public engagements preferred to go barefoot at home. She always kicked off her expensive high heels the minute she returned to her apartment. When going out off duty, she chose rather ordinary shoes. Diana liked to wear Marks and Spencer footwear and walked into the George Street salon where her stylists worked one day wearing a pair of black M&S slippers.

'Do you realise what you are wearing on your feet? They're slippers,' she was told.

'Oh, I didn't know, but they're so comfy I don't care,' Diana replied.

Over the months and years she visited her royal client at the palace, Natalie began to realise that the Princess, who once had such a passion for fashion, was a changed woman. Glittering jewels and glamorous outfits no longer delighted her. She had reached a stage when many of her clothes represented her old life as the heir to the throne's wife.

Soon after her divorce from Prince Charles, she also decided to rid herself of many of the dresses she had worn as Britain's future queen. These elaborate, delicately embroidered, beaded and sequinned creations were her Windsor wardrobe, and each was a reminder of a life she no longer wanted to lead. So she symbolically gave away 79 of her most magnificent designer gowns. On 25 June 1997, they were auctioned for charity by Christie's in New York.

The next morning, she looked exhausted but exultant. 'I've been up all night getting reports by phone on the money the auction has made,' she explained.

The upheaval in her life as she embarked on a new, solo existence had given Diana many sleepless nights. 'She told me she had too much on her mind to get any rest,' Natalie remembers. 'So she had acupuncture needles stuck inside her ears to make her relax. As she got ready for the Christie's London preview of her dress auction, three weeks before their sale in America, she asked me to brush her hair so that the needles wouldn't show. I couldn't believe she was going to walk out the door with these needles sticking in her ears. But she said she couldn't take them out because she was desperate for a good night's sleep.'

For big, glitzy dates like the Tate Gallery dinner, Diana could still pile on the glamour and become the dazzling Princess everyone expected to see. But, increasingly, it was all an act, just like the one staged by another beautiful blonde, whose death at 36 inspired Elton John to write the song he would perform at Diana's funeral

To those who really knew her, Marilyn Monroe played out a similar performance for the public. Like the Princess, she suffered from deep feelings of worthlessness and self-loathing. Born Norma Jean Baker, she would wistfully ask curious friends, 'Do you want to see me turn into her?' Then the famous pout and sexy wiggle would appear and the depressed, unhappy girl would be transformed into Hollywood's legendary movie star.

In much the same way, Diana was switching on another personality when she appeared in public. The performance would begin when police motorcycle outriders screeched to a halt, their sirens wailing a warning of her approach. A Jaguar would pull into the kerb behind them and the ragged cheers from crowds held back by barriers would turn into silent, star-struck stares.

An electronic storm of photographers' flashguns would erupt on all sides as Diana slid elegantly out of the back seat. She would straighten up, turn and wave, then glide straight towards the open door ahead. The babble of conversation inside would die away as she sashayed into the room, with head half lowered, looking up smiling from under her silky long lashes. The whole effect was sexual dynamite. Every other woman in the room would be outclassed and every man mesmerised.

On dozens of occasions, Natalie Symons would return in the evening to prepare the Princess for big dates like these. She vividly remembers that quite often Diana did not look forward to being the centre of attention. On 1 July 1997, her thirty-sixth and last birthday, she was scheduled to attend a dinner at the Tate Gallery. Natalie asked if she planned to drink some champagne to celebrate. Diana looked glum.

'I never drink alcohol,' she said. 'There's been too much of it in my family.' Then she added that she was not looking forward to the night ahead. 'I am spending the evening of my birthday in a room full of people I don't know and don't even like. The only person there that I know will be my brother. What a way to enjoy my birthday!'

Her apartment was filled with the scent of 90

bouquets which had arrived from famous friends around the world, including dozens of magnificent Casa Blanca lilies from Italian fashion designer Giorgio Armani. But Diana was depressed, as she always was on every birthday. She revealed that the only bright spot in her day had been a phone call early in the morning from Prince Harry. He had phoned with all his classmates to sing 'Happy Birthday' and she had loved it.

The only time she smiled as she got ready to go out was when she tried to wriggle into a brand new Jacques Azagury dress. It was so tight across the bust that she couldn't fit into it. This was surprising because Azagury had been designing for Diana since 1985 and knew her measurements exactly.

When she first wore one of his evening gowns, her figure had lost a lot of its former shapeliness, as she herself admitted. That year on a visit to Australia, she was chatting to a group of journalists about bygone days before her marriage and asked them, 'Do you remember how I was then? I used to have lots up top, remember? Well, it's all gone now I've had my boys, hasn't it?' she sighed. And with both hands clasped across her bosom, she indicated exactly what she meant.

More than ten years later, her figure had dramatically and mysteriously regained its former lush curves. Even the most ingenious exercise regime could not work such magic and cleverly designed corsetry could only achieve so much. What was the reason for her miraculous new shape?

Tossing the dress aside, Diana giggled and with mock seriousness said, 'I just can't understand what's happened. It's amazing! I'll wear something else.'

Natalie had noticed she had gained an astonishing

new cleavage and suspected that the Princess had undergone a breast enhancement operation. She knew that clever plastic surgeons can transform a woman's silhouette in hours, recovery takes only a few days and, hidden beneath layers of clothing, the operation can remain a total secret. Later, Natalie heard that someone else in Diana's circle had plucked up the courage to ask a member of the staff about the Princess's amazing new figure, only to be told, 'We don't talk about that.'

The Princess's battle with the eating disorder bulimia had convinced her that a healthy, well-toned body was more important than the most expensive outfit. So she concentrated more on the woman beneath the designer dresses and dispensed with many of the fripperies which had once thrilled her.

When George Michael sent her a diamond-studded wrist watch, she dangled it in front of Natalie and said, 'This is very expensive, but I couldn't possibly wear it.' It was not her style, she explained, so the gift was left in its box. She adored the singer and sighed, 'He's gay — what a waste!'

Glossy magazines were always piled up in her sitting room, but Diana did not actually read them.

'She used to flick through *Vogue* looking at the photographs of the supermodels then toss it aside,' Natalie remembers. 'She never examined the text between the pictures or seemed interested in information on new trends.'

Always more interested in the faces than the fashions, Diana was glancing through a magazine one day when she spotted a picture of black supermodel Naomi Campbell. 'That girl is truly beautiful,' she said. 'She is so exotic and glamorous that an old black binliner would look good on her.'

While Natalie blow-dried her hair, Diana chatted

on the telephone to friends or read newspapers, usually the *Daily Mail*, the *Express* and the *Telegraph*. When a particular story touched a chord, she would always comment on it. In September 1996, Princess Stephanie of Monaco's marriage broke up after her husband, former bodyguard Daniel Ducruet, was photographed cavorting in compromising circumstances with a nightclub dancer. Diana devoured every word printed about their split. 'I feel so sorry for her. She must feel so humiliated. It's just like my story all over again,' she told Natalie.

Despite this reference to the pain of her own marital break-up, she no longer felt any animosity towards Camilla Parker Bowles by the time she was divorced in the summer of 1996. Natalie recalls, 'I could tell because she would never read a story about anyone she disliked; she always quickly turned the page. But when she noticed a report on James Hewitt or Camilla, whom she felt had both betrayed her, she would read all of it. She had moved on with her life and no longer felt strongly about either of them.'

Natalie never heard her utter an unkind word about Camilla, but she never referred to her by name, jokingly calling her 'the Rottweiler'. Sometimes, when she spotted an unflattering picture of her ex-husband's mistress in the press, she could not resist mentioning it. Then with her face twisted into a crocodile smile, she would say, 'Just look at that!'

She was also scathing about Sophie Rhys-Jones, who would marry Prince Edward in 1999. Diana referred to her as 'my clone' after Sophie had her hair cut into a short blonde style, and quickly turned the page whenever she saw a press report about the girl many thought vaguely resembled the Princess.

PD, as Natalie called her, was usually on the

THE TRUTH

telephone laughing when the hairstylist arrived. 'I could tell at once that she was talking to Fergie, who called from her car after dropping her daughters off at school. No one else could make Diana giggle as much as the Duchess of York. The Princess had a real, dirty laugh and I had to stop myself breaking into gales of laughter myself.'

When she hung up, Diana told Natalie that Fergie was trying to persuade her to go out and party. The Princess was worried that the paparazzi would find out and chase them, so Sarah had suggested she should stick on the dark wig she used to avoid being recognised. Diana was not keen. 'I'd rather stay home and watch *Brookside*. It's my favourite soap,' she explained.

Once, while looking at photographs in *Hello!* magazine of Fergie and Andrew at a golf tournament with their daughters, she asked, 'Why did they bother to get divorced? They shouldn't have done it because they'll never really split up.'

Sadly, the close friendship between the Duchess and the friend she called by her childhood name 'Duch' (inspired by Diana's perfect manners) ended when Sarah published her autobiography in 1996. In it, she explained how grateful she had been before her marriage to her future sister-in-law. 'When I lived in Clapham, Diana helped me by giving me all her shoes (and, less happily, her veruccas).'

Diana was furious at the suggestion that her footwear was less than hygienic and did not speak to her again. As months went by, the Duchess attempted to heal the rift but the Princess refused to accept her phone calls, ignored her apologetic letters, and cut her completely out of her life.

This abrupt ending to what Sarah once called their

'mutual aid society' caused Diana considerable pain. She admitted that she missed the Duchess and was sad that she could no longer see her nieces Beatrice and Eugenie. 'I adore those little girls so much,' she told Natalie. 'I'd love to see them again.'

Her dressing room was adorned with pictures lovingly drawn by the small girls, and letters signed with love and kisses. Proof that the Princess treasured their handiwork came when the room was redecorated and the childish paintings were immediately pinned back up on the walls again.

Although Diana had broken off her friendship with Sarah, she still followed advice from her former sister-in-law. Every morning she gulped down a full glass of fresh carrot juice and each evening drank another tumbler of celery juice. When her butler Paul Burrell walked in saying, 'Here's your medicine, drink it all down,' Diana wrinkled her nose in disgust. 'I hate that stuff,' she said, but forced herself to drink the lot. 'Fergie says it's a great way to de-tox the body and boost the immune system,' she explained.

When she conquered her eating disorder, Diana became concerned that if she ate normal meals she would pile on pounds. As a result, she lived on a permanent diet and so did Natalie. Both were constantly comparing notes about nutrition and food fads. One morning, the Princess claimed that she had lost four pounds in a week by replacing some meals with a liquid food called Herbalife. She suggested that Natalie could do the same and asked her dresser to give her some from her own supply. As Natalie left, an anxious Angela Benjamin was waiting at the bottom of the stairs. 'I've given you the very last jar of Herbal Life we've got and it's very hard to get, so can I please have it back?' she pleaded. 'The Princess will go potty if we haven't got any left for her.'

Diana was always determined to look her best but was certainly not vain. The cupboard beneath her dressing table was crammed with make-up jars, tubes and bottles. Asked which cosmetic she liked best, she replied, 'I like all of them. I like trying different ones.' She liked to keep two of almost every product, but the one she used most often was an inexpensive tinted moisturiser from the Body Shop range. For official appearances she carefully made up her face, but while off duty she did not usually bother with much more than a little lip gloss and mascara.

Unlike many celebrities, she was not at all concerned about being seen in public without make-up — well, almost.

Once, when woken by a security alarm in the middle of the night, she jumped out of bed but refused to go downstairs to assure royal protection officers that she was all right.

'I was half asleep and couldn't find my mascara, so I couldn't go down because I never let anyone see my face without my mascara. No one would recognise me like that, anyway,' she explained to Natalie. 'I'd rather be blown up or grabbed by terrorists than brave the world with naked eyes.' Then she added, 'If I was ever washed up on a desert island, the one luxury I would crave would be my mascara.'

After trips to the United States, Diana would always return with a jokey American accent. 'Don't I look *gorrjuss?*' she would say, pulling faces at her reflection in the dressing-table mirror.

'She never took herself seriously and didn't believe she was glamorous at all,' Natalie reveals.

Diana painted her nails every morning but one day Natalie Symons arrived to find her using Chanel's Rouge

Noir nail polish, which had been very popular for months. 'You can't wear that. It's too dark for a summer day. It's a winter colour,' Natalie told her. 'OK,' said the Princess, and instantly switched to a clear varnish instead.

'It's not hard to understand why Diana took so little interest in the world of fashion,' Natalie says. 'She came from the kind of aristocratic, country background in which women dress conservatively and look their best in riding clothes. Diana was not born with, and did not have any experience of, the instinctive style which sets Continental women apart. Of course, she loved wearing designer dresses, but they were her work clothes. At home, where she could simply be herself, she reverted to her upper-class type. She relaxed in Laura Ashley or Marks and Spencer creations, the kind of clothes she had worn when she was a London working girl and first started dating Prince Charles.'

It is astonishing to learn that the most influential fashion figure of her time was not really very interested in expensive clothes for their own sake. Of course, Diana had once adored trailing around town on endless shopping sprees. Until her engagement, she had owned only one pink evening gown, one good pair of shoes, a silk shirt and a few woollen and cotton skirts, as well as some colourful sweaters. So it's hardly surprising that after marrying one of Britain's wealthiest men, she went on a decade-long shopping spree. Her royal status required that she needed dozens of ballgowns, suits, dresses and separates. But she bought hundreds and eventually thousands of outfits. She would buy not one cashmere sweater, but a dozen in different colours. She owned so many clothes and shoes that she would occasionally have a clear-out, toss a pile of clothes on the floor then load them into the boot of her car and

THE TRUTH

take them to one of her sisters' homes.

When Diana died, almost 40 different, black cocktail dresses alone were found in her wardrobes, apart from the dozens of formal, full-length evening gowns and countless outfits for day wear.

Throughout the Eighties, Diana experimented wildly with different styles, and a downstairs room formerly used for staff meals at Kensington Palace was converted into more wardrobe space for her clothes.

Her sensational designer creations boosted British fashion around the world, but they also labelled Diana as a frivolous shopaholic. Clothes were her only interest, the press reported, claiming she was never happier than when cruising through department stores like Harrods and Harvey Nichols, or visiting top designer salons scattered around the Knightsbridge area. Palace advisers began worrying that her glitzy image could trivialise the monarchy.

At the same time, Diana realised that people paid more attention to what she wore rather than what she did. Something had to be done. Diana became determined to find a look that would not distract from her official duties.

This new approach to her image coincided with the time when Charles and Diana began leading separate lives. Asserting her independence for the first time, she began to realise that she could rise to the occasion on solo engagements. Encouraged by the warmth and affection that greeted her everywhere, she slowly developed a sense of self and realised that she could, by example, redefine the monarchy through her sons, bringing it more in touch with the people.

When she suggested lending her support to AIDS victims, royal officials advised against it, warning that she should not associate with such people. Diana refused to listen and went ahead without their approval. Her compassion and concern would soon transform attitudes to AIDS and HIV-infected patients around the world.

Her new-found confidence was evident when she began wearing higher heels, towering over her shorter husband. She also threw off the old frilled, flounced fashions she had once favoured, along with her ribboned, veiled hats. They were girly styles no longer appropriate for a sleek, sophisticated woman. Diana was finally learning the greatest of all fashion rules — less is more.

These sartorial changes reflected the Princess's inner resolve and growing maturity. Clothes became signals which she used like semaphore to send messages to the world. She wanted to appear more businesslike and that is what she achieved with one favourite style, the coat-dress, which appeared both in summer and winter. This loose-fitting, double-breasted outfit was extremely comfortable and practical, allowing Diana to bend down or kneel when greeting children. She had dozens in wool, linen and cotton, as well as plain, checked and striped fabrics. These were designed by French-born Catherine Walker, who created the great majority of the Princess's outfits for 15 years.

Along with a number of tailored suits, the coat-dresses provided the perfect working woman's uniform. Instead of jewellery, the only adornments on these outfits were a number of large buttons. Quite often, Diana would carry a briefcase rather than a handbag to emphasise this more serious look.

It may seem difficult to understand why a high-maintenance woman whose wardrobe was created by the world's top designers would privately show so little interest in high style, and come to rely on people like her hairstylist for fashion tips. But Diana knew that Natalie, who worked daily on fashion shoots with supermodels and celebrities, was in touch with every changing trend and had a wealth of useful information.

Natalie had first been summoned to Kensington Palace on a particularly busy day when she had clients booked every half hour, including several who had become good friends. When she walked into Diana's bedroom she was told, 'You've got exactly 20 minutes.'

Instead of looking flustered or disappointed, the hairstylist smiled. 'That's great. I've got to rush back to the salon as soon as possible.'

The fact that she was not at all impressed by a princess in a palace seemed to please Diana and soon she was calling on Natalie's services regularly.

'I was always thrilled when I walked through the front door of PD's home,' the hairstylist recalls. 'It was so beautiful and peaceful. At the end of the hall was a bronze bust of the Princess lit by spotlights, and as you walked up the stairs, the walls were covered with drawings of the christenings of Prince William and Prince Harry. On the landing was a magnificent portrait of Diana in a white blouse and green skirt, which I think was the work of the American artist Nelson Shanks. The walls and the carpets were all pale green, a perfect background for the marvellous flowers that were everywhere. What I liked best was that the place was not at all grand, just wonderfully cosy. It's so sad to think that this lovely home no longer exists.'

Upstairs, Diana's bedroom was unimpressive by comparison. Far from luxurious, the large room had yellow walls and was dominated by an enormous, carved wooden four-poster bed with a floral coverlet in a rather chintzy, country-style print. At one end stood an enormous 40-inch television set. Apart from bedside tables, the room was uncluttered and spacious.

Diana's yellow dressing room was a surprise, more suited to a teenage girl than a princess. The white dressing table was topped with glass beneath which Diana had stuck dozens of photographs of her sons. On the wall above was an oval mirror framed in white-painted cane. Around the walls were long, fitted wardrobes.

'She had a gold crucifix on a chain which had come from Italy and was always in the centre of the dressing table. One morning, when it had been moved, she became very upset and was not happy until it was returned to its proper place,' Natalie recalls. 'It was an extremely plain room with no decoration. I was astonished because it lacked any personality of the woman who lived there.

'Her sitting room was totally different, jam-packed with knick-knacks, framed photographs and souvenirs of her trips around the world. I almost had to walk sideways to get across the room and was always frightened of knocking things over,' Natalie says. 'On her desk was a 2ft-tall amethyst crystal, which she believed had healing powers, and a wooden statue of Christ which she had been given in South America. The walls were covered with so many photographs and sketches of ballerinas that it was difficult to see the colour scheme beneath.'

This was her inner sanctum, the place where she removed all traces of the public Princess and became her true self. 'I think she was quite lonely, especially at weekends,' Natalie says. 'When I visited her on Saturdays she used to keep me talking for ages, as if she did not want to be left alone in the house.'

As their working relationship deepened into

x x

friendship, Diana increasingly turned to the young woman, almost ten years her junior, for advice. 'I like the scent you're wearing,' she remarked to Natalie one morning, and was informed that it was a new line from the Sloane Street store Joseph. The following day when she returned, Diana held up a large bottle of exactly the same scent crowing, 'Look what I've got.'

Natalie was always in a rush with clients backed up all day and half the night. One morning, she was complaining that she had so much styling to do she couldn't find the time to do ordinary jobs like changing the sheets on her bed. Diana laughed and said, 'Why don't you sleep on one side for a week then switch to the other side? That way, your sheets will last two weeks instead of one.' Natalie smiles at the memory. 'She was only joking — I think!'

When an IRA bomb alert caused traffic chaos in London one morning, Natalie started to panic as her taxi crawled towards Kensington Palace. She was worried that she would be late for her appointment with the Princess, who would be leaving home at mid-morning for a job in aid of the British Lung Foundation. Suddenly she heard a car horn and spotted Diana at the wheel of her stationary car in the next lane. She was waving and beckoning the hairstylist to jump into her BMW. Natalie was so relieved to see the similarly delayed Princess that she hopped into her car as fast as she could.

A few minutes later, Diana asked, 'Why is that taxi driver staring at us?'

Natalie shrieked, 'Oh God! I forgot to pay him.' The only solution, Diana decided, was to stop at the next traffic lights while Natalie jumped out and handed over some cash to the amazed cabbie. Diana giggled as they turned into the private road to the palace. 'He must think I go around stealing fares from taxis!'

Soon, the Princess began to divulge more about her thoughts and feelings. One May morning, she revealed that she was furious with her chef. 'I had some friends round for lunch yesterday and chose lobster for the main course,' she explained. 'But I was terribly embarrassed because there wasn't enough lobster and I thought it looked so stingy. I don't want my friends to think I'm mean.'

When she was angry with someone, she didn't care who knew it. On 30 May 1997, Natalie remembers that Diana was hopping mad with Tiggy Legge-Bourke, the woman Prince Charles had chosen to keep a motherly eye on his sons when they were with him.

Diana was not at all pleased about another woman becoming so close to her boys, but could do little about it. For months, she had been convinced, without the slightest foundation, that Tiggy was having an affair with Prince Charles and, when Diana visited her hair salon to have her blonde highlights touched up, she passed on this information to the staff, urging them to spread it around.

On this occasion, she was angry because she had stayed away from the Fourth of June, as the parents' picnic day at Eton College is known, to avoid stealing the spotlight and spoiling everyone's fun — then she had discovered that Tiggy had taken her place. She was particularly upset that Tiggy turned up with a boozy picnic for her son, bringing bottles of champagne and offering drinks to anyone she knew. 'That bitch!' Diana screamed.

Eventually, she calmed down and decided to issue a statement to the press, more or less denying that she had objected to Tiggy's presence at the picnic. Not sure

THE TRUTH

about what to say, she asked Natalie and Paul Burrell to help her write it. The stylist recalls, 'She scribbled down what we dictated and by the time she had finished she had convinced herself she wasn't furious with Tiggy any more.'

In the last months of her life, Diana began turning to Natalie for advice more frequently. In particular, she was constantly seeking guidance on the subject of men. She loved to flirt with a number of men as if seeking reassurance that she really was desirable. These included opera stars Placido Domingo and Luciano Pavarotti; pop singers George Michael, Elton John and Brian Adams; and Christopher Whalley, a businessman she had met at her fitness club.

They all telephoned regularly and she had a secret code to identify each one as the men went up and down in terms of their popularity. One week Brian Adams was at the top and was coded Number One, the next he was Number Eight on her list. Paul Burrell used the code when Diana had a visitor. He would simply say, 'Number Two is on the telephone,' to keep the caller's identity a secret. There were other not-so-famous men who also called. One was a European prince who failed to be impressed by Diana's charms, much to her chagrin, and she pined for quite a while.

On a few occasions, she met film star Tom Cruise and thought he was extremely fanciable. She once reported that he had offered her some chewing gum at a film première.

'What will I do with it when I've finished?' Diana asked.

'Just stick it under your chair,' Cruise had replied.

Diana repeated this story giggling but revealed that she had not liked the film star's wife Nicole Kidman.

'She kept shooting me hostile looks as if to say,

"Keep your hands off my man".'

Another regular caller was a media man who often rang offering his help when she had received a bad press. Diana sweet-talked him whenever he phoned but when he hung up she often made two-fingered gestures and mimed throwing up to indicate her true feelings. The poor man never realised what she really thought of him and remained her devoted swain. Diana always quickly saw through people who enjoyed reflected glory or were trying to exploit her friendship in some way.

Placido Domingo was another who used his charm on her down the telephone and did not impress her at all.

'He perhaps fancies his chances with me,' Diana remarked after one ardent call. 'Huh!'

She was more receptive to Pavarotti who seemed to have no romantic ideas about the Princess. After her death, he was so distraught he felt he would be unable to travel to London for her funeral, but eventually he summoned up the courage. 'I knew her as the sweetest of people,' he recalled that week. 'I knew her as a person who was a symbol of the modern woman, who was sweet and intelligent with regal manners.'

One very important man in her life was Prime Minister Tony Blair. On 2 May 1997, the Princess was celebrating his victory at the polls. 'I like Blair a lot,' she confided and sought Natalie's advice about what to wear when she went to Chequers for lunch. 'It was a lot of fun,' she reported the following day.

At the end of her life, she was making plans with him to take on a new role as a roving ambassador for good causes. Blair's predecessor John Major had not won her admiration in the same way. 'I don't like him. He snubbed me,' she explained vaguely.

THE TRUTH

Powerful men always fascinated her and she was thrilled when she met President Clinton.

'He's got a Southern drawl that sounds incredibly sexy,' she reported, adding that she was not so keen on Hillary Clinton, whom she found quite cold.

Prince Charles, the source of so much upset throughout her married life, had long ago been forgiven. They were very friendly in the months before the Princess died, 'just like brother and sister', Natalie remembers. 'She was thrilled when Prince Charles turned up wearing a sweater she had given him for his birthday. She thought it was a very nice gesture.'

One man on whom she relied totally was her butler Paul Burrell, the Coal Board lorry driver's son from Grassmore, near Chesterfield, who ran her household with great efficiency for nine years. For Diana's sake, he uprooted his wife Maria and sons Alexander and Nicky from their happy life at Highgrove to move to London after the royal couple separated.

But even he, perhaps, never realised exactly what the Princess thought of him. Although kind and generous, Diana was a demanding boss and expected him to dance attendance on her night and day. When he was guilty of the occasional lapse or she was in a low mood, she would conveniently forget his years of devoted care.

One morning he failed, for some reason, to bring her breakfast tray into the dressing room and left it outside in the corridor. Diana snapped, 'For Heaven's sake, what's he doing?'

Just before her death, she vowed to sack him. 'He's got to go,' she told Natalie. 'I'm going to get rid of him soon.'

One minute she liked someone, and an hour later she would be irritated by the same person, the hairstylist explains. 'She worked totally on instinct and if she was in a foul mood, nothing pleased her.'

Paul Burrell was not mentioned in Diana's will, which she had rewritten after her divorce. Her family rectified this by granting him £50,000 for his loyal service from the Princess's estate. Burrell should have known that sooner or later he would be out of favour because there was a relatively high turnover of staff at Kensington Palace.

Many of the domestics resented being frequently asked to work overtime and often asked Natalie, 'Will you find out if the Princess is going away this weekend? We'd like some time off.'

When Natalie suggested they should ask Diana themselves, they always replied that they didn't dare. A chart was kept in the kitchen with the days of the week listed against employees' names. 'If Diana put a tick against your name on Saturday and Sunday, that meant you had to work the whole weekend,' Natalie explains.

Although she expected the highest standards from everyone in her service, Diana could also be softhearted at times. Once, when she advertised for a new dresser, a Portuguese girl called Clara turned up for an interview crying with nerves.

'I felt so sorry for her that I gave her the job straight away,' Diana later revealed.

Despite her threats, Paul Burrell survived longer than anyone else and he was still devotedly serving her after her death when he dashed over to Paris to take care of arrangements to bring her body home until Prince Charles arrived.

The Diana Natalie knew was not the glamorous royal covergirl renowned for reaching out to the sick and the needy. Instead, she got to know someone who sought what most ordinary women want — a man who would come home to her at the end of the day and banish the unbearable loneliness she felt after her separation from Prince Charles. And in the last two years of her life, there was one other very special man who telephoned almost every day, often late at night.

'After his calls, I'm so excited I can't sleep,' Diana confided. But she had no thought of subordinating her life to his, believing instead that he should understand that she could never abandon those who needed her help.

Natalie watched as a battle for supremacy raged between the two Dianas. Would the emotionally deprived girl who longed for a happy marriage and more children overwhelm the dedicated charity worker who needed the oxygen of the public's adoration to survive? If she married a commoner, would she have as much influence as Princess of Wales?

What she really needed was a man who would respect both sides of her character, someone with whom she could form a partnership dedicated to serving those most in need. In 1997, Diana was sure she had found him.

He was the man who had set her on a new path to fulfilment, which had taken her half-way around the world to Australia on a mission which has never before been revealed.

1

The first time Diana flew to Australia, she arrived at Sydney Airport on a warm February morning in 1981 and promptly disappeared. She had slipped out of London with her mother Frances Shand Kydd when speculation about her romance with the Prince of Wales was at its height.

From the day in September 1980 when the *Sun* newspaper discovered the name of the girl who was watching Prince Charles fishing from a riverbank at Balmoral, Lady Diana Spencer's life had become a nightmare. The newspaper's story claimed, with astonishing foresight, that she had all the 'perfect qualities for a future queen'.

By the following day every other newspaper was in hot pursuit of the Prince's new sweetheart, dispatching teams of reporters and photographers to dig up any information available about her.

The relentless hunt for news of Lady Di, as she soon became known, made normal life impossible, not just for her but for her three flatmates and her family, too. A jostling throng of cameramen crowded around Diana everywhere she went. Photographers, hoping to get a different picture, even followed her younger brother Charles, Viscount Althorp, who was then a pupil at Eton College, because Diana often took him out to lunch.

Only once did Diana break down under this intense pressure. One day, she emerged from the Young England kindergarten where she worked in London to find that foreign paparazzi had boxed in her car with some heavy oil drums. Unable to shift them, she broke down in the street and sobbed. Just then, the *Sun* newspaper's royal photographer Arthur Edwards appeared on the scene. Rolling away the oil drums, he offered some fatherly advice to the vulnerable girl who was trying to cope all alone.

'Listen, love,' he said with genuine concern, 'stop crying because that's just what those Continental boys want. Hold your head up and remember who you are. Don't let them catch you crying again. I'll tell you something else. I've met all Prince Charles's girlfriends and you're better than any of them. If he doesn't marry you, he's out of his tiny mind.'

Diana laughed, climbed into her car and drove home, still chuckling.

Every time she left her flat in Coleherne Court, South Kensington, an elaborate system using decoys and diving through back exits had to be employed. Sometimes, Diana borrowed a car belonging to her grandmother, Lady Fermoy, a lady-in-waiting to the

Queen Mother. Occasionally, she made a performance out of packing her own car with suitcases as if leaving London for a weekend in the country.

Fleet Street's finest newsmen would wait nearby, believing she was heading for a reunion with Prince Charles at his country estate. Then their quarry would disappear back inside her flat and leave through an entrance at the back of the block where a taxi would be waiting.

The inexperienced 19-year-old managed to outsmart the wily members of the royal Rat Pack, as the newsmen were known, just as she outmanoeuvred all the worldly blondes who had set their sights on Prince Charles before her. It was an early indication that, despite her lack of educational qualifications (she had gained not a single O-level), Diana was resourceful and quick-witted. In years to come, when her adversaries were not newsmen but members of the Royal Family, she would once again display an ingenious ability to outwit them all.

Six months earlier, she had been unknown outside her family and small circle of friends. Lady Diana Frances Spencer was then just another rather aimless, aristocratic young woman, working for pin money in London. The most interesting thing about her was her ancestry, which was loaded with royal connections on a family tree which linked her to more than one king. Genealogists would later work out that Charles and Diana were actually sixteenth cousins once removed through their joint ancestor Henry VII.

The Spencer family motto — God Defend the Right — dates back to the sixteenth century when Warwickshire-born John Spencer, who founded the family fortune through sheep farming, was knighted by Henry VIII. A hundred years later, Robert Spencer, one of the wealthiest men of his age, became the first baron. His grandson Henry was created the first Earl of Sunderland by Charles I after lending the king money to fight the Civil War. His heir became adviser to three kings in succession — Charles II, James II and William III.

The senior branch of the family went on to become the Dukes of Marlborough, while the lesser branch retained the Spencer name. So Diana had plenty of history, but just as importantly, she had no past.

Charles, like every Prince of Wales before him, was in need of a wife, a mother for the sons he hoped would one day inherit his throne. But he was searching for a very special woman beyond reproach, a woman with all the right attributes for a queen. It was not something in which the head could be ruled by the heart, he told one interviewer.

He explained, 'Marriage is rather more than just falling madly in love with someone and having a love affair for the rest of your life. It is basically a very strong friendship. Creating a secure family unit in which to bring up children and give them a happy, secure upbringing — that's what marriage is all about.' So said the bachelor Prince.

He had met Diana when both were children, but their first adult encounter came in November 1977, when, as Diana's elder sister Sarah's boyfriend, he joined a shooting party at the Spencer stately home Althorp in Northamptonshire.

Charles was introduced to his future wife in a ploughed field near Nobottle Wood and later recalled that he thought, What a very jolly and amusing and attractive 16-year-old.

Diana Frances Spencer had been born at Park House on the Royal Family's Sandringham estate near

THE TRUTH

King's Lynn, Norfolk. At the time, her father Edward John, the eighth Earl Spencer, known to everyone as 'Johnnie', was serving as an equerry to the Queen who had allowed him to lease the house next door to her own for his growing family.

Johnnie Spencer farmed beef cattle on 650 acres he and his wife had acquired near their Norfolk home. They first had two daughters — Sarah, born in 1955; and Jane, who arrived two years later. A son and heir called John had been born in January 1960 but lived for only ten hours. Depressed and desperate to give her husband the boy he longed for, Frances became pregnant again the following autumn, giving birth to another girl on 1 July 1961. The little girl weighed 7lb 12oz and, according to estate worker Ernie Smith, who saw her when she was less than 24 hours old, 'she had lovely long legs, the best I've ever seen on a baby'. The following month, her parents christened her Diana Frances.

Later in life, the child came to believe that she was a disappointment to her parents. After the death of their first son, they longed for another boy. A third daughter, no matter how lovely, did not generate much excitement in the Spencer household.

In May 1964, when the young Diana was almost three years old, her mother finally gave birth to the boy who would inherit the title and all the family estates. While Diana had been baptised in the village church, her more 'significant' brother was christened with great ceremony at Westminster Abbey. The Queen was one of his godparents.

In 1969, when Diana was eight years old, her world was rocked by an event which would have repercussions for the rest of her life — her parents divorced after a bitter court battle for the custody of their children. Diana's mother was named as co-respondent in the divorce of wallpaper millionaire Peter Shand Kydd and his wife Janet. In the Sixties, long before divorce law reform, the other party in a divorce was looked upon as a rather immoral person. Even Frances' own mother took her husband's side in the custody fight.

Frances soon married Peter Shand Kydd but was permitted only limited access to her three daughters and son in their school holidays. Johnnie Spencer also remarried. To the reported dismay of his children, he chose as his second wife Raine, Countess of Dartmouth. Sarah, Jane, Diana and Charles did not warm to their new stepmother and, behind her back, used to sing their own version of the old nursery rhyme 'Raine, Raine, Go Away'.

The three sisters lived in flats in West London. Newsmen quickly discovered Diana's address — a first-floor apartment in Coleherne Court, South Kensington, and staked it out. Interest in the royal romance was so intense that television crews from around the world began to converge on London.

When Prince Charles left for his annual winter holiday in Switzerland, he found an Australian TV crew waiting for his arrival, hoping Diana would be with him. One day, TV reporter Ray Martin wished the Prince 'Good morning' and, noticing his accent, Charles asked, 'Where have you come from?'

Ray replied, 'Australia.'

The Prince looked amazed. 'Bloody hell!'

Two days after he returned to London, Charles invited Diana to dinner at his apartment in Buckingham Palace. Her flatmates Carolyn Pride, Virginia Pitman and Ann Bolton later revealed that Diana had guessed he was about to pop the question. As she excitedly

THE TRUTH

prepared for her big date, she told Carolyn, 'He's going to propose tonight. I just know he is!'

Diana's instinct was absolutely correct. That night, Charles asked her to be his Princess. He knew she was leaving for Australia the following day, and as he later explained, he wanted to give her some time to consider what the future would be like with him, 'to think if it was all going to be too awful'.

But Diana did not need time to reflect. She believed she was wildly, deeply in love for the first time and she had no doubts that she wanted to marry Charles. To leave him for two weeks was heartbreaking, but it was her last chance to enjoy a break before their engagement was announced.

It's not surprising that she chose Australia as her refuge from the storm that surrounded her in London. First, it was the country where her mother Frances and her second husband Peter Shand Kydd had a holiday home. The couple farmed a property near Yass, New South Wales, called Good Hope Farm — not far from Canberra — and left their main property in Scotland to spend the cold British winters in the warmth of the Australian summer.

Second, Prince Charles was well known to have a deep affection for the land down under. When he was 16, he had spent two terms at Timbertop, an outback offshoot of Australia's most prestigious school, Geelong Grammar, in Victoria. He had later described it as one of the happiest periods of his life. It seemed sensible for his fiancée to learn something about the country that meant so much to Charles.

With a complicated plan, she managed to leave her flat undetected, stay at a friend's home overnight, and next morning reach London's Heathrow Airport, where she boarded a Qantas jet for Sydney. This was not as easy as it seems. Britain's largest airport is the base for a whole team of news photographers who cover the arrivals and departures of celebrities every day of the year. With a network of contacts in all areas of the airport, they rarely miss a VIP passenger, but this time they failed to catch Lady Diana.

After the plane touched down at Sydney's Kingsford Smith Airport, Diana simply vanished. This caused pandemonium back in London. Royal reporters could only guess what Diana's disappearance meant. Was the romance with Charles over?

The newshounds of Fleet Street immediately contacted reporters in Australia, hoping they could trace their quarry, but not one of them managed to pick up Diana's trail. Television news helicopters hovered over Good Hope Farm near Yass, but no trace of the missing Lady Diana Spencer could be found.

When Frances Shand Kydd was contacted at her farm, she tried to protect her daughter with a well-meant fib. 'Diana is not here and is not coming here,' she said. 'She is certainly on holiday, but not in Australia. I know where she is but, of course, I'm not saying where. Diana has gone somewhere sunny. We are here for six weeks and we do not expect to hear from any of our children except by mail until we return.'

As if her denial was not strong enough, her husband Peter Shand Kydd added, 'Lady Diana is on a different continent.'

Later, Frances admitted, 'I lied through my teeth. I have no regrets. I was determined to have what my daughter and I knew to be our last holiday together. I chose Australia because it's a country for which I have a great affection. The people there were marvellous — they succeeded in concealing us for ten days.'

THE TRUTH

Eventually, as days went by without any news at all of the tall, blonde beauty, the press gave up and went away. As it turned out, they had all been looking in the wrong place. Diana was nowhere near her family's country property. She was well hidden many miles away on the south coast of New South Wales.

Frances Shand Kydd had rented a modern beach house tucked away among tall gum trees overlooking Mollymook Beach some 200 kilometres south of Sydney.

Almost 20 years after Diana discovered it, Mollymook is still a quiet, peaceful place and the beach is rarely crowded. A nine-hole golf course is situated at the southern end of the sand and this is where most of the social activity takes place.

Set on the edge of a prosperous agricultural area, this tiny seaside haven is now fast developing into a popular tourist resort. In this sub-tropical paradise, rolling, green hills reach down to the sea and the only sounds are the crashing surf and drumming of cicadas. With the Pacific Ocean to the east and the dominating escarpments of the Southern Tablelands to the west, the south coast around Mollymook and the nearby larger town of Ulladulla is a region of dramatically beautiful vistas. One green headland follows another in an endless emerald chain along the sea-washed coastline to create an area of outstanding natural beauty.

Forests of cedar in the surrounding hills first drew settlers here. In 1828, Thomas Kendall, grandfather of the Australian poet Henry Kendall, settled at Kendall Dale nearby.

This idyllic spot inspired another poet, Mary Dunlop, in the 1930s. In *Our Heritage*, she wrote of a beachside cottage just like the one in which Diana stayed.

*By the beach the white golf house has feet
  near the waves
The surf club stands back from the surf
And up on the rise in the lee of the trees
Is the cottage surrounded by turf*

*The cottage of slabs sits snug with red roof
It overlooks Mollymook beach
And down in the hollow a wild garden grows
Amid fruit trees, pear, persimmon, peach*

Few Mollymook residents know that the world's most famous woman once holidayed among them, but one local historian has recorded an apocryphal story that, during her stay, Lady Diana was a regular at the golf club and played a few rounds almost every day. Unfortunately, this is not true. Not only was Diana totally uninterested in the game, she stayed close to the beach house, afraid that she might be recognised and her holiday ruined.

Clinging to the hillside, Diana's dark-stained timber beach house had a wonderful view of the surf and miles of dazzling white sand below. It was situated at the end of a winding, dirt track which made it invisible from the road. On this totally secluded and private property, she was able to relax for the first time in more than six months.

As the sun set behind the hills at the end of another hot day, the future princess and her mother enjoyed a cool drink on the wooden, elevated deck facing the sea, watching the silvery light fading over the ocean. They discussed the enormity of Prince Charles's proposal and its impact on all their lives.

Mollymook was the perfect place for Diana to retreat from the world and consider what lay ahead.

THE TRUTH

While the press were searching all around the Australian capital, Canberra, and nearby Yass, the girl who loved to swim was revelling in the peace and solitude of a tiny coastal resort.

Glenda Cartwright, property manager for local estate agent Ian Cowley, helped Frances Shand Kydd find the house. She has never before talked about Diana's hideaway, but agreed to for this book. She remembers that Diana never ventured far from the beach, afraid that someone would recognise her by-now famous face.

Occasionally, says Glenda, Diana's mother climbed into her Volkswagen and drove into the larger town of Ulladulla, one kilometre away, to buy food and supplies. With a sarong over her swimsuit and flip-flops on her feet, she easily blended in with the locals, but Diana did not dare to accompany her.

Instead, she went surfing each day, skipping down a path to the beach then repeatedly diving beneath the waves. She never seemed to tire of the water, popping up to scrape her hair back from her forehead then turning to dive back beneath the water again.

The lone girl splashing about in the surf attracted no attention whatsoever. The Christmas and New Year holidaymakers had left long ago. The beach was deserted and there were no curious onlookers. To anyone who passed by, Diana was just another swimmer cooling off in the pounding surf on a hot day.

Sometimes, Frances Shand Kydd spread a beach towel out on the hot sand and sunbathed as she watched Diana surfing, although usually she also took a dip. There would be other holidays in the years ahead when they visited Richard Branson's Caribbean hideaway Necker. But they would be accompanied by Diana's children, their police bodyguards and a whole retinue of hangers-on.

Mollymook was the very last opportunity for mother and daughter to enjoy simply being together. As Diana later explained, 'My mother told everybody I wasn't in Australia to protect me. She wanted me to have a rest, to get away from people. Whatever I may feel, I know why she did it.'

Glenda Cartwright remembers when she first met Frances Shand Kydd on that 1981 holiday. She told her, 'It's an honour to meet you.'

Frances replied, 'It shouldn't be. I'm just an ordinary person like anyone else.'

Many years later, Glenda still feels privileged to know Diana's mother. Sitting in her local office, she explained, 'She is the most wonderful person and was very kind to my daughter when she visited England. That's where Diana got her wonderful down-to-earth nature and her way of treating everyone as an equal. She learned it from her mother.'

Mollymook became Diana's paradise, which she would later remember almost as if it was part of a dream. She was never to enjoy such solitude and contentment again.

Prince Charles stayed in touch by phone but had some difficulty tracking Diana down. When he called the Shand Kydd homestead, he was firmly told that no one had any information about his sweetheart. He protested that it was the Prince of Wales calling but, after dozens of press enquiries at the house, no one believed him.

Diana existed in a happy daze as she lazed around in the sunshine, day-dreaming about life back in London with her prince.

For a brief period, there were no pursuing paparazzi, no gawking crowds, no pompous palace

THE TRUTH

officials, and no police bodyguards. It was the last time Diana felt truly free.

Later, as Princess of Wales, she looked back at those few carefree days in Mollymook and said, 'For the rest of my life I was constantly followed — either by the police or by the paparazzi. But no one found me or followed me on that holiday. I'll always remember it was the last time I walked alone.'

Diana flew back to London and, once again, managed to avoid detection at Heathrow Airport. When her Qantas jet landed, she was taken off first and a private car was waiting on the tarmac to whisk her away to London. Prince Charles was making sure that she would be spared the ordeal of walking through the Arrivals hall crowded with other passengers — and the media.

Special clearance had been arranged for her with Customs and Immigration, another clue that this young woman was assuming more and more importance. She was reunited with Prince Charles at his country home Highgrove on Friday, 20 February 1981 where Diana, glowing with happiness, excitedly told him all about her escape to the sun. Australia, she reported, was just as wonderful as he had said it was.

Early the next morning, Diana accompanied the Prince to the Lambourn, Berkshire home of his trainer Nick Gaselee. Then a keen amateur jockey, Charles was in training for a three-mile steeplechase the next day at Chepstow. But as he was out riding on the Downs, his 11-year-old hunter Allibar had a heart-attack and died. The Prince felt a tremor run through the horse's body, and dismounted. A second later, Allibar collapsed in front of him.

As Charles kneeled down, cradling the stricken horse in his arms, Diana, sitting in a Land Rover nearby, watched with tears pouring down her face. She knew how much the horse meant to him and, although not a keen rider herself, she shared his sorrow.

They had been hotly pursued to Lambourn by a group of pressmen, who were unaware of Allibar's sad end until much later. They were puzzled when Charles drove off alone looking upset. Diana, more determined than ever not to be photographed with the Prince, was eventually driven away from the Gaselee's home hiding under a rug on the muddy floor of a Range Rover.

The death of his favourite mount almost ended Charles's career as a jockey. He did carry on with a brown gelding called Good Prospect, who threw him twice in successive races, and discouraged the Prince from another National Hunt season. Good Prospect simply could not compare with the wonderful Allibar and Charles's heart was no longer in the sport. The tragedy may also have helped to bring forward the engagement of Diana and her prince.

Both Charles and Diana were growing weary of the secrecy, the detailed planning and the time-wasting involved in hiding their love for each other from the public. Many royal observers believe that the betrothal was originally planned to take place in March.

Diana had been telling her friends that she was planning to return to work at the Young England kindergarten in Pimlico after her holiday in Australia, and there is no reason now to doubt that she meant what she said.

But the speculation surrounding the couple was becoming intolerable and Allibar's death only intensified the feeling that they needed to put an end to the harassment. It was unacceptable that a girl who had won the Prince's heart should have to hide on the floor of a station wagon to avoid the media. That was no

THE TRUTH

way to treat a lady, never mind someone who could become Britain's future queen.

Back in London, Diana disappeared from her flat, leaving her flatmates to fend off questions from the press. Lady Diana was not there, they declared. When would she be back? 'Well, er, I'm not sure when she's coming back.' Her loyal friends were trying to be polite yet protect their landlady at the same time. The royal newshounds began to feel certain that something was up!

In the event, the teams of tabloid reporters and photographers were all scooped by the *Times*, which exclusively revealed in a small paragraph on page one of its 24 February edition that the royal engagement would be announced later that day.

By breakfast time, every radio station, newspaper office and television company was buzzing with the story.

At 10.00am, Prince Charles was due to pay a visit to the Foreign and Commonwealth Office in Whitehall. It was part of his preparation for the throne to learn about the workings of government.

A large crowd of photographers, reporters and TV crews gathered outside to await his arrival, but by 10.05am he had not appeared. Just then, a senior official appeared to announce that 'the Prince of Wales has decided to postpone his visit'!

To a man, the whole contingent decamped from the Foreign Office and rushed over to Buckingham Palace. They were not to be disappointed. At 11.00am, the Palace released the news everyone had been waiting for. The simple statement declared: 'It is with the greatest pleasure that the Queen and the Duke of Edinburgh announce the betrothal of their beloved son, the Prince of Wales, to the Lady Diana Spencer, daughter of the Earl Spencer and the Honourable Mrs Shand Kydd.' Royal officials also revealed that a wedding would follow in the summer.

In his palace apartment, Charles and Diana toasted each other with pink champagne. It seemed the worst was over. Diana was now enclosed within the secure walls of Buckingham Palace, installed in what had once been the nursery suite. It seemed a lifetime of happiness was now within her reach.

She could have no inkling that, from then on, Diana Spencer would need to draw on every ounce of the strength she had gained during her seaside holiday down under.

2

Five months later and 30lb lighter, Diana floated down the aisle of St Paul's Cathedral to marry her prince. The healthy, round-cheeked girl who had sunned herself in Australia had become an almost gaunt shadow of her former self.

Her waist, once an average 26, was now a waspish 21 inches. And her billowing silk and lace wedding gown seemed almost to overwhelm her. The girl inside it had lost so much weight that she seemed to be drowning in yards of voluminous fabric and veiling. No one noticed this, of course. It is only in retrospect that the destruction of the real Diana Spencer and the creation of a new goddess can clearly be seen.

With pounding hearts and misty eyes, the world watched a twentieth-century fairytale come to life. In this atmosphere of universal euphoria, who wished to be reminded that the greatest fairytales, like those of the Brothers Grimm, often feature violence and grief? Rapunzel was imprisoned in an ivory tower; Snow White lost her mother, and then was poisoned by her envious stepmother.

As author Suzanne Lowry wrote in her book *Princess in the Mirror*, 'Every ancient golden fable had a darker, even cruel, flip-side — which helped to give it force and meaning. And, whether we — or they — like it or not, the members of the Royal Family are part of a living, breathing fairytale upon which we pin, and on to which we project, our hopes and fantasies.'

Whether she wished it or not, Diana was *our* dream princess, a national treasure, the most prized jewel in the Crown. Naturally, this paragon had to be exploited.

The sound of wedding bells had barely faded before plans were under way to get the Royal Family's new golden couple out working for Britain.

In fact, Charles and Diana were still enjoying the second half of their honeymoon at Balmoral in Scotland when a highly placed palace sourced tipped me off that a tour of Australia was being organised.

The trip was pencilled in for late summer 1982, when the new Princess of Wales wrecked everyone's plans by becoming pregnant. It was more good news and the whole world rejoiced with the happy parents-to-be. Meanwhile, Charles's hopes of introducing his bride to the people down under had to be postponed for a year.

Little thought seems to have been given to whether the new Princess of Wales was ready to undertake such an arduous trip. The huge machinery of the monarchy ground on and Diana somehow had to find a way of avoiding being crushed by its relentless momentum.

Unfortunately, she was having difficulty adjusting to her strange new life. Morning sickness plagued her throughout the pregnancy and post-natal depression followed her first-born son's safe delivery on 21 June 1982.

In retrospect, it is clear she was suffering from stress. Within the space of little more than a year, she had been transformed from an unknown nursery school assistant to the world's most famous wife and mother. The Royal Family believed that the unprecedented interest in the new Princess would quickly die down, but as Diana began to return to public life after her pregnancy, the stampede for news about her only increased.

On the first occasion Diana reappeared in public after the birth of Prince William, she was still a little overweight and, self-conscious about the way she looked, she began to lose the extra pounds as quickly as possible. By November 1982, her astonishing weight loss was obvious to everyone when she arrived at a Guildhall fashion show wearing a one-shoulder dress which exposed her protruding shoulder blades and painfully thin arms.

Newspaper editors were soon publishing endless features about the Princess of Wales's disturbing appearance. She seemed astoundingly thin, prompting the *Daily Mirror* to splash the front-page banner headline CONCERN FOR DI'S HEALTH. Its rival, the *Sun*, also published a similar story, which we now know to be totally accurate.

However, Palace spokesmen condemned the stories as 'grossly exaggerated'. The Queen's press officer

Michael Shea declared, 'The fact that the Princess of Wales was in sparkling form on two public occasions yesterday for millions to see speaks for itself.' Cleverly, the Palace never once categorically denied that Diana was suffering from any form of eating disorder, issuing statements such as, 'We do not get involved with the personal affairs of the Royal Family every time a distasteful rumour is started.'

Behind Palace doors, the word 'spoilt' was bandied about and there were fears that Diana sometimes vented her feelings of isolation on those closest to her. One courtier remarked rather callously, 'Perhaps the Princess does not have the intellectual capability to come to terms with what she so blithely took on.' Patronising comments like this only heightened Diana's feelings of inadequacy and desperation.

The switch from carefree teenager to future queen had sent Diana's stress levels rocketing way past the danger point. As well as bulimia (the illness which had transformed a chubby girl into a stick-thin new mother), she was suffering not just from the normal post-natal baby blues, but also from clinical depression.

Clearly, she was in dire need of help and her husband arranged for treatment by a psychiatrist. Despite this, she was expected to shape up and do her duty. Plans for the tour of Australia were dusted off and rescheduled for March 1983.

Buckingham Palace officials continued to play down Diana's problems believing that there was nothing wrong with her which patience and time could not cure. But they grievously underestimated the extent of the difficulties the Princess was having in adjusting to her new life. Her despair only increased when another startling allegation was made about the Princess. Nigel Dempster, a columnist on the *Daily*

THE TRUTH

Mail, gave an interview to the US TV show *Good Morning America*, in which he called Diana 'a fiend and a monster'.

He declared, 'Suddenly getting this enormous power, having people curtsy and bow and do everything she wants, she has become a fiend. She has become a little monster.' He also claimed Prince Charles was desperately unhappy because he knew he could never divorce Diana. The Palace dismissed Dempster's story as 'ridiculous'.

It was equally crushing about an American psychiatrist's warning in January 1983 that the Princess of Wales stood an 80 per cent chance of becoming ill as a result of her stressful life. 'An obsessive compulsive illness could definitely be a possibility,' claimed Dr Thomas Holmes from the Department of Psychiatry at Washington Medical School. He had devised a stress scale which indicated how dramatic changes in a person's life could create high levels of stress and lead to ill health

Any change in a person's life may be stressful, even if it is a happy one. Diana had become engaged, married, a mother and moved into two new homes in little more than 12 months. She was simply a princess living under horrendous pressure.

Diana had shown signs of an obsessive compulsive disorder as far back as 1973 when she broke the rules at West Heath boarding school by sneaking into the bathroom after lights out to have more baths than other girls. 'She also had a compulsion about washing clothes,' author Penny Junor recorded in a 1982 biography. She was fastidious about her surroundings, constantly tidying her drawers and cupboards in a compulsive way. When she went to visit her sisters she spent a great deal of the time doing their washing and cleaning their flats.

Was this an indication of her need to exert control over her life after becoming the child of a broken home? Or was it a sign of some deeper mental disturbance? Whatever the explanation for Diana's manic conduct, the psychiatrist was more accurate than even he could have imagined. Public concern about Diana's appearance was mixed with her puzzling behaviour during official duties. Despite her scrawny looks, the Princess carried out her royal duties faultlessly. She smiled endlessly and gave every indication of being happy. It was only when away from the public eye that royal insiders revealed she was 'difficult and disturbed'.

Occasionally, a private holiday brought this out into the open. In January of that year it seemed unlikely that the insecure Princess would be able to cope with a demanding tour of Australia.

Her erratic behaviour worried many people when Charles and Diana went on their first skiing holiday together. They stayed in the tiny principality of Liechtenstein with Prince Hans Adam and his family at their castle in Vaduz, but spent most of their time skiing over the border in nearby Austria.

One afternoon, when they had finished skiing in the Austrian resort of Lech, they were trapped in an alleyway while they were waiting for their car to turn up to take them back to Vaduz. Diana tried to hide her face inside the collar of her ski jacket and began to cry.

Just then, around 20 more photographers turned up and began blazing away at the couple. Charles and Diana were completely surrounded with no hope of escape. By this time, Diana was hysterical. She clamped her hands over her ears and began to scream, 'I can't stand it! I can't stand it!'

Her worried husband tried to comfort her as best he could. 'Please, darling, please, don't be stupid,' he begged. Fortunately, Prince Hans Adam's car arrived at that moment and they were able to escape in it back to Liechtenstein.

If the new Princess could not cope with a dozen or more cameramen on a single afternoon, how would she deal with hundreds day after day on their forthcoming trip to Australia and New Zealand? Diana was only 21 and had had no special preparation or training for her exalted role.

Charles was an old trouper who had represented Britain on around 50 international tours. Diana had rarely travelled outside Britain, apart from a brief stay at a Swiss finishing school and her 1981 secret holiday in New South Wales. But the planned tour could not be postponed a second time. Diana would simply have to conquer her nerves and get on with it.

There appeared to be no consideration for her inexperience and her difficulties in adjusting to her extraordinary new position. It now seems unthinkable to expect a royal novice to undertake a six-week slog around Australia and New Zealand, but that is what lay ahead of Diana when an RAAF 707 jet touched down at Alice Springs Airport at 7.54am on 20 March 1983.

Wearing an aquamarine silk dress, the Princess of Wales appeared in the aircraft doorway with her husband, who was kitted out in what is known locally as 'Territory rig' — beige bush shirt, beige trousers and a maroon tie.

At the happy suggestion of the Australian Prime Minister, the couple had brought their nine-month-old son Prince William with them.

But within an hour of her arrival, Diana was forced to say goodbye to her baby who, in the care of his nanny Barbara Barnes, was travelling on to Woomargama, a sheep station in Victoria, where he would stay until his parents could join him on their rare days off duty.

As the royal visitors stood on the tarmac posing for more than 150 journalists, a familiar winged insect landed on the baby prince's head. 'Oh look, his first fly,' Charles chuckled, as if nothing could be a more appropriate introduction to Australia.

Then they said goodbye to their son and climbed into a car to travel to their hotel in Alice Springs. At that moment, Francis Cornish, a member of their staff, leaned forward and whispered to the Princess, 'Good luck, Diana.' He knew she would need all the good fortune and nerve she could possibly find.

Jet-lagged, separated from her baby for the first time and feeling totally out of her depth, Diana embarked on her first official overseas tour. There were 80,000 kilometres to cover, thousands of hands to shake and up to seven official engagements each day.

There was the unaccustomed heat to cope with, along with the unseasonal rain — Australians claimed Charles and Diana had brought 'Pommie' weather with them. At first, it seemed the trip would be a complete wash-out. The most arid region of Australia had been lashed by heavy rain the week before the tour was due to begin. The Todd River at Alice Springs, normally little more than a trickle, had been turned into a torrent by a flash flood and three people had been drowned.

But the wet weather had transformed the red heart of Australia into a green oasis. Desert flowers bloomed and the sky, washed clean by days of non-stop rain, made the scenery sparkle in the clear air. The white trunks of the eucalyptus trees stood out starkly against the red earth and deep blue sky, creating a spectacular

THE TRUTH

introduction to the Australian Outback.

Unfortunately, the heavy rain also caused some last-minute changes of schedule. The luxury Alice Springs Casino, where the royal couple had planned to stay, was cut off by floodwaters, so they were hurriedly rebooked into a rather more modest motel situated on a drier patch of land. The motel was immediately staked out by the press who kept a watch for any movement by their quarry.

The reporters among them were thrilled when they discovered that the suite of rooms hastily redecorated for the royal visitors had a hot tub in the bathroom. British newspapers splashed the news of this quite unusual luxury (at that time) fitting in the predictable headline RUB-A-DUB-TUB, TWO ROYALS IN A TUB.

If Diana thought longingly of her previous visit to Australia, when she had enjoyed blissful solitude, it would be easy to understand. In the dead heart of the continent she could not have been further from the sea and the surf, where she had found such solace only two years earlier.

Royal tours are no vacation. In fact, they are non-stop hard work designed to promote local organisations and strengthen links with Britain. So Charles and Diana were introduced to the wonders of the Outback's School of the Air, and children on far-flung properties hundreds of kilometres away were able to speak to them by radio.

The royal tourists were also given a chance to climb Ayer's Rock, now known by its Aboriginal name Ulurulu, the vast, brooding monolith rising above the desert. Although not equipped for climbing in their city shoes, they managed to scale around 20m or more.

They were then driven a short distance away so they could watch the desert sunset change the colour of the sandstone rock from red ochre, to fluorescent orange, then to burnt sienna, pale lilac and deep purple. Unfortunately, the recent heavy rains had washed from the air the thick desert dust that, reflecting the rays of the setting sun, normally brings about this transformation. A bemused Diana sat on the stump of a fence post waiting patiently for the technicolour display which never came.

The royal couple also attended a Northern Territory government reception, opened a new St John Ambulance Centre and, on a subsidiary trip to Tennant Creek in temperatures soaring up to 115°C, gained a greater understanding of how harsh Outback life can be. Their only escape from duty was a private visit to a swimming pool at the home of an Alice Springs businessman. After unwisely sunning herself for some hours, Diana returned to her motel suite sunburned and a little sore.

After a break, when they were reunited with Prince William at Woomargama homestead, Diana and Charles were off on the road again. Aware that his wife found the whole experience very daunting, the Prince tried to guide her through tricky procedures.

At the Australian War Memorial in Canberra, as they placed a wreath on the memorial stone, he quietly gave his wife instructions.

'You take two steps forward, pause, then two steps back.'

Diana obediently did as he suggested.

Later, on a walkabout among well-wishers, her lack of experience showed when she blurted out some very candid remarks. A young mother with babe-in-arms told Diana that she envied her because she had a nanny to help take care of her son.

'Oh no, I envy you,' the Princess replied. 'You can

be with your baby all the time.'

It was clear that she was missing Prince William. The high price of becoming the globe's most gawked-at celebrity was beginning to show. In the years ahead, Diana would learn to be more guarded when talking to the public. But on that first tour of Australia, she said what she thought and her comments made front-page news around Australia every day.

Diana was elated by the Australian public's overwhelming adoration, but simultaneously bewildered and fearful. She relied heavily on her husband for support, often clutching his hand for reassurance when crowds of people surrounded the couple.

On walkabouts, schoolchildren tugged at her skirts, trying to get her attention, adults clutched her hands, often unwilling to let go, while besotted young men declared their undying devotion. Each time Diana felt unable to cope, Charles was there beside her, ready to extricate her from the situation. He diplomatically made light of such incidents but, privately, was deeply concerned about the pressure his wife was under. As Jonathan Dimbleby revealed in his biography of the Prince, Charles wrote to a friend from Australia: 'How can anyone, let alone a 21-year-old, be expected to come out of all this obsessed and crazed attention unscathed?'

The wildest welcome awaited Charles and Diana in Sydney. Crowds jammed the city streets to see the Prince and Princess arrive at the Opera House in an open-topped Rolls-Royce. The steps leading up to the world-famous concert hall became a makeshift stage where schoolchildren greeted them with a medley of Welsh songs, and teenage girls in leotards put on an athletic performance. Australia's two most famous landmarks — the Harbour Bridge and the Opera House

— set against a clear blue sky — formed a dazzling background for the ceremony.

The Prince delighted the vast crowd in a speech of thanks. He said, 'It is now 17 years since I first set foot as a hesitant Pom in this vast and fair land, and I will never forget the open and forthright way I was made to feel at home.' Loud cheers greeted his words.

He added that his wife had been enveloped in warmth and affection from the moment she arrived, and he sincerely hoped that his small son would also experience the same. 'A small portion of his impressionable conscious will be filled with the sights, sounds and smells of Australia — the Lucky Country.'

The next morning, Charles took an early morning dip at Bondi but managed to avoid the predatory, bikini-clad girls, who, on earlier visits, had stolen kisses as he surfed. He was now a married man and his days of flirting with beach beauties were over.

The most glittering event on their schedule in the Premier State was a ball held at the Sheraton-Wentworth Hotel in Sydney. The orchestra played 'The More I See You, the More I Want You' and Charles whirled his wife around the dance floor watched by a thousand eyes.

It was the first time the glamorous royal couple had ever danced together in public. It cannot have been easy to put on a show for the curious onlookers but, somehow, Charles and Diana managed to stay in step and to laugh as they spun around the parquet floor. A few minutes later, they were joined by guests anxious to rub shoulders with the future King and Queen.

Sydney socialites had paid the then considerable sum of $75 each to attend the most eagerly-awaited event of the year, which had been organised to benefit the Benevolent Society. Naturally, Diana was the belle of the ball in a dazzling blue gown embroidered with silver thread, which made her a shimmering figure beneath the bombardment of press flashguns.

As she walked in, the electronic onslaught was blinding. But Diana swanned through the door, head up, smiling through the blitz as if the hordes of cameramen were not even there. A thousand eyes were on her, checking her make-up, valuing her jewellery, taking her sumptuous blue evening dress apart at the seams. Her poise, her posture and her glossy hair all got non-stop scrutiny all night, even her hands were examined for signs of nervous nail-biting.

Everyone in the room had wondered what the woman then thought destined to be a queen was really like. At last, they had a chance to find out. And she did not disappoint them.

The marathon tour continued to attract enormous crowds throughout the state. When Charles seized the chance to play his favourite summer sport — polo — at Warwick Farm, Diana was reunited with her former flatmate Ann Bolton, who had developed a keen interest in the game since moving to Australia.

Ann noticed that her friend had lost a great deal of weight, but told the press she was not surprised. In their days as flatmates, they had all lived on Mars Bars and baked beans, she revealed.

Last year's concerns about a possible eating disorder had been forgotten. No one seemed alarmed that the pencil-slim Princess was growing steadily more slender. Even the eagle-eyed members of Britain's Royal Press Rat Pack saw nothing to worry about. Harry Arnold, leader of the pack, wrote, 'Two years of marriage have changed Diana. The rounded figure and the glowing health of the courting days have been replaced by a slim elegance and an air of vulnerability.'

The public wanted a fairytale and newspapers, magazines and television all conspired to give it to them. No one wanted to tell the Princess's devoted fans that all was not well in this storybook romance. Besides, who could have guessed what was really happening as the tired centre of attention turned out each day and smiled, smiled, smiled?

Diana staged an award-winning performance throughout the tour. She seemed deliriously happy to be down under. She never frowned, never looked tired and never ever appeared bored. She lived up to everyone's expectations magnificently.

Although emotionally and physically exhausted, she was buoyed up by the overwhelming admiration of the Australian public. She found it terrifying yet magical, and did her best not to let everyone down.

A trip to the famous wine-growing Hunter Valley Region of New South Wales, which included Newcastle and Maitland, brought out more cheering, ecstatic crowds. At a civic reception, the Prince and Princess were introduced to a certain Bill and Marie Sutton. In her typically candid way, Marie shook hands with Prince Charles and jokingly said, 'It's your wife I want to meet, not you.' She was only expressing what everyone felt, that Diana was the big attraction. This deliciously pretty blonde was a dream princess come to life and no one realised she was living a nightmare.

Who wanted to make small-talk with Charles when you could chatter to the woman *everyone* wanted to meet?

It was a comment the Prince was to hear constantly throughout the tour. Although born to be a king, he was no longer as important to the public as his wife, a commoner until her marriage.

THE TRUTH

Diana and Marie exchanged pleasantries and, a minute or so later, the Princess moved on. Neither woman could have imagined then how close they would become 15 years later.

The island state of Tasmania, known as the Apple Isle, played host to the royal visitors for just 29 hours, but they managed to pack a great deal into a tight schedule and were swept away on a tide of goodwill.

A State Reception in Hobart provided perhaps the worst moment of the tour. A crowd of local dignitaries, forgetting their manners, pressed forward to stare at the royal couple, who were seated on a dais, examining them just as if they were animals in a zoo. Not one of the organisers made any attempt to prevent this appalling conduct as Diana sat like a trapped fawn in front of a horde of hungry hyenas.

At that moment, the cost of becoming a royal ambassador for Britain must have seemed far too high. Diana was just 21 years old, but the masterminds who organise such tours seemed to give little consideration to her extreme youth and inexperience. It was left to Prince Charles to defuse the awkward atmosphere. Noticing his wife's discomfort, he made an effort to distract attention from his embarrassed wife by standing up to make a light-hearted speech.

He mentioned that on his last visit to Australia, when newly engaged, he had promised to return with his wife. 'My goodness, I was lucky to marry her,' he declared. Sitting behind him, Diana pulled a wry face at his words and the audience roared. Realising that his wife had made a jokey gesture he could not see, Charles laughed. 'It's amazing what ladies do when one's back is turned.'

Two days in South Australia followed in deteriorating weather, but thousands of people waited in rain and strong winds to welcome the royal couple at an RAAF base. In the evening, Diana was the star of a disco at Adelaide University. She had changed from the beige, cream and white silk dress in which she had arrived into a patterned blouse and black skirt. She had no shortage of partners but took time out for a breather when she sat on her husband's knee.

The following day, the gruelling schedule continued. They set off for Renmark and Port Pirie where they were greeted by an enormous sign fixed 40m above the street on a grain silo: 'Port Pirie Welcomes Charles and Diana'. Some of the thousands of youngsters who lined the streets to see them had travelled up to 500km.

More excited crowds were waiting for them in Perth, capital of Western Australia, along with wintry British weather. It had not rained in the area for a month but Charles and Diana had delighted the farmers once again.

In Fremantle, the Princess carried out her first solo engagement in Australia when she toured Fremantle Hospital. Charles was busy back at Government House holding an investiture.

At a garden party, the Prince recalled fond memories of his first WA visit in 1977 and a second for the State's 150th anniversary two years later. 'And you don't look a day older,' he joked with the crowd.

The royal couple set off in different directions on a vast semi-circular path around the garden to meet as many people as possible. When they met half-way round, Charles came face to face with his wife, and charmed the crowd when he picked up her hand and kissed it Continental-style. 'Keep it up, darling, you're doing a great job,' Charles told her.

Their last duty in Western Australia was a trip to

THE TRUTH

Bunbury where the Prince made a royal gaffe when wind whipped away a speech he was planning to make. 'God, my bloody bit of paper,' he exclaimed. There was a ripple of laughter among his audience of schoolchildren and Diana giggled.

It was still raining when they returned to Perth. A soaked crowd of around 1,500 well-wishers had braved the chill, damp weather to say goodbye as the Prince and Princess left to spend another weekend at Woomargama with Prince William.

Queensland, the Sunshine State, turned on a welcome that almost overwhelmed Diana. Crowds lined the streets 20-deep and police had to link arms to keep excited well-wishers from closing in on the couple as they walked through the City mall. At one point, the Princess felt rather faint and had to be ushered into a side room in Brisbane City Hall for a rest and a glass of water.

Prince Charles called it a 'boiling welcome' and told guests at a reception, 'We always knew Brisbane people were warm and friendly but they have really shown it today.' The crowds returned that evening to see Diana, wearing a tiara and a pink organza gown, arrive for a Queensland government reception.

The next morning, they hit the tourist trail, embarking on a mind-numbing tour of local industries including a visit to the Yandina ginger factory, where they watched macadamia nuts whizz along conveyor belts and took a ride on a 'nutmobile' — a five-carriage green train — to the Sunshine Plantation, also known as the Big Pineapple. There, they got a real taste of tropical Queensland with a buffet lunch of pawpaw, prawns, avocado and salad.

The last leg of the Australian tour took Charles and Diana to Melbourne where the Garden State provided a stunning climax to their 28-day visit. The royal couple visited a housing estate in Altona, then at lunchtime they strolled through the City mall, where crowds estimated at up to 200,000-strong cheered their arrival. 'Being in Melbourne today means I have introduced my wife to every capital city in Australia,' the Prince announced. He did not mention, but no doubt thought, that this appallingly long and exhausting itinerary was an ordeal no human being should be expected to fulfil, never mind a novice princess.

In the afternoon, he and his wife managed to snatch a few hours of rest so they could prepare for a gala show that evening at the new Melbourne Concert Hall. The following day, they set off for the country on a four-hour journey to Ballarat.

At the Sovereign Hill tourist village, they had their first brush with the law in the shape of a sword-waving trooper who stopped them in the street. He declared, 'You're wanted in these parts for bringing the township to a complete standstill and causing the abandonment of commerce. In pursuance of my duty, I should arrest you both. However, as I can see I am vastly outnumbered by your supporters, I shall let you off with a warning.'

Diana popped into a dry goods store and emerged with a few grammes of extra-strong mints to nibble on the rest of her trip. A ride in a reproduction stagecoach once owned by Cobb & Co also helped to give the royal visitors some insight into the Colonial days of old.

The Princess had learned a great deal during her month in Australia. Her initial nervousness disappeared as the crowds in every state took her to their hearts. The naïve girl who had arrived in Alice Springs had been replaced by a more confident woman and Diana demonstrated her new self-assurance on her last night in Melbourne.

She arrived at a charity ball in aid of the Mental Health Foundation wearing a slinky, sequinned gown that moulded itself to her figure like a glittering second skin, and drew gasps of admiration from all the guests. 'She saved the best for last,' whispered her bodyguard Graham Smith as he watched the electric effect the Princess had on her audience.

Gone were the girly, swirly gowns Diana had favoured at the start of the trip. Here was a sophisticated lady, who was no longer just a decorative support to her husband, but the star of the royal show.

Crossing the Tasman next morning, the royal couple began a two-week tour of New Zealand. The weather was cold and rainy and both Charles and Diana were completely exhausted by the crowds, chaos and the cameras, but cheered by the astounding welcome they had received all over Australia.

It had been a punishing experience for a beginner, but Diana had faced the worst that the flood, fire and drought-ravaged country could throw at her. Somewhere along the way, she had also learned to face the harsh reality of life as a future king's wife. Nothing she had ever encountered before equalled the stress of spending every day of a two-country tour under the searing spotlight of the media. Charles and Diana were never asked to undertake such an arduous journey ever again. It had lasted six weeks. By the time their marriage drew to an end, their trips did not even last six days.

Ostensibly, the Princess's very first tour abroad had been a great success. From Alice Springs to Auckland and from Brisbane to Gisbourne, the trip had been a total triumph for Diana. At least, that's the way it seemed to the press and public. Privately, the trip had piled even more stress on to the mentally fragile Princess. She was far too young and far too frail to tackle such a taxing tour. The Foreign Office officials and Palace courtiers who had arranged it must have been close to inhuman to subject a newcomer to such an ordeal. Yet two months later, they sent the royal couple off again on another exhausting trip across Canada.

The thought that the rest of her life would be just like this must have been extremely depressing.

These journeys proved to be a steep learning curve for her husband. On every previous visit, he had been the centre of attention. As the world's most eligible man, he had been the one everybody wanted to see. Now he was virtually ignored while Diana was adored. The Prince was slowly forced to realise that he had been totally eclipsed by his wife. Although Charles had never sought the spotlight, it was disconcerting to find that it had switched away from him to someone else.

Although proud of Diana's success, he also naturally resented being overshadowed by her. It was a feeling that would fester and grow, until it slowly poisoned the love they shared.

3

It's one of the the last great royal mysteries — was the Princess of Wales as paranoid and neurotic as her detractors have always claimed? Or did she have good reason for her obsessive belief that Prince Charles never gave up his first love, Camilla?

Only Charles, Camilla and a handful of royal protection officers who accompanied the Prince everywhere know the answers to these questions. Looking back, it is not difficult to discover just when the happiness Charles and Diana briefly shared became poisoned by distrust and disillusion.

While Diana was expecting her second baby, she and Charles shared the closest, most loving months of their marriage. It seemed that they had settled down after the early years of difficult adjustment. Following the birth of Prince Henry, known as Harry, on 15 September 1984, something changed. Perhaps motherhood had brought maturity, but the once nervous and insecure girl began to assert herself more often. She expected her husband to play a greater part in bringing up their children, and he was delighted to do so.

As always, he entered into the job with such enthusiasm that he was soon acting as if he knew more about parenting than anyone else. He stayed at home, spending long hours in the nursery with his little boys. He read countless books on childcare and wanted to be involved in every aspect of his sons' lives. This prompted Diana to half-seriously complain, 'He knows so much about having babies, I think I'll let him have the next one.'

Devoting more time to being a father meant less time for his royal duties and his office staff found that work piled up and nothing was sorted out. Always indecisive, Prince Charles drives his private secretaries demented with his inability to tackle paperwork. He hates anything that keeps him working at a desk and makes no secret of it.

To the public he is a mild-mannered, kindly character, but his staff know a stubborn man with a very short fuse. One after the other, his private secretaries, infuriated by the Prince's procrastination and bad temper, left his service. Michael Colborne, who had served Charles for ten years, left at the end of 1984 and, a few months later, Michael Adeane also departed.

Assistant Private Secretary David Roycroft took on the duties of both but was not confirmed in the top job and soon left to become an executive at Independent

Television News. Sir John Riddell, an international banker, then took on the prestigious post as Private Secretary and, although it was hoped he would remain to become chief adviser to the next king, he stayed for only five years.

Diana was feeling restless and resentful. Despite the joy of caring for her two little sons, she felt trapped behind palace walls. She could not go out without a Scotland Yard bodyguard, and when she did venture out on official duties her commitment to good causes seemed to count for nothing.

The press paid more attention to what she was wearing than what she was doing.

The insecurity, which had plagued her ever since her mother left home when she was six years old, threatened to overwhelm her. She had never been able to shake off the feeling that Prince Charles was still involved with his old friend Camilla Parker Bowles, despite his repeated reassurances to the contrary. Her conviction had the opposite effect to what she intended. In a classic case of jealousy's destructive effect, instead of enlisting her husband's sympathy, she drove him further away from her.

Were her suspicions unfounded as Prince Charles's supporters have always claimed? Members of his circle have regularly insisted that, when he married, he ceased all contact with his closest friends and devoted himself to his young wife. The Palmer-Tomkinsons, Lord and Lady Tryon, and Camilla and Andrew Parker Bowles were no longer a part of his life. In 1994, in an authorised biography of the Prince of Wales, Jonathan Dimbleby claimed that the Prince had cut Camilla out of his life when he proposed to Diana.

'Following his engagement to the Princess in

February 1981, the Prince had made virtually no contact with Camilla Parker Bowles for over five years,' he wrote.

He added that the couple met only fleetingly on social occasions, apart from the time shortly before his marriage when he gave Camilla a farewell gift of a bracelet. Dimbleby also insisted that the Prince made only one phone call to her in the years after his marriage, when he rang to say he and his wife were expecting their first child. 'Like his other close friends, she had been wholly excluded from his life,' he alleged.

In a television interview with Jonathan Dimbleby, the Prince himself also declared that he had not resumed his love affair with Camilla until his marriage had 'irretrievably broken down'.

Was this the truth, the whole truth and nothing but the truth? Not according to the Prince's late valet Stephen Barry, who remained on his staff until April 1982. A bachelor who enjoyed the nightlife in London, Barry did not wish to be stuck in the country when Charles and Diana began spending most of their time at Highgrove in Gloucestershire and handed in his resignation. Proof that the Prince regarded him highly was the offer of a Duchy of Cornwall flat into which the valet moved when he left the Palace. Barry was also lent a car until he could arrange to buy one of his own.

Long before Andrew Morton exposed Camilla's relationship with Charles, Stephen Barry recalled in his 1983 memoirs *Royal Service* that the Tryons were dropped after Charles married Diana, but the Parker Bowles were not. He described meeting Lady Tryon at a wedding, who was mystified by her banishment from Charles's life. 'I can't understand why we're never invited,' she told him. Barry, who later died of AIDS, recalled that the other couple with whom the Prince had been close, Andrew and Camilla Parker Bowles, were still very much on the scene.

'The friendship, unlike the Tryons, seems to have survived his marriage,' he revealed. Stephen Barry had no reason to invent this story. He and the Prince had remained on good terms at that time.

Years later, after the couple separated, Diana's bodyguard, Chief Inspector Graham Smith, who later died of lymph cancer, revealed, 'The trouble was Camilla. It was always Camilla. Forget all the others, Kanga and the rest. They didn't mean a thing. Camilla was the only woman he ever loved.'

A former friend who once spent a great deal of time with Charles and Diana when they first married recalls, 'I felt very sorry for her because Camilla always seemed to be around.'

In the spring of 1985, the growing gulf between Charles and Diana became evident when they toured Italy, a trip originally planned for October 1984, which had been postponed when Diana was expecting her second baby. It was the Prince's first visit to the country about which he had heard so much from his grandmother, Queen Elizabeth the Queen Mother. He was enraptured by the architectural glories of Italy and its antiquities. He soaked up the sunshine and the Mediterranean scenery and was entranced by the alluring, sophisticated women he met. In particular, he seemed to be fascinated by the Marchesa di Frescobaldi, a tall, elegant Diana lookalike. She played hostess to the royal couple at her family's magnificent palazzo, enchanting Charles with discussions on Florentine art and architecture.

The tour of Italy was, for Charles, the start of a love affair with the country which continues to this day. On his return to London he hired an Italian chef, Enrico Derflingher, and, even as recently as March 1998, his staff insisted that all his favourite dishes were Italian. He has a particular fondness for risotto with truffles.

Diana did not enjoy Italy quite so much and it was there that the very first signs of her despondency were noticed by journalists. When they visited monasteries and palazzos, she trailed around in her husband's wake, apparently unimpressed by her magnificent surroundings. The girl who had never managed to pass a single exam in her life felt patronised by the toffee-nosed dignitaries who accompanied them. They made it dazzlingly clear they thought the Princess was no culture vulture. 'The Princess did ask some questions but it was obviously all new to her,' was one blunt comment to the press after the royal couple were shown around Florence Cathedral.

Her simmering annoyance boiled over one day as she was led around yet another architectural glory. As they walked through a low arch, Charles warned, 'Mind your head!'

Diana replied bitterly, 'Why? There's nothing in it.'

Her comment was a symptom of her increasing resentment. She was bored by dinners with elderly royal officials that dragged on for hours. She was irritated by antiquated royal rules and angry about the lack of personal freedom she was given.

Diana was also irritated by reports that she had spent a Queen's ransom on stylish new clothes for the tour. It seemed the whole world believed she was a hopeless shopaholic and nothing more testing than what to wear ever crossed her mind.

So a few months later, the couple seized an opportunity to knock such ideas on the head when Independent Television News asked them to do the first television interview since their marriage. 'My clothes are not my priority,' Diana declared. 'I enjoy bright colours and my husband likes me to look smart, presentable, but fashion isn't my big thing at all.' Few people believed her.

Her predicament was summed up by the *Sunday Times*: 'How is she ever — short of abandoning her blonde highlights, gaining a couple of stone and slobbering around in unprincesslike clothes — to be taken as anything more than an exquisitely coiffed airhead?'

Unfortunately, the common perception of the Princess as a delightful dimwit increased the feelings of worthlessness which fuelled her bulimia. By the end of 1985, Diana's eating disorder was almost out of control.

A sailor who had joined them aboard the royal yacht *Britannia* at the end of the Italian tour revealed that the Princess made late-night trips to the ship's galley to gorge herself on industrial-sized tubs of strawberry and vanilla ice cream. Later he recalled, 'We all knew what she was doing but we couldn't understand why she didn't put on weight. None of us had ever heard of bulimia.'

While they continued to put on a show of togetherness in public, Charles and Diana made no secret of their growing hostility in private. One man on their staff remembers, 'As I arrived for work on summer mornings, I could hear them arguing through the open windows of their bedroom. The Princess would scream hysterically and slam doors. We all tippy-toed around the house until she calmed down again.'

The only joy the couple seemed to share was being with their children. They were both besotted by their little boys and relished every minute with them.

That summer, Diana was marooned once again at Balmoral, far from her friends in London, and unwilling to join Charles in his favourite outdoor pursuits — fishing and stalking. She became increasingly lonely and restless. Accustomed to a daily dip in the Buckingham Palace pool, she missed the regular exercise which kept her in good shape mentally and physically.

The Queen had little sympathy for Diana's ill-concealed irritation. She would not consider building a private pool at either Balmoral or Sandringham, believing that her family could get plenty of exercise walking, stalking and on shooting parties.

To fill her empty hours, Diana began spending a lot of time with Sergeant Barry Mannakee who had been promoted to guard her after spending some months with Prince William. They were often seen strolling through the grounds of Balmoral Castle. The handsome police officer pushed Prince Harry in his pram while Diana chatted away at his side. Any passer-by might easily have mistaken them for a young married couple out for a walk with their own baby.

Their friendship sparked off speculation in the press when Jim Bennett, a freelance photographer, spotted them speeding along the road between Braemar and Crathie, not far from Balmoral Castle. He followed them for 30 miles along the road to Aberdeen. When the Princess finally noticed who was coming up fast behind her, she slammed on the brakes, did an expert handbrake turn, just the way she had been taught by the SAS, and zoomed back the way she had come. It seemed a very strange way to behave and the photographer quickly told all his colleagues about it.

Although only a sergeant, Mannakee seemed extremely popular with the Princess. He was a good-looking charmer from the East End of London and he was married. No one was surprised when, less than a year later, the likeable protection officer was transferred to other duties. At the time, Mannakee claimed he had requested the transfer for personal reasons. 'The job meant long hours away from home,' he explained, but his roving eye was considered to be the real reason for the loss of his much-prized position.

His marriage was going through a rough patch and he had become involved with an attractive housemaid at Kensington Palace. One night, when Charles and Diana's staff were invited to tour the studios at Independent Television News in London, he chatted up another woman on his bosses' payroll and took her home. This caused a flare-up between the two girls fighting for his attention and the romeo bodyguard got his marching orders.

Since then, several royal observers have claimed that Diana was also romantically involved with Mannakee. This seems doubtful when he was already entangled with two other women apart from his wife.

Tragically, in May 1987, Barry Mannakee was killed in a road accident. He was a passenger on a motorbike driven by a colleague which was in a collision with a car. This was enough to start wild allegations that he had been murdered by mysterious forces to protect the Princess's reputation. This conspiracy theory soon collapsed when it was revealed that the vehicle which smashed into Mannakee was driven by a 17-year-old novice girl driver.

Prince Charles was informed of the accident next day, and he broke the news to his wife as they were on the point of leaving London to attend the Cannes Film Festival. Diana fled from the room in tears but, by the time she arrived at the festival, she had regained her composure. In public, she had learned to mask her true feelings and present a wonderful impersonation of a happily married woman.

Malicious gossip continued to circulate whenever Diana spent time with another man. For some months it centred on Philip Dunne, an old Etonian banker and the son of the Lord Lieutenant of Hereford and Worcester. The Princess had spent a weekend at Dunne's family home, Gatley Park, in Herefordshire. His parents were not at home but there were others in the house party including Philip Dunne's sister Millie, who had become close to Diana.

In 1987, Diana monopolised Dunne at the wedding of the Marquis of Worcester to Tracy Ward, creating a great deal of comment in the press. It was noticed that Prince Charles left the reception in the early hours of the morning but his wife stayed on dancing and flirting with Dunne. Was she really interested in the handsome banker? Or was she merely trying to annoy Prince Charles, who spent a great deal of the evening talking to Camilla Parker Bowles? The gossip soon petered out when Dunne married Domenica Fraser, the daughter of a former chairman of Rolls Royce, and Diana was there to wish them both every happiness.

When the Prince and Princess set off on their second official visit to Australia in October that year, Diana was alarmingly thin. *Sun* photographer Arthur Edwards recalls, 'As I photographed her, I realised for the first time how much weight she had lost. Her dresses hung loosely on her skeletal frame and her shoulder blades were protruding through her skin. Her lovely face had not an ounce of spare flesh on it.'

But Diana's reputation as a dedicated follower of fashion convinced the public that she was only trying to do justice to her designer clothes. By the mid-Eighties she was regarded as the greatest ambassador the British fashion industry had ever had.

The Palace's repeated denials that the Princess had an eating disorder had been believed simply because Diana appeared so cheerful and energetic. She joked with the public and the press on walkabouts and carried out her duties faultlessly. Apart from her slender figure, there was no outward sign of any inner difficulty.

This was the era of 'Dynasty Di', when the Princess favoured power dressing with sharply tailored suits featuring large shoulder pads, partly inspired by American TV soap operas.

Her slim shape was essential to fly the flag for British designers, or so everyone imagined. Only a very few realised that Diana was suicidally depressed and her despairing husband was at his wits' end.

Once again, Palace officials seemed to ignore the problems Diana was experiencing and committed her to undertake a double tour. After Australia, Charles and Diana would go on to visit Washington, the first time they had appeared together in the United States.

The Prince and Princess arrived in Melbourne to help Victorians celebrate the 150th anniversary of the state. To all appearances, it was just like a re-run of their first visit two years earlier — with one exception. Diana no longer smiled endlessly. When she was bored, she didn't bother to hide the fact.

On a visit to Rotamah Island, the Princess took little interest in her surroundings, and the photographs taken there show she could not wait to escape. She enjoyed visiting the children's ward of a hospital but, understandably, was not so entranced by an aluminium smelter at Portland. The Victorian government had spent a lot of money on it and the royal couple were expected to give it the seal of approval.

Both Charles and Diana had little interest in flat racing. Since ending his days as a National Hunt jockey, Charles now rarely visits racetracks, and has even cut down the number of days he attends Royal Ascot week, the highlight of the summer social calendar in Britain. In the early years of their marriage, Charles and Diana used to accompany the Queen to Epsom in Surrey to watch the Derby, one of Europe's greatest horse races, but the Prince always sat in the back of the royal box working on official papers and didn't take the slightest interest in any of the races.

In Victoria, he and Diana dutifully attended Australia's premier sporting event, the Melbourne Cup. Apparently unaware that there is generally as much interest in the fashions on the field as there is in the starters and riders, Diana turned up in a black and white Bruce Oldfield outfit she had worn before. Cries of disappointment from fashion editors greeted her appearance. Diana had snubbed the Australian fashion industry, they decided.

In Canberra, they attended the obligatory state dinner and sweltered in soaring temperatures on a trip to Mildura and Echuca.

The most memorable night of the trip came when Charles and Diana attended a dinner dance at the Southern Cross Hotel in Melbourne. Diana had chosen a beige silk gown to wear with a diamond tiara. Through an oversight, the tiara was left behind in London and the Princess had to quickly cobble together another formal look for her big date.

Searching through her jewellery case, she found an emerald choker which had been a gift from the Queen. Tossing aside the beige evening dress, Diana tried on a vivid green gown and asked her hairstylist to help her transform the choker into a headband.

Her ingenious fashion trick wowed press and public alike and it diverted attention away from her scrawny figure. But once again, Diana had strengthened the impression that fashion was her main preoccupation.

Prince Charles often groans when he finds out what he is expected to do on tour. 'The things I do for England,' he complains when some particularly inane idea is suggested. In Victoria, he and Diana were invited to give a boost to road safety by squeezing themselves into cramped toy cars.

Despite this, Diana generally put on a dazzling performance, especially when the press were around. As she strolled through Melbourne Botanic Gardens, an official pointed out exotic plants and flowers. Then, as they walked past a posse of pressmen, Diana giggled, 'And these are the weeds, I presume,' she said pointing to the cameramen.

To the casual observer, she was as much in love with her husband as ever. When she presented Charles with a trophy after he took part in a polo match at Weribee Park, she giggled and blushed.

She donned a hard hat when visiting the building site of Canberra's new Parliament House and chatted away in an animated manner with the Australian Prime Minister Bob Hawke and his wife Hazel. Then it was time to fly off to the United States. Along the route, they stopped to refuel in Fiji and later landed in Honolulu to rest overnight before their American début.

Around this time, Diana's bulimia was so rampant that she was making herself vomit more than five times every day. According to one former employee, she spent a great deal of time on aeroplanes losing her lunch in the loo she shared with Prince Charles. 'The smell of sick revolted him,' says the informant. 'He didn't want to be anywhere near his wife. Like many men, he could not understand her compulsion to gorge then throw up. The Princess refused to seek treatment for the eating disorder and he was beyond caring by that stage.'

Diana arrived in the US capital feeling light-headed and jet-lagged. 'The room is going around and around. I just don't know how I am going to stay upright tonight,' she told me as we chatted at the British embassy. But there was one great bonus involved in the Washington visit, which gave her a boost. At a White House banquet, Hollywood superstars could not wait to cut in when President Reagan led her on to the ballroom floor. While her husband did a majestic waltz with America's First Lady, Diana changed partners to boogie with John Travolta and Saturday Night Fever broke out all over the US capital. A few minutes later, Clint Eastwood whirled her away in his arms and later reported, 'She made my day!'

The man she really wanted as her partner, Russian ballet star Mikhail Baryshnikov, was forced to sit quietly beside her all night. He had injured a leg and was banned from the dance floor. All her life, Diana had been obsessed with ballet and had once hoped to become a ballerina until she grew too tall. For years, she had been a devoted fan of the Bolshoi star who had defected to live in America. So she showered him with sympathetic smiles and compliments, showing him she knew just what she was missing.

Diana revelled in the knowledge that men competed for her attention on other occasions, too. In a desert camp an hour's drive from the Saudi Arabian capital Riyadh, during a tour in November 1986, she acted like a modern-day Sheherazade. Lounging against rich brocade cushions dressed in harem pants and a blue silk tunic, she sat cross-legged on a carpet.

In a scene straight out of *The Arabian Nights*, tribesmen in traditional robes wielding swords with solid gold handles whirled like dervishes in a wild dance. The Princess sat watching, saying little and sipping the thick black coffee offered to welcome all guests on arrival according to Middle Eastern custom. Peeping over the rim of her porcelain cup, she smiled at an Arab prince.

When the royal party moved into another marquee where a sumptuous banquet had been spread out, the dazzled prince decided to honour the slender blonde wife of Britain's future king by serving her himself. He ripped off a chunk of meat from a whole roast sheep with his bare hands and gave it to her. Diana smiled demurely and said, 'It's delicious,' and her eyes sparkled. No diplomat could have made a better impression.

In the Arab world, women are born to serve men and to see this tradition overturned astonished everyone present. Diana and Charles's host in Saudi Arabia, then the world's richest potentate King Fahd, amazed the British contingent by inviting the Princess to his palace. The only other female to have received this high honour was a woman astronaut whom he was obliged to have as his guest because she had rocketed into space with a Saudi prince in her crew.

Diana's flirtatious act continued when she met the President of Portugal, Dr Mario Soares, at the Ajuda Palace, Lisbon, in February 1987. She arrived flaunting bare shoulders in a revealing, strapless dress. Then she proceeded to turn on the charm. She twanged the President's braces, fluttered her eyelashes and joked, 'If I get cold will you help warm me up?' In less than a minute, she had won a new admirer. The only person who did not seem astonished by, or even aware of, the Princess's coquetry was her husband.

It seemed significant that Diana's amazing *femme fatale* routine happened more often when Charles was around. It looked to many observers as if she was trying to remind the Prince how desirable she was.

If so, her efforts were in vain. He publicly put her down on one occasion after a game of polo at Smith's Lawn, Windsor. A loud wolf-whistle split the air as Diana walked out of the royal pavilion to present cups to the winning team. Prince Charles seemed more than a little annoyed by the whistler's cheek, but he gave his wife a kiss to thank her for his prize. As if to get even, she immediately wiped it off her lips with the back of her right hand.

Moments later, they began to slap and push one another in the car park. The battle royal began when Diana gave Fergie's father Major Ronald Ferguson, then Charles's polo manager, a warm goodbye kiss and Prince Charles playfully hit her on the head saying, 'That's enough!'

Diana was not about to let him get away with that and kicked out at her protesting husband, then gave him a hefty push. In return, he shoved her back against her car. Diana then ducked for cover but, as she jumped into the driving seat, he brought one hand down on the back of her neck. Realising that people were staring in amazement, the couple laughed, but no one was in any doubt that the pushing and shoving looked too forceful to be funny. The rows that were regularly taking place inside their home were now spilling out into public view.

In the first six months of 1987, Charles deserted his wife on five different occasions to enjoy holiday breaks

THE TRUTH

without her, resulting in the first press reports that they were leading separate lives. In February, he had stayed on alone, skiing in Switzerland, after she flew back home to work. In March, he had returned to the Alps to spend a long weekend in Gstaad with friends. Then, in early April after a tour of Southern Africa, he had disappeared into the desert with author and mystic Sir Laurens van der Post. A month later, he left his family once again to spend three days salmon fishing in the River Dee. To most people, it seemed a strange way to conduct a marriage.

By the time their sixth wedding anniversary arrived, Charles was deserting his wife at every opportunity. She had to find her own fun going out with a younger crowd. Then a story leaked out that sent shockwaves through Fleet Street. Charles and Diana had attended a weekend house party and insisted on separate bedrooms!

This astonishing news was given credence by several statements from the Princess. She fuelled the fires of gossip by telling a large number of people that she was taking a long break from pregnancy. 'I'm not a production line, you know,' she said tartly when a woman on a walkabout asked if a third baby would come along soon.

At a meeting with the media in February 1987, she backed this up by rubbing her stomach and declaring, 'By the way, I'm not.' Two months later she said it again. 'I'm too busy to have any babies for at least a year. I have to go to Australia next January.' Then she added mysteriously, 'You see, I'm safe,' again gesturing towards her stomach. Privately, she was telling friends, 'Fat chance of that happening!'

Their arrival in Sydney the following January would become their last together down under. Members of the

53

Royal Family never visit Australia in high summer because it is simply too hot. Charles and Diana had had no choice. They had been elected to represent the Queen at the Bicentennial celebrations of the country's foundation.

The highlight of their schedule on 26 January, Australia Day, was a naval parade at Sydney Harbour. A heatwave had hit the city of Sydney and Diana was growing increasingly uncomfortable in her dress and broad-brimmed hat. From the deck of *HMAS Swan*, from which Charles was due to take the salute, she gazed enviously at people aboard pleasure-craft on the harbour who were dressed in shorts, swimsuits and little else.

It had been planned that she would return to Admiralty House where they were staying to cool off. But Diana declared she was too hot to move and had to have a shower immediately. Startled officers on board the warship were in a quandary. There were no facilities on board suitable for a Princess, but Diana would not listen.

She wanted a shower and she wanted it *now*! Eventually, she was led down to the crew's quarters and stripped off to freshen up under a cold stream of water.

Meanwhile, Prince Charles, embarrassed and not quite sure what to say, chatted with the Captain and his officers. While he waited for his wife to reappear, the fleet of ships taking part in the naval salute was diverted to circle endlessly around Goat Island in the middle of the harbour.

The entire grand naval parade was thrown into chaos because Diana could not stand the heat. Officials were sympathetic but commented that the Queen had frequently endured much higher temperatures on her

Australian trips. Royal princesses were not expected to look bored, tired or hot.

Incidents such as this made Prince Charles, who always stuck scrupulously to his schedule, grow weary of working with his unpredictable wife. He was broiling in a woollen suit, shirt and tie, yet he showed no sign of feeling the heat.

At a reception in Adelaide, Diana looked sulky and tearful, according to one onlooker. On another engagement in Goolwa, she did not hide the fact that she was wilting in the fierce sunshine. Years of frustration had forced Diana to take a stand. Tired of being ordered to undertake one gruelling trip after another, she had decided to rebel.

4

At 1.00pm on Wednesday, 9 December 1992, the television monitors around the House of Commons and MPs' offices flashed up an urgent message: 'PRIME MINISTER'S STATEMENT AT 3.30pm'. Puzzled MPs began to ask one another what this might mean. Was some international incident imminent?

When John Major rose to speak at the appointed time, the House was as packed as it would have been for the twice-weekly confrontation of Prime Minister's Questions. Members were crammed into the benches, standing in the aisles and sitting on the carpeted stairs.

With a solemn expression, the Prime Minister looked around the chamber then began: 'With permission, Madam Speaker, I wish to inform the House that Buckingham Palace is at this moment issuing the following statement. It reads as follows: "It is announced from Buckingham Palace that, with regret, the Prince and Princess of Wales have decided to separate."'

He went on to explain that the royal couple had no plans for divorce and to declare somewhat inexplicably that their constitutional positions were unaffected. Then, on a personal note, he added, 'I am sure that I speak for the whole House — and millions beyond it — in offering our support to both the Prince and Princess of Wales. I am also sure that the House will sympathise with the wish that they should both be afforded a degree of privacy.'

There was a stunned silence as the significance of what he had said sank in, then gasps of incredulity swept the chamber. John Major then repeated that the decision to separate had no constitutional implications and declared that 'there is no reason why the Princess of Wales should not be crowned Queen in due course'.

The former Conservative Prime Minister Sir Edward Heath, the member for Old Bexley and Sidcup, stood to add a few words.

'I think that the House would wish me, as Father of the House, to express the understanding of the whole House of the action which has been taken.' He added, 'It must be one of the saddest announcements made by any Prime Minister in modern times.'

Senior backbencher Robin Corbett, the Labour member for Birmingham Erdington, recalls the amazement he and all his colleagues felt. 'We had no inkling of what was to come when the Prime Minister began to speak. The news dropped like a bombshell over the House. Perhaps a few members of the Cabinet knew what was happening, but most of us didn't. We were totally shocked. It was the only topic of conversation in the tea rooms and bars later. A seismic shock had rocked the throne and we were all wondering what this separation would mean for Britain, as well as for the monarchy.'

His astonishment was echoed by millions throughout the country and the rest of the world, who had assumed that the Waleses' marriage simply had to work, despite Charles and Diana's well-publicised differences.

Visiting a school for children with special needs in Tyne and Wear that day, Diana put on a brave face, but journalists covering her visit noted that for much of the time her mind was not on her job. She had a distant look in her eyes that implied she was not in a mood to celebrate the declaration of her liberty.

It should have been the day that Diana had longed for, the day she imagined when the gates of freedom would spring open at last. Yet it was not turning out to be the happy release she had expected. Just days earlier, she had spent the weekend of the Windsor Castle fire removing the bulk of her remaining belongings from Highgrove House, the country home she had shared with her husband. No matter what had passed between them, they had planned this home together and had shared many happy memories there with their children. In 1981 she had called Highgrove 'my dream home'. Now she was leaving it for ever.

While Prince Charles toured the smouldering ruins of his family's most ancient home, his wife was busy stuffing the last vestiges of her married life into suitcases. She had chosen to return to Highgrove while Charles was away enjoying a shooting party at Sandringham, but he had interrupted it to rush to Windsor after the inferno.

Diana's move was carried out with the aid of her sister Lady Jane Fellowes, wife of the Queen's then Private Secretary, Sir Robert. Staff who watched the departure, reported that Diana used an old Land Rover to remove her belongings, as well as her own car. She took away photographs, correspondence, mementoes, some wedding presents and a small amount of clothing. The bulk of her designer wardrobe had always been kept at Kensington Palace.

The Buckingham Palace announcement, which the Prime Minister delivered so dramatically, marked the end, not just of a royal marriage, but of a process which had really begun three years earlier.

On a frosty morning early in 1990, the Princess had learned that a telephone call she had received from her car dealer friend James Gilbey, speaking from a mobile in his car parked in an Oxfordshire lay-by, had been bugged. It was an extremely intimate conversation, punctuated with kisses, in which Diana talked about the 'torture' of her marriage to her ardent admirer, who repeatedly declared his love for her and called her by her pet-name 'Squidgy'. The couple discussed a planned rendezvous when the Princess returned to London from Sandringham, and she warned her caller, 'I don't want to get pregnant.'

A tape recording of their electrifying phone conversation had been passed to the *Sun* newspaper by a Mr Cyril Reenan, a retired bank manager from Abingdon, Berks, who claimed he had recorded the conversation on a £900 scanner linked to an aerial in his garden. An amateur radio enthusiast, he regularly used his equipment to tune in to police and air traffic control transmissions.

Investigations by security firms later revealed that amateurs like Mr Reenan would not normally have been able to record such high-quality conversations in which both voices were at the same level. And there was no doubt that he had not, in fact, recorded the phone call 'live', as it had actually occurred. The couple made clear they were talking on New Year's Eve, 1989, but Mr Reenan had taped their chat five days later on 4 January 1990. This suggested that someone with advanced technical know-how had monitored the original call on highly sophisticated equipment, and then rebroadcast it for amateurs to pick up. Conspiracy theorists would later claim that the only organisations with the means to do this would have been MI5, GCHQ or the CIA. Within hours, Downing Street dismissed this as 'nonsensical'. A later investigation by Cellnet, the mobile phone company used by James Gilbey, indicated that electronic eavesdropping had occurred on the landline Diana was using at Sandringham.

After checking the tape's authenticity, journalists from the *Sun* newspaper confronted Gilbey outside his flat in Lennox Gardens, close to Kensington Palace. His jaw dropped open with shock, but he refused to make any comment, flinching only at the mention of the word 'Squidgy'. Then he jumped into his new Saab, and quickly drove away.

It seems safe to assume that, as soon as possible, panic-stricken Gilbey told Diana what had happened. He would have been desperate to warn her that an eavesdropper had listened in to their late-night call.

From then on, Diana knew that a time-bomb with her name on it was waiting to explode. She naturally expected that the newspaper would publish its red-hot revelations imminently and lived in dread of what this would do to her reputation. At the time, she could do no wrong in the eyes of the world and was sarcastically known as 'the one who walks on water' at Buckingham Palace. Now, here was a phone call in which the adored Princess talked about masturbation, used four-letter words and made spiteful comments about her friend Fergie. What would her adoring public think if it was published?

Instead of rushing into print, *Sun* executives decided it would not be wise to expose the Princess to such brutal humiliation and locked the incriminating tape away in the office safe. Such discretion no doubt puzzled the mystery person or persons who had recorded and released what became known as the 'Dianagate' tape. Some months later, another newspaper also received a copy of the taped phone call but, once again, it declined to publish the Princess's indiscretions.

Unaware of this, Diana realised that she had to launch a pre-emptive strike to defend herself. This is no doubt one of the main reasons she decided to co-operate with Andrew Morton on his Palace-quaking bestseller *Diana: Her True Story*. Since 1986, when she had begun an affair with cavalry officer James Hewitt, Diana had been fantasising about escaping from the Royal Family.

They had met at a Mayfair drinks party towards the end of summer 1986. Learning that he was a Staff Captain involved in running the Household Division stables, she told him about her fear of riding and he offered to give her lessons at the Knightsbridge Barracks. Within days, the Princess telephoned him and Hewitt became her instructor. It wasn't long before they were involved in a passionate affair which, on and off, would last for five years.

It seems almost certain that Prince Charles knew of his wife's liaison with the red-haired riding instructor

THE TRUTH

and gave it his tacit approval. James Hewitt certainly seems to believe that the Prince was happy to have his tiresome wife otherwise involved. There is no doubt that officers from the Royal Protection Squad would have known about it as they guarded the Princess and accompanied her everywhere. They would automatically have informed their superiors of the relationship, who would have felt it their duty to warn Prince Charles.

The romance did provide Diana with a great deal of solace and the passion that had been missing from her life — at least for a while. In 1989, Hewitt had been posted with his regiment to Paderborn in Germany and an angry Diana had accused him of abandoning her. Suddenly she stopped taking his phone calls and claimed she was too busy to see him. While he was away, she renewed her friendship with James Gilbey, whom she had known before her marriage, when they met at a dinner party. But when Hewitt returned to London and soon afterwards was sent to fight in the Gulf War, Diana was so concerned for his safety that all her old feelings for him returned.

This reawakening of their romance was not to last. Her own desire for self-preservation forced her to be more careful about her private life. Hewitt had begun to enjoy approaches from the press. He had become used to being wined and dined by executives and he talked to one or two about his affair with the Princess. His lack of discretion made him too dangerous to have around at a time when the unexploded Dianagate bomb was still waiting to go off. Hewitt was soon just a part of her past.

Learning about the incriminating tape recording undoubtedly spurred Diana into defensive action. During the summer and autumn of 1991, she sat in her

Kensington Palace sitting room pouring out all the anguish of her unhappy marriage into a tape recorder. The tapes were passed on to Morton via go-between Dr James Colthurst, and published as a book in June 1992. He republished the book with transcripts from these tapes within weeks of Diana's death in 1997.

Suddenly, the dark side of the fairytale marriage was exposed in all its ugliness. At last, the world could learn how Charles's affair with Camilla had driven Diana to attempt suicide.

The girl whose life had seemed so golden was actually plagued by the eating disorder anorexia, loneliness and despair.

The entire book read like a petition for divorce. It was extremely one-sided and, in places, rather inaccurate, as Diana had left gaps in her narrative which the author had somehow to fill. Millions immediately voiced their sympathy for the Princess betrayed by an uncaring husband, and denounced Prince Charles.

Officially, Buckingham Palace did not react or work out any strategy to counteract this devastating blow to the heir to the throne. A senior aide declared, 'We are not going to dignify it by making any comment at all.'

Privately, it was a different matter. When Charles confronted Diana about her part in the blockbuster she stood her ground and yelled at him, 'Now try and get rid of me!' The future king's top advisers perceived the book as a brilliant public relations exercise carried out by a vindictive woman. They were convinced Diana was behind the bestseller, not just because it portrayed her as a saint-like heroine, but because several of her best friends had been interviewed for it.

Diana turned up on the doorstep of one of

THE TRUTH

Morton's principal informants, Carolyn Bartholomew, just three days after the first extract from the book was serialised in the *Sunday Times*. Press photographers were there in force to capture this endorsement by Diana of her friend's inside story because newspapers had been tipped off about her arrival by a mystery woman caller.

The message was quite clear — the Princess was grateful that her supporters had spoken out in her defence. The fairytale had ended to be replaced by a Gothic horror story.

Just days after Morton's controversial opus hit the bookstores, the Princess visited a hospice in Southport, Merseyside. The enormous sympathy felt by everyone there can be gauged from a welcoming speech delivered by the chairman Bill Davidson.

'God bless you and may you always remain, Ma'am, just you,' he told her.

Diana bit her lip, fighting to hold back tears and kept her eyes fixed on her posy as he went on to pay tribute to her 'tender, loving, care'. But after struggling to control her emotions inside the hospice, she burst into a flood of tears on a walkabout outside. The following day, newspapers reported that the pent-up emotion she had been determined to hide spilled out when she was overwhelmed by the love and support of well-wishers.

The truth, never before revealed until now, was somewhat different. A keen young girl reporter, standing in the crowd, managed to confront Diana and ask the question that was in everyone's mind: 'Did you really help Andrew Morton to write his book?'

In the middle of what Diana imagined would be a crowd of sympathisers, these daring words were totally unexpected. It was the question she could not answer, so an embarrassed Diana evaded a reply by breaking down. It was not difficult. She had been shaking with nerves when she arrived, wondering how people would react to the book's revelations of her suicide attempts, self-mutilation and bulimia. Covering her face with her hands, she turned to her Scotland Yard bodyguard Dave Sharp, who quickly escorted her to her car.

The *Sun* newspaper ran this story with an exclusive photograph of Diana's tearful face, which was syndicated to newspapers all over the world. Photographer Mark Tattersall had earlier arrived at the job and attempted to join the pen reserved for the press. As another photographer from his newspaper was already in it, he was turned away. Walking down the street, feeling he was wasting his time, he spotted a gap in the crowd and decided to try to snap the Princess if she came his way. By an incredible stroke of luck, he was standing very near Diana when her tears began to flow. The photograph he never expected to get earned a fortune in foreign rights and a £500 bonus for Mark Tattersall.

Every member of the Royal Family also suspected that Diana was behind the book's revelations but they could not prove it and, when questioned, she categorically denied any involvement. Despite this, her in-laws reacted by forcing Diana into permanent internal exile. No one spoke to her; she became a non-person in royal circles. The evil Empire was striking back.

Two months later, when she travelled to Balmoral with Charles and their children for the annual summer holiday in the Highlands, she was totally cut off from the friends who had supported her in London. In the glorious scenery of Deeside, where generations of Windsors have found peace and inspiration, Diana

THE TRUTH

experienced only alienation and misery. She was isolated in the enemy camp, constantly watched yet disregarded.

One evening, a troop of entertainers from the Edinburgh Festival travelled to Balmoral to stage a private show for the Queen and her family. A member of the cast reported afterwards, 'I could not help noticing that the Princess sat on her own, quite a distance from the rest of her relatives. Even her son, Prince William, was sitting on a cushion at the Queen's feet, not with his mother.'

When the programme ended, the actors were invited to enjoy supper with their hosts and noted that no one went near to or spoke to Diana. 'She was totally excluded from their company,' the entertainer reported.

On 24 August, this distressing situation was made worse when the *Sun* finally published extracts of the 'Squidgygate' conversation. An American supermarket tabloid, the *National Inquirer*, had just gone on sale with an article based on the astounding telephone conversation. Hoping to gain a beat on its rivals, the *Sun* ran a transcript of the phone call, deleting only what were described as 'more intimate' exchanges between the couple.

For two-and-a-half years, Diana had been living in fear of this exposure. The strain of worrying whether each day would bring this explosive relationship to light can only be imagined. She no longer knew who to trust and was convinced that she was under constant surveillance.

Many royal observers were convinced that the Princess's army of admirers would be disillusioned by the Dianagate tape, which so clearly suggested that she had also broken her marriage vows. Diana herself was sure it would destroy her. Nothing of the kind happened.

Surprisingly, the public did not lose faith in its adored Princess. The general reaction from the public was that Charles's neglect had driven his wife to find comfort in the arms of another man. He had become an even blacker villain than before. The Morton book had fulfilled its purpose extremely well. The world wished only to believe that Charles was a monster and Diana a martyr.

At Balmoral, of course, her relationship with Gilbey was not forgiven so easily. Diana was shunned by everyone but, by an extraordinary stroke of luck, her discomfort did not last long. On 20 August, the spotlight switched to her sister-in-law the Duchess of York, when photographs of her cavorting with her financial adviser John Bryan in St Tropez were published in the *Daily Mirror*. Now it was Sarah's turn to experience the hostility of the Royal Family gathered at their Highland home.

The beleaguered Princess received yet another boost when the *Daily Mirror* published reports of a far more sensational taped telephone conversation between Prince Charles and Camilla Parker Bowles. When the full extent of this explicit call became known in January 1993, the Dianagate tape seemed tame by comparison. A transcript of the recording emerged in an Australian magazine and 24 hours later appeared in a British tabloid.

The Prince of Wales had been metaphorically caught with his trousers down, declaring his love for his mistress and discussing various ways he wished to satisfy her. He fantasised about coming back in the next life inside Camilla's trousers, but guessed that, with his luck, he would return as a tampon. Astonishing in its adolescent crudery, the 'Camillagate' tape heaped more humiliation on a prince already regarded as a treacherous scoundrel. It also confirmed that Diana had been right to walk away from her sham marriage. For months, the world wondered how the Prince of Wales could ever recover from these shameful revelations.

But Diana was not totally vindicated. She came under further pressure for deceit over her dealings with the media. When the Morton book went on sale, she misled the Queen's secretary, her brother-in-law Sir Robert Fellowes, by denying that she had been involved with it. She also insisted she was not using the press to make her marriage problems public, when, in fact, she was briefing friends who passed on the information.

When informed by editors of Diana's clandestine co-operation with newspapers, the Press Complaints Commission chairman Lord McGregor declared that 'the Princess had, in practice, been invading her own privacy.' Film director and columnist Michael Winner would later sum up the situation more bluntly. 'She is a publicity junkie addicted to the fame of her job.'

Slowly and inevitably, Diana was being downgraded and shoved on to the royal sidelines. Despite this Establishment hostility, the public's demand for the fairytale marriage to continue was such that few people outside Whitehall, Fleet Street and Court circles suspected Charles and Diana were desperate to be rid of each other.

For a month or two, it looked as if the worst was over, then the Queen insisted that a reluctant Diana should undertake a tour of Korea with her husband in November. The look of misery on Diana's face throughout the four-day trip revealed more eloquently than any words that the charade had ended. Until then, most people had imagined that this marriage was the one that would stagger on for the sake of their children and the monarchy. Somehow, the couple would muddle through. Then Diana's agonising look proved there was no hope left. Not once did she gaze at her husband or even speak to him. Instead, her determined indifference was splashed over every front page.

On the morning after their arrival in Seoul, I sat down with a group of other reporters covering the trip and predicted, 'This must be their last tour together. They cannot go on like this.' Each day brought more evidence of the cold war each waged against the other. None of us had ever seen such behaviour by members of the Royal Family before. We could not believe our eyes.

They seemed to be on two different tours. When they walked down a staircase, Diana stuck to one side with her entourage while he stayed on the other with his. They appeared to be separated, not just by a few metres but more than 1,000 miles.

True to his training, Charles kept his private feelings under a tight rein, but Diana could not disguise her distress any longer. Each day, photographers and reporters gawped with astonishment at the tricks Diana used to indicate her loathing for her husband. During an official welcome at the Blue House, the Princess looked utterly miserable until it was time to leave. Then she looked over at photographer Mark Stewart and gave him a wink. Her 'unhappiness' was being deliberately staged for the media.

When they arrived at the de-militarised zone separating North and South Korea, the Princess silently stood to one side refusing to join in while Prince Charles chatted to Korean War veterans. Then, just when the visit was ending and her husband was making for their car, she decided to approach the old soldiers and kept him waiting while she talked for some minutes. At a banquet in Seoul, she rolled her eyes to

Heaven, giving every sign of being thoroughly bored when he delivered a speech. Her message was unmistakable — I didn't want to come here so don't expect me to pretend I'm enjoying it.

It was still a shock three weeks later when John Major declared the couple had legally separated.

Ever since the late Eighties when Charles had begun spending weeks away from his wife, the public had known the marriage was under strain. Still, most people hoped the couple would work out some kind of reconciliation. Ordinary people separated and got divorced but future kings and queens did not, or so we wanted to believe. Monarchs existed to set an example to the rest of us. The fairytale union of the dashing prince and his lovely bride had symbolised all our hopes.

How could the vows made before millions in a round-the-world TV spectacular be broken? Charles without Diana was unthinkable. What did this mean for the monarchy, for the nation and, in particular, for their two young boys?

The statement issued by Buckingham Palace following their official separation only confused the issue further and led to weeks of heated debate. It repeated the Prime Minister's declaration that 'there is no reason why Her Royal Highness should not become Queen'.

Within hours, leading pundits were disputing this. How could a couple who could not stand each other share a throne? It seemed unlikely that Palace advisers would ever permit a woman they regarded as a traitor to become Queen. No doubt, a divorce would inevitably follow which would make it impossible for Diana to reign alongside Charles.

The statement also stressed that the separation was

'amicable', adding, 'They are still fond of one another.' Just weeks after the hostility evident on the Korean tour, this seemed hard to swallow. It went on, 'There have been no third parties involved, on either side, in this decision.' To everyone who knew of Camilla Parker Bowles' role in the marriage break-up this seemed ludicrous.

At first, Diana had been elated when the news broke. All alone, she had confronted her husband's family and won. Everything would go on as before, she assumed, only without the presence of her husband. A new life seemed to be opening up before her. She had hinted at this on a trip to Paris just days before her separation was made public. While chatting with *Sun* photographer Arthur Edwards, she appeared quite different from the unhappy woman who had flown home from Korea less than a week earlier.

She looked triumphant as if she was celebrating a great personal victory and talked excitedly about her plans for the future. 'I'm going to Nepal next year with the Red Cross,' Diana declared.

'Will the Prince be going with you?' the photographer asked.

Shaking her head, she gazed straight at him. 'No, it's time to spread my wings.'

The message was unmistakable. Diana was about to break away from the Royal Family and go her own way.

Almost immediately, a campaign to rehabilitate Charles was orchestrated. At the same time, with cruel efficiency, the diminishing of Diana in the eyes of the public began.

The Queen's advisers did not once publicly attack the Princess, but the sound of axes being sharpened seemed to be echoing down every corridor in

Buckingham Palace. The number of foreign tours she planned to undertake was mysteriously cut to one — a four-day visit to Nepal — and Charles's sympathisers began spreading pro-Prince propaganda. They agreed to co-operate with author Jonathan Dimbleby on a sycophantic biography of the Prince.

Soon, more revelations leaked out about Diana's relationship with James Gilbey and on her arrival in Katmandu she was given a rather second-rate welcome on what was claimed to be advice from London. The Establishment was closing ranks against Diana, as it had once ostracised Wallis Simpson when she had shaken the foundations of the monarchy almost 50 years earlier.

1993 proved to be far more testing than Diana had ever imagined, but she did herself no favours by behaving erratically. Just after Easter, she secretly flew off to spend a weekend on the Costa del Sol with her friends Catherine Soames and Kate Menzies. Photographers quickly tracked her down to the Hotel Byblos in Fuengirola, which was soon packed with paparazzi. Although she was aware of their presence and ordered the hotel management to throw them out, Diana decided to sunbathe topless by the swimming pool in plain view of other guests.

One of the Spanish paparazzi hidden in a hotel room snapped her from his balcony and, within hours, was offering his pictures to the highest bidder. A Spanish guest sitting just yards from the Princess later described her amazement. 'I could not believe it when Lady Di dropped her top. After two children, gravity had taken its toll and she was not looking her best. Apparently, this didn't worry her. She seemed to want to be photographed. There was no other explanation.'

To save the Princess's blushes, Eduardo Sanchez

Junco, publisher of Spain's top magazine *Hola!*, gallantly bought the shots of a topless Diana to keep them off the market. Instead of being grateful, the Princess never forgave him, believing he did it in order to put her in his debt. Today, the rather unflattering photographs remain locked away in a safe in Madrid.

As her conduct continued to astonish and dismay courtiers, it was not difficult for Charles's friends and supporters to denigrate her openly, and there were accusations that she was planning to set up a rival court. If Charles and Diana carried out engagements on the same day, hers was reported extensively by the media and his was ignored. Despite the separation, Diana was still overshadowing him.

To prevent this, Charles insisted that she must submit all her official engagements to his office for approval. 'He pays the piper, so he calls the tune,' a member of his staff commented. Weary of this constant criticism, Diana made up her mind to walk away from the spotlight and leave the stage to Charles.

Her resolve was strengthened when Peeping Tom pictures of her exercising in a gym were published in November 1993. Despite Palace advice to ignore this wounding intrusion, Diana declared her 'distress and deep sense of outrage'. The knowledge that an unseen eye had been watching her as she had worked out seemed to increase the Princess's paranoia. She believed she was not safe anywhere and could trust no one.

She quickly won a High Court ban on further publication of the pictures taken with a hidden camera, but some time later an out-of-court settlement was agreed.

As the year drew to an end, Diana was under an intolerable strain. Many of her formerly loyal staff were deserting her. Her chauffeur, Simon Solari, swapped sides to work for Prince Charles; her favourite Scotland Yard bodyguard Ken Wharfe asked for a transfer to another job and, six weeks later, his deputy Peter Brown was also removed from her side. Unwilling to be guarded by strangers, she asked for and received permission to dispense with all police protection in a desperate attempt to lead a normal life. After months of relentless strain, Diana was living on the edge.

On a bitterly cold December day, she arrived at the Hilton Hotel in Park Lane for a charity lunch at which she announced her decision to retire completely from public life. Word had quickly spread through the media what the Princess was planning and television crews from all over the globe had flocked to this sensational event. Independent Television News, aware that this was a story of major public interest, decided to run it live.

Press photographers were lined up four-deep, perched precariously on their ladders, jostling for the best picture. But Diana did not give them a single glance as she swept through the glass doors.

For two-and-a-half hours, she sat making small-talk with her hosts while she tried to eat her lunch and sipped sparkling mineral water. Then she stood up, took a prepared speech out of a plastic holder and dropped her bombshell.

'When I started my public life 12 years ago, I understood that the media might be interested in what I did. I realised then that their attention would inevitably focus on both our private and public lives. But I was not aware of how overwhelming that attention would become, nor the extent to which it would affect both my public duties and my personal life, in a manner that has been hard to bear.

'At the end of this year, when I have completed my diary of official engagements, I will be reducing the extent of the public life I have led so far. I attach great importance to my charity work and intend to focus on a smaller range of areas in the future.

'Over the next few months, I will be seeking a more suitable way of combining a meaningful public role with, hopefully, a more private life.'

From now on, she declared, her first priority would be her children, to whom she wished to give more love, attention and an appreciation of the tradition into which they were born.

'I hope you can find it in your hearts to understand and to give me the time and space that has been lacking in recent years,' she pleaded.

Her stunned audience leapt to its feet applauding as she walked back to her seat, her flushed face and heavy breathing indicating it had been the most difficult speech of her life.

All too soon, Diana realised that her attempt to escape from the limelight had backfired. As she scaled down her public engagements, each became of much more interest to the media and the public. The demand for news of the popular Princess seemed insatiable.

By the time summer arrived, she had given up all hope of leading a life out of the spotlight and was regularly appearing at events arranged to raise funds for the six charities she was continuing to support. One of these was the Serpentine Gallery in Hyde Park.

At the end of June, she was scheduled to attend a dinner at the gallery. By a fortunate 'coincidence', on the same night, a much-hyped television interview with the Prince — *Charles, the Private Man, the Public Role* — was due to be broadcast. It was planned as the climax of his year-long rehabilitation campaign, a revealing look at the life of a hard-working prince.

The charity dinner gave Diana a superb opportunity to prove that she certainly was not glued to her TV set, waiting to hear what her husband had to say. It also proved that in the game of one-upmanship, the Princess of Wales was a world-class champion.

Looking confident and totally unworried, she stepped from her car wearing a midnight-blue, off-the-shoulder dress that clung to every curve with a skirt slashed to the thigh. It was undoubtedly the most provocative and revealing gown she had ever worn. That night, when newspaper editors had a choice between running a picture of the sober-suited Prince or the seductive Princess on their front pages, there was no contest. Diana had vanquished her husband on the very night he had hoped to score a new victory in the War of the Waleses.

To compound his failure, the Prince rather foolishly confessed that he had committed adultery, an admission that would hinder his attempts to improve his tarnished image for years to come.

Two days later, Diana had every reason to celebrate on her thirty-third birthday. Once again, she had eclipsed Charles and the public had cheered. But Diana knew that the Prince's camp would not forgive her PR success. Soon, the pro-Charles camp would be on the offensive once again.

Throughout this stressful time, Diana was living in limbo, estranged from the Royal Family but not yet divorced. She felt abandoned and very much alone. She was free to start dating again but was afraid of damaging gossip. There were many men keen to be her escort, but what she really needed was a friend she could trust. And she thought she had found one in art dealer Oliver Hoare, whom she had known for several years.

He and his wife, the French heiress Diane de Waldner, were close friends of Prince Charles, who often enjoyed holidays at their family villa in the South of France. An expert on Islamic art, Oliver Hoare was an extremely knowledgeable and sophisticated man whom the Princess seemed at first to regard as a father figure, gradually becoming more dependent on him.

She began visiting his West London home when his wife was away. One night, they were photographed driving into her home at 10.30pm, a strange hour for a married man to visit a princess. When Diana learned that the incriminating photograph would appear in a Sunday tabloid, she made a point of very publicly enjoying a Saturday lunch date with William van Straubenzee, an old family friend. Making no attempt to hide, they both walked down a London street, allowing photographers to shoot dozens of pictures. When one cameraman, bolder than the rest, asked who her companion was, she replied, 'He's a friend. I have lots of men friends.'

Diana believed she had deftly deflected attention from Hoare. To a certain extent, she was correct, but their closeness was finally revealed when Mrs Hoare began to receive nuisance telephone calls and her husband contacted the police. Most of these were traced to Diana's Kensington Palace apartment, although she denied that she was responsible. Hoare distanced himself from the Princess and their meetings ceased.

Worse followed in October 1994, when James Hewitt published the story of his five-year affair with Diana in a book called *Princess In Love*. His account, related by writer Anna Pasternak, told of passionate love-making under Charles's roof at Highgrove and also at Kensington Palace.

Diana's response came in contemptuous statements from Buckingham Palace and her lawyer Lord Mischon. Privately, she told friends, 'We never made love. His account is a fantasy created just to make money.'

A year later, on BBC TV's *Panorama* programme, she would retract this. When asked if they had had an affair, she replied, 'Yes, I was in love with him ... but I was very let down.'

In her loneliness, Diana often reached out to the nearest man who befriended her. None could give her the status she enjoyed as wife of a future king, but this soon ceased to matter. The royal outcast was looking for an outsider like herself, someone who did not live by the rigid rules of the British Establishment, yet someone strong enough to take her on with all her entanglements.

She did not have to wait long before he walked into her life.

5

As 1995 unfolded Princess Diana was at a low ebb. She had been officially separated from Prince Charles for two years and was under increasing pressure from Palace advisers to grant her husband a divorce.

Her past still clouded her new solo existence and her future looked bleak. The press, once so flattering, now seemed to seize every petty excuse to attack her. When a gust of wind had lifted her overcoat, revealing a skirt split to the thigh, on her way to church on Christmas Day at Sandringham, the *Daily Mail* screeched that she looked cheap.

Why did she favour a style that was already two seasons out of date? writer Lydia Slater asked. 'The answer can only be that the recent spell out of the public eye has proved less attractive than she originally imagined,' the journalist wrote. 'And, like a showgirl, she's making the most of her physical assets to lure back the spotlight.'

This was no ordinary comment on Diana's fashion sense. The story went on to claim that the sight of her wind-blown skirt revealed 'not just legs exposed by her choice of attire. It's her naked ambition.' Describing the Princess as 'a mistress of manipulation', the newspaper added, 'She probably knows better than anybody — except Liz Hurley — how the paparazzi love a glamorous outfit.'

Just a few weeks later, a report in the London *Evening Standard* claimed Diana had used a medium to contact her dead relatives. Diana had 'dabbled' with the occult as often as once a fortnight, the paper alleged, as 'she fought with mental instability'. It seemed a blatant attempt to ridicule her and warned that her interest in spiritualism would almost certainly cause anger in church circles.

Such diatribes added to Diana's increasing cynicism about the media. For years she had been the newspapers' favourite celebrity; now many were more sympathetic to her estranged husband. No longer destined to share his throne, she had become mere Nikon or Canon fodder for the cameramen, simply an easy way to fill columns of newsprint.

Worse was to follow in March when she went skiing with her sons in Lech, Austria. Continental photographers stalked her constantly until she complained that she felt as if she was being 'raped'. To stop and pose for pictures might have been easier, but Diana was aware that this would bring accusations that she was using her children to gain publicity. Whatever she did would invite criticism.

To add to her private torment, Diana believed her phone was tapped, her home watched and her every move logged. She would later reveal she knew that certain people were deliberately making her life difficult 'by visits abroad being blocked, by things that had come naturally my way being stopped, letters that got lost and various things ...'

Camilla Parker Bowles and her husband Andrew had divorced in January, and Diana was in no doubt that her own husband wished to be rid of her soon, so that he could start a new life with the woman he had always loved.

Diana's withdrawal from public life the previous year had done little to achieve her greatest aim, the chance to lead a normal life. Forced to admit that this was an impossible dream, she began to reconsider her future. Diana was convinced that she needed to find a new role, one that would exploit her worldwide fame to benefit others. She was determined to be taken seriously.

A visit to Tokyo in February briefly lifted her spirits as the Japanese people gave her an overwhelming welcome. The trip, along with another to Russia, had been cancelled a year earlier while Whitehall mandarins decided if she should be allowed to venture into such politically sensitive areas. Two previous trips to Japan in 1986 and 1990 had been traffic-stopping triumphs with more than 100,000 people lining the streets at every event she attended. Since then, Dimania had dwindled after her separation from Prince Charles shocked and disappointed her Eastern fans. This third journey to the Land of the Rising Sun was regarded as a new test of the Princess's popularity.

Finally, she was given the green light and Diana left London hoping that her four-day visit would be just the first of several goodwill missions which would put her firmly back on the international stage.

From the moment she touched down at Tokyo's Narita Airport, she worked hard to charm her way back into oriental hearts. At the suggestion of her friend, television host Clive James, she had taken a four-week, crash course in Japanese and spent the long flight from London practising her pronunciation. At a luncheon at the National Children's Hospital, staff and patients alike were surprised and pleased that she greeted them with a speech that began with a few phrases in Japanese.

Moments later, she made a point of mentioning the subject which, at that time, overshadowed everything else in Japan — the Kobe earthquake.

'In the last three weeks, our thoughts have been with the children and families of Kobe and the surrounding area — victims of the most terrifying earthquake,' she said. 'Yet in the midst of the most dreadful devastation, it was wonderful to see neighbours come to the help of those who needed it, and to witness the great sense of commitment in the rescuers and relief-workers.

'The resilience and optimism of the Japanese people has been much in evidence during this tragic time. My heart goes out to the victims of this savage natural disaster and, of course, to their families.'

As each day passed, the crowds grew larger at each venue at which Diana was scheduled to appear. Back in London, her success was splashed across the press and featured in every television news bulletin. Surely, she had proved her worth as a roving ambassador for Britain?

While fighting to establish her independence from the all-powerful Establishment, she was still eager to represent Britain abroad. As a result, she was compelled to toe the Establishment line, to avoid venturing into political minefields and stick strictly to charity work. If she didn't, there was the ever-present fear that the backing for her goodwill trips would be withdrawn.

In April, another short trip to Hong Kong followed, arranged in aid of the Red Cross and cancer and leprosy charities. Diana visited a rehab centre for 300 heroin addicts and was wolf-whistled when she presented prizes at a tennis tournament.

With apparent ease, she managed to put on a show of unity with Prince Charles when they played their part in the 50th Anniversary celebrations of VE Day in May. As they parted in Hyde Park at the end of a day commemorating the outbreak of peace, Charles and Diana exchanged a kiss. It was a temporary cease-fire in the War of the Waleses, which appeared to be staged mostly for the benefit of their two watching sons.

In June, the Princess's delayed visit to Moscow went ahead. Diana had long been a private supporter of the Tushinskaya Children's Hospital, which was severely under-funded and poorly managed, a dire legacy of Communist rule. She had donated money from her own Princess of Wales Trust to help set up a school of paediatric nursing at the hospital, which she flew over to open.

It seemed that Diana was slowly re-establishing herself on the international scene as a campaigner for good causes. At each public appearance, she looked confident and cheerful. Her skirts were shorter, her heels higher and her well-toned figure shown off to perfection in revealing, clinging dresses.

At home, in the privacy of Kensington Palace, she was an entirely different woman. Suffering from chronic back pain, she felt depressed and anxious. On 1 July she had little reason to celebrate her thirty-fourth birthday. Andrew Morton's *Diana: Her New Life*, a sequel to his original bestseller, was being serialised in a newspaper. 'Hasn't he made enough money out of me already?' Diana said bitterly when discussing it with the author of this book.

Feeling isolated and depressed, she had turned to England rugby captain Will Carling, whom she saw frequently at her Chelsea health club. Their friendship began when he offered advice on her fitness programme. As Carling recalled in his autobiography, 'She used to work out really hard on the weights and that was the subject of our first real conversation.'

He told the Princess that she did more weights than any other woman he knew. Diana's fitness trainer who was standing nearby, said, 'She looks good on it, doesn't she?'

Carling looked doubtful and said, 'Not really.'

Diana was surprised and amused. 'You cheeky bastard,' she replied.

At another training session she walked up and asked if Carling fancied a coffee.

'I found her immensely attractive and I was flattered that, once or twice a week, she sought me out,' he explained in his memoirs.

Carling was fascinated by the Princess's gossip about the famous people she met, but he also found her a good listener. He was invited to lunch at Kensington Palace and brought along the Welsh rugby player Ieuan Evans whom Diana wanted to meet.

Soon, she asked him if her sons could attend a training session at Twickenham. William, Harry and their mother went into the changing rooms afterwards and chatted to the players. Their visit soon came to the attention of the Rugby Football Union committee members who were furious that they had not been present.

Too many people now knew that the not-yet-divorced Princess of Wales had struck up a very chummy relationship with the rugby captain who had been married for just a year. But no one realised just how close the two had become until Carling's former PA, Hilary Ryan, leaked the full details to a Sunday newspaper. She told of furtive meetings, long, secret phone calls and pet names they used.

None of the previous allegations about Diana and other men had had quite the same impact as this torrid tale. Diana was branded a 'marriage-wrecker' and became the butt of new press attacks. Under the headline DIANA'S DANGEROUS GAMES, the *Today* newspaper declared, 'No longer is Diana the revered saint. Suddenly she's the target of everyone's cheap jibes.'

It was referring in particular to comments made on the BBC's news quiz *They Think It's All Over*, when sports stars David Gower and Gary Lineker laughed at snide remarks about Diana and men made by comedienne Jo Brand.

Lineker, asked by presenter Nick Hancock if he'd had lunch with Diana, shot back, tongue-in-cheek, 'That woman's too much trouble.'

Will Carling insisted that it was only a harmless friendship, and gave a newspaper interview in which he confessed that his meetings with the Princess had been a mistake and regretted the distress caused to his wife Julia.

At the time, Julia Carling was a rising television star and rather expert at dealing with the media. She told the newspaper that she did not want her husband to see the Princess again.

'She picked the wrong couple this time,' she declared, and was immediately surrounded by a wave of public sympathy.

Despite this, her husband made the mistake of visiting Kensington Palace once again to drop off some rugby shirts for William and Harry. Diana was not at home, but this did not seem to matter. The press was hot on his trail and, despite his protestations, it seemed he could not leave the Princess alone.

Soon afterwards, Diana broke down in tears at her health club and sobbed uncontrollably. Her outburst came just minutes after she had spoken to Carling, who had approached her as she was working out. They had spent 15 minutes in deep conversation before he walked away. Friends later explained that the Princess was in an emotional mood after saying goodbye to her sons who had just left for a holiday with their father. Few people believed this was the real reason for her tears.

The *Daily Mail*'s Rhoda Koenig claimed that by meeting Carling in such a crowded place, Diana had been naïve and childish. Her motive was clear to any female, the writer added. 'Her action was not aimed so much at Carling as at his wife, to show her that no little commoner was going to get away with telling the popular Princess what she could, and could not, do.'

Once again, it appeared that Diana had taken up with a man who was another lightweight, just like James Hewitt, someone who craved attention.

The searing publicity surrounding her relationship with the rugby star alarmed Diana, especially when, some time later, the Carlings announced that their marriage was over.

The criticism of her reckless behaviour continued. No one could understand why a woman who had been so furiously resentful of her own husband's relationship with Camilla Parker Bowles could appear unconcerned about the feelings of her men friends' wives.

'Having seen her own marriage founder under a wave of accusation and counter-accusation, how can she now interfere — even peripherally — with the relationships of others?' royal writer Ingrid Seward asked.

Such critics did not realise how deeply she had been affected by the separation from her husband. The Princess had been left in a kind of royal limbo, forced to endure difficulties and restraints which no ordinary person had to face. Her privacy was constantly invaded and every action scrutinised and analysed, often producing newspaper reports that were wildly inaccurate. Every meeting was an assignation, every friendship a sizzling romance.

It is surprising therefore that Diana was not more discreet about her friendships with men, especially married men, but she continued to arrange trysts in London, where she was constantly watched.

Did her desire for a fulfilling love-life overcome her common sense? Or was she simply so self-obsessed that she did not think she was playing a dangerous game?

Normally, Diana shrugged off such red-hot gossip, but now it made her anxious. All of her relationships with men had seemed to be disastrous and none had offered her the support she so desperately needed.

Her main worry was that these attacks on her reputation might have a damaging effect on her fight to retain custody of her sons. She was very much aware that her boys belonged to the nation, not just to their parents.

The Queen herself was one of the main influences on their upbringing and, after the Waleses' divorce, their mother feared that the power of the Palace over William and Harry would become ever more evident.

Diana felt lonely and beleaguered. Her boys spent most of each year at boarding school and she now had to share their holidays with Charles. Prince William was set to begin his first term at Eton College in September and his parents were expected to deliver him to his new housemaster, Andrew Gailey. Diana was not looking forward to spending the day with her estranged husband.

When William and Harry were with her, the Princess's empty apartment became a home once again. The silent rooms were filled with pop music on their blaring television set and the shouts of the young princes crashing around in the first-floor sitting room. They often invited school friends for meals, at which time the noise level went even higher.

The boys used to get up at around 9.30am in the holidays and bounce into their mother's bedroom for a kiss still wearing their pyjamas. It was noticeable that William's always seemed to be at half-mast because he was growing so rapidly. Diana would fling her arms wide and hug them to her. When her hairstylist was present, she would remind her sons of their manners. 'Say, "Good morning, how are you?"' she would tell them.

Diana normally introduced William as 'my DDG' (drop-dead gorgeous). Blushing furiously, he would protest, 'Oh, Mum!' She also called him Wombat, the nickname Prince Charles gave him as a baby (inspired by an Australian storybook *Willie the Wombat*). When he walked out of the room, his proud mother would rave, 'Isn't he gorgeous? He's so tall.'

When he was at school, she was constantly declaring, 'I must phone William. I need his opinion.'

At times, it almost seemed their roles had been reversed with her son becoming the parent. She was constantly seeking his advice, which proved to be quite sensible. Once, she told him that a certain MP had telephoned asking her to make a speech with him. William suggested it would not be wise to do so, as the man had recently been accused of sleaze.

After ringing to warn him that photographs of her and Dodi on their first holiday were about to appear in the press, she reported that William had said, 'I don't mind about that, Mum, as long as you're happy.'

William talked to his mother's hairstylist about his longing to visit Ireland, but said he wasn't allowed to go there. He added that he had heard from his relatives how beautiful the Irish countryside was and hoped that one day it would be possible to spend some time there.

He walked in very excited one morning because he had just received a Harrods gold card in the post.

'Are you going straight down there to do some shopping?' his mother asked.

'I'd love to, but Mohamed Al Fayed probably wouldn't let me pay for anything, so I'm going to Selfridges,' he said.

While William was thoughtful and mature for his age, Harry seemed a lot more than two years younger. He was in the habit of jokily introducing himself to visitors, 'I'm King Harry. If William doesn't want the job, I'll do it.'

William, at that stage, was at that sensitive age of adolescence when he did not enjoy being different from his friends and was constantly uneasy about being seen in public. 'Why can't I just be normal?' he would often ask. Harry had no such qualms and gleefully told everyone that he would be happy to swap places with his big brother.

Like most mothers, Diana constantly urged her boys to be tidy. One morning she was chasing Harry who had a pile of clean laundry waiting to go upstairs to his room.

'Harry, put your washing away,' she chided him.

Half-an-hour later, when it was still there, she reminded him again. 'Harry! I've told you to please put your washing away.'

The cheeky youngster simply replied, 'Will you stop nagging? I'll do it in a minute.'

Harry had sent a Valentine card to his favourite supermodel Cindy Crawford and waited each morning for the post expecting a note of thanks. He was devastated when Cindy failed to reply. Eventually, Diana fibbed that she had received a phone call from the famous blonde expressing her gratitude and Harry was placated.

When the princes went back to school, life seemed to fade from the palace. At times, the Princess found the silence of her Kensington Palace home to be unbearable, yet each time she left its shelter she was hounded by roving bands of paparazzi cameramen.

It was at this low point in her life that, one morning in September 1995, Diana received a phone call from her acupuncturist Oonagh Toffolo, who told her that her husband Joseph had been admitted to hospital for heart surgery.

Diana had known Oonagh for six years and had become her friend as well as her patient. This was not Oonagh's first experience of royalty. She had nursed the Duke of Windsor on his deathbed when she was working in Paris during the Seventies.

A mutual acquaintance had introduced the Irish nurse to the Princess, believing she could not only relieve her constant back pain but help to heal the rift between Charles and Diana. Although an eternal optimist, Oonagh soon realised that this plan was hopeless.

When her husband became seriously ill, she informed the Princess that her regular acupuncture and meditation sessions would be interrupted. Diana at once offered to visit architect Joseph Toffolo, then 70, who had undergone a triple heart bypass operation at the Royal Brompton Hospital in Fulham, only a mile from Kensington Palace. She was sitting by his bed chatting when a tall, dark-eyed surgeon, still wearing his operating theatre gown, arrived to check on the patient.

He did not recognise the Princess and barely acknowledged her presence. As a senior registrar, Hasnat Khan was an extremely busy man and, within a few minutes, he had moved on to see another patient.

Born in Lahore, Pakistan, Hasnat Khan, then 35, was the son of a glass factory owner who had studied at the London School of Economics. A member of the proud Pathan tribe he is a devout Muslim whose whole life has been dedicated to pioneering heart and lung surgery.

As he walked away, Diana noticed his name printed on the back of his operating theatre shoes. Immediately impressed, she later confided to a girlfriend, 'When I saw it, I thought I must remember that.' Here was a man so immersed in his life-saving work that he did not even notice her.

Diana did not waste any time in following up their first meeting. The next day, she was back at Joseph Toffolo's bedside and struck up a conversation with the handsome doctor, known to his colleagues as an Omar Sharif lookalike. He was flattered by her interest in his work, as Diana asked endless questions about heart surgery, especially heart transplants which Khan carried out with the hospital's famous Professor Sir Magdi Yacoub.

The Princess invited the doctor and his medical team out to dinner and returned almost daily to the hospital to visit her architect friend and other patients in his ward.

She became such a frequent visitor that Joseph and Oonagh were quite overwhelmed. Mr Toffolo said later, 'She used to pop in practically every day. It was a great morale booster, but I didn't expect to see her so often.'

As Diana and the dark-eyed Pakistani doctor got to know each other better, she became totally engrossed in his world. It was a world of secrecy. Diana was not then divorced and she realised that if their relationship became public knowledge it could complicate matters. She also feared that Hasnat would have difficulty continuing his work undisturbed. He had a natural fear of publicity and was determined to make his mark in the world as a surgeon, not as the latest man in the Princess's life. So, when he insisted on discretion, Diana was happy to go along with his wishes.

Anxious only to please him, she agreed to be careful. Bitter experience had finally taught her to be more circumspect about friendships with men. Late at night she would slip into his home a few yards from the hospital entrance, but they never went out in London together, although he began to visit her at Kensington Palace. His arrival always took place late at night after the paparazzi had given up and gone home.

Frequently, he hid on the floor of her car under a rug — and he always left Diana's apartment very early the following morning.

Occasionally, they drove out of town to have quiet dinners in out-of-the-way places. Once or twice they dined at the Greek Connection, a rather unpretentious establishment in Stratford on Avon.

They walked in one night without a prior booking, sat at a table in a quiet corner and stayed four-and-a-half hours, leaving together at around midnight. Diana chose moussaka for her main course, while Mr Khan had a vegetarian dish. Both had fresh strawberries for dessert. Restaurant boss Lazarus Seferidis said, 'The staff were as amazed as the customers when Diana walked in. We had no idea she was coming. She and the man looked to be enjoying each other's conversation. At times, they seemed quite intense and very wrapped up in each other's conversation.'

Two weeks later, delighted that they could meet well away from the lenses of the London paparazzi, Diana and Hasnat were back again. Not long afterwards, they also had dinner at an Italian restaurant nearby.

When Natalie Symonds turned up early in the morning to style her hair, the Princess could not wait to tell her all about the new man in her life. Within days she was completely captivated and started singing his praises to Natalie.

'He's such a brilliant surgeon and so dedicated,' she raved. 'He has saved so many people's lives. I admire him so much.'

The stylist soon began to notice that Diana had developed a new interest in everything Asian. She began burning pungent incense in her palace apartment, and watched any Pakistani films she could find on video. One Saturday morning, Natalie arrived to find Diana all alone upstairs in her bedroom watching a video of a black-and-white Pakistani film. 'Aren't they a good-looking race of people?' she sighed.

The besotted Princess also began wearing Eastern

dress, especially the *salwar kameez*, a long shirt worn over billowing trousers.

Natalie Symonds later recalled, 'She was wildly in love, totally obsessed by Dr Khan.' Diana confided, 'He works so hard and can't see me as often as I'd like, so I just live for his late-night phone calls. But after I've talked to him, I can't sleep because I'm so happy and excited.'

At last, she had found a man who was not trying to exploit her in any way, someone uninterested in reflected glory. This was a new experience for the Princess, who had so often been used by men in the past.

Within a few weeks she was a different person; light-hearted and more content than she had been for many years. Like a carefree girl, she began roller-blading through Kensington Gardens, the public park adjoining her London home. Dressed in a baggy black sweatshirt, black-and-white shorts with a blue baseball cap pulled down low over her eyes, she passed unnoticed in the crowd of people enjoying the sunshine. After just four weeks on roller-blades, she felt so confident that she did not bother to strap on a crash helmet or knee pads.

Encouraged and inspired by her new happiness, Diana felt she could achieve almost anything. It wasn't surprising, therefore, that she accepted an invitation to answer questions from reporter Martin Bashir on the BBC TV documentary *Panorama*. It was to become the most extraordinary interview in royal history.

With astounding frankness, the Princess talked about the men in her life, her eating disorder, self-mutilation, the husband who had betrayed her and the courtiers who had plotted to discredit her.

Diana also savagely attacked her husband. 'I think

THE TRUTH

that I've always been the 18-year-old girl he got engaged to, so I don't think I've been given any credit for growth. And, my goodness, I've had to grow.' She added that she had never received any approval or credit for the work she did. 'Nobody ever said a thing, never said, "Well done" or "Was it OK?" But if I tripped up, which inevitably I did, because I was new at the game, a ton of bricks came down on me.'

With her eyes heavily ringed with dark make-up, Diana sadly explained that her husband's friends said she was 'unstable, sick and should be put in a home of some sort in order to get better'. Asked if Prince Charles agreed with them, she hedged, 'Well, there's no better way to dismantle a personality than to isolate it.'

Had Mrs Parker Bowles played a part in the breakdown of the royal marriage? Diana answered with an acid comment that was to become the most memorable statement she would ever utter. 'Well, there were three of us in this marriage, so it was a bit crowded.'

She admitted that she had wanted the true story of her unhappy marriage to be made public. 'I was at the end of my tether, I was desperate. I think I was so fed up with being seen as someone who was a basket-case, because I am a very strong person and I know that causes complications in the system that I live in.'

Diana also confessed that her relationship with James Hewitt had gone beyond a close friendship. Asked if she had been unfaithful, she replied, 'Yes, I adored him. Yes, I was in love with him. But I was very let down.'

She declared that rather than become queen, she would like to be queen of people's hearts, although many people did not want her to be queen. 'I mean the Establishment that I married into,' she explained. 'They have decided that I'm a non-starter. Because I do things differently, because I don't go by a rule book, because I lead from the heart, not the head.'

Returning to the subject of Prince Charles, she hinted that he would not make a good king. 'It's a very demanding role, being Prince of Wales, but it's an equally more demanding role being king,' she observed. 'And because I know the character, I would think that the top job, as I call it, would bring enormous limitations to him, and I don't know whether he could adapt to that.'

In a grand finale to this compelling performance, Diana suggested that she was speaking out merely for her husband's own good. 'My wish is that my husband finds peace of mind,' she declared. The House of Windsor might have been desperate to get rid of her, but she would not, in her own words, 'go quietly'.

The reaction to Diana's devastating interview immediately divided the nation. Many women who had also been betrayed by their husbands, and those who had battled to overcome a lack of self-esteem, were full of admiration. They felt the Princess's searingly honest disclosure of her problems was impressive. In just a few minutes, her image had been transformed from thick to thoughtful. Even while admitting that she had committed adultery, Diana managed to elicit sympathy from her audience.

Newspapers immediately ran phone polls asking readers if they believed the Princess was right to speak out so fearlessly. The fact that the overwhelming vote was in her favour was due in no small way to Diana herself who ordered some of her staff to man the telephones all day voting thousands of times to support her. They dialled and redialled endlessly until the Princess was satisfied that she had done her damndest to rig the poll.

The feminist sisterhood hailed the Princess as one of their own, praising her courage in speaking out as a wronged woman still deserving of the public's affection. In general, women viewers saw her as a brave victim, while others were shocked by her discussion of distasteful subjects such as post-natal depression, self-mutilation and eating disorders.

There were fears that Diana had delivered a death blow to the monarchy. As the *Guardian* newspaper commented, 'When an institution depends entirely on mystique, it cannot survive the mystique being stripped away. Diana sat there demurely, but she might as well have had a blow-torch and scraper in her hands.'

No sooner had the programme ended than her husband's close friend, Tory MP Nicholas Soames, announced on the BBC current affairs TV programme *Newsnight* that the Princess was suffering from 'the advanced stages of paranoia'. While many people agreed that Diana had been close to, if not quite over, the edge, it was equally obvious that her enemies had underestimated her. She was a woman with the power to wield great influence, and her devastating critique of a dysfunctional dynasty would linger long in the minds of the public.

The earlier attacks on her reputation were suddenly forgotten as Diana enjoyed a new respect for coping so courageously with a role for which she had been so pitifully unprepared. Hasnat Khan would have been an exceptionally hard-hearted man if he had failed to be impressed.

In February 1996, she found an excuse to learn more about the homeland of the doctor she adored. She jetted out to Pakistan to raise funds for a cancer hospital founded by cricket idol Imran Khan, husband of her close friend Jemima Goldsmith. There is no doubt she sincerely wished to help the Khans raise money for the hospital in Lahore, but the chance to find out about life in Pakistan also proved irresistible.

Diana was impressed by the closeness and support Jemima enjoyed in her extended Pakistani family. By the time she returned to London, she was totally captivated by the Muslim lifestyle.

When Hasnat's grandmother, Nanny Appa, visited London, Diana welcomed her to Kensington Palace and they exchanged presents. From then on, the old lady described the Princess as 'my daughter'.

Her friendship with the surgeon had, by then, turned into a passionate affair, but both were wary of making their relationship public. They kept furtive roadside rendezvous after he finished work. One amazed passer-by spotted the couple meeting near the Royal Brompton Hospital.

'It was like a scene from a spy film,' he said. 'Her car pulled up and suddenly a man dashed out of a nearby doorway. She wound down her window and he leaned in to talk to her. It was obviously all arranged.'

Both were dressed up as if going out on a special date and chatted for about 15 minutes. Just as it seemed Hasnat was about to open the door of Diana's car and get in, she spotted a photographer watching them and roared off down the street.

Later, when questioned by a reporter, the doctor claimed it was a coincidence that he happened to walk out of the hospital just as Diana drove past. He said he was with three ward sisters who briefly spoke to the Princess then they all left. However, the newspaper's informant claimed that Hasnat was alone, and insisted there were definitely no nurses with him.

On another occasion, in the early hours of a

Diana arriving at the Victor Chang gala in Sydney in 1996. By this time, Diana was no longer strictly a royal, and was not protected from the demanding attentions of an adoring public. *Inset:* Hasnat Khan's god-daughter, Lucy (daughter of Khan's close friends Paul and Erin). Khan himself only met Lucy a year after Diana's death and, sadly, Diana never met her.

Top: Natalie Symons and Tess Rock, who were Diana's personal hairstylists for several years and who saw the private Diana rather than the public persona.
Below: Sydney 1996: Diana is accompanied by Marie Sutton.

Diana is pictured here at the London Lighthouse, the AIDS and HIV charity. Diana's face shows the exhaustion that she was suffering from. She was even using acupuncture to help her sleep. Despite her tiredness she continued to be dedicated to her work.

Top: The dirt track leading to Diana's hideaway in Mollymook, Australia.
Below: A glimpse of the hideaway itself.

Top: Charles and Diana in Australia in 1983. The author of this book is visible in the background.
Below: Diana became tired of the constant demands of touring. Here, she is meeting Boris Becker at a royal engagement.

This picture shows how close the press could once get to the Princess. Diana i
pictured here on a walkabout in the North of England at the time when she wa
pregnant with William. Behind her is Judy Wade, along with her lady-in-waiting and a
policeman.

An elegant figure, always noted for her impeccable style: Diana is pictured here in a Catherine Walker coat dress.

Diana in Tyne and Wear the day her separation from Charles was announced

Saturday morning, a *News of the World* photographer caught Diana leaving what he believed was a wing of the Royal Brompton Hospital. When he approached the Princess, she panicked, afraid that her secret was out, and she asked to speak to the newspaper's royal reporter by cellphone.

She explained that she had begun visiting critically ill and dying patients late at night to avoid publicity. Diana was so desperate to conceal her relationship with the handsome surgeon that she invented the story to cover her tracks.

The newspaper soon realised that the Princess had been more than economical with the truth, when both patients and hospital workers began telephoning the News Desk to insist that they had never seen Diana wandering the wards late at night. In a way, Diana's explanation was not too far from the truth. Her obsession with Hasnat Khan had awakened an interest in pioneering heart surgery. The more complicated the case, the more Diana wanted to know about it. Several times she watched Hasnat operate and was wide-eyed with amazement at the way people who seemed doomed could be brought back from the brink of death.

The surgery fascinated yet appalled her. 'Sometimes, I want to throw up but I keep watching,' she told Natalie Symons.

At home, she reported in detail the complex operations she had seen to Prince William. 'You wouldn't have believed it,' she told him on one occasion. 'I saw this man's chest cut open from the top to the bottom.'

William protested that these gory stories made him feel quite sick, but Diana was unrepentant, totally enthralled by the life-and-death dramas enacted every day in the operating theatre. She also read medical textbooks so that she could increase her understanding of this highly specialised area.

Carried away with enthusiasm for the miracles performed by cardio-thoracic surgeons, in April 1996 she invited Britain's Sky satellite television company to film her at Harefield Hospital, Middlesex. Standing by the operating table, she watched as Professor Sir Magdi Yacoub performed a life-saving operation on a seven-year-old African boy called Arnaud Wambo. A week earlier, she had seen the same medical team remove a cancer sufferer's breast.

In an interview which accompanied the film, Diana explained why she watched so many operations.

'It motivates me — it brings purpose and meaning to my life,' she said. 'I do gather information much more from visual contact — not from reading books. So when I stand up and speak about the various subjects, whatever it is, I find it much more beneficial if I have seen it myself.'

The real reason, of course, was that she wanted to learn more about the work of the man she loved.

Although the Princess was wearing a mask, hospital gown and cap, she was also heavily made-up and wearing earrings. Nursing authorities criticised her for this, alleging that she had breached hygiene regulations in an operating theatre.

The hospital programme sparked off other gossip. One columnist, Philip Norman, writing in the *Daily Mail*, pondered, 'Does she nurture a secret hankering to study medicine? Does the spectacle of people being carved up provide cathartic relief to her own private pain and confusion? Or does she have some inexorable, ghoulish need for the sight of blood or the smell of anaesthetic? Or has she even — far from impossible — taken a fancy to some dashing young Dr

Kildare lookalike, and is longing to be the one who mops his brow?'

He was more accurate than he knew. But some of the paparazzi cameramen who regularly spotted the Princess leaving the Royal Brompton Hospital where Dr Khan spent most of his time began to suspect that her visits to the wards were not entirely altruistic.

When news of her passion for the Pakistani surgeon finally appeared in a tabloid, it caused few ripples. Most royal watchers were sceptical. Hasnat Khan simply did not seem Diana's type. He certainly did not resemble the slender and rather effete young men like James Gilbey and James Hewitt, with whom she had been romantically linked in the past.

Hasnat was tall, dark and solidly well-built. Although vegetarian, he existed mostly on hospital canteen food and had a tendency to put on weight. Even more surprisingly, he was a chain-smoker and Diana was vehemently opposed to smoking.

For once, this did not seem to matter. The Princess was in love and she talked endlessly to Natalie about Hasnat. 'He hasn't any money, I'll have to keep him,' she joked. 'But I've got a thing about doctors!'

By the summer of 1996, Diana was so deeply involved in the medical world that she devoted most of a visit to Chicago to raising funds for medical organisations. She visited Cook County Hospital, renowned as the inspiration for the hit TV series *ER*, and attended a symposium on breast cancer at Northwestern University.

The trip was a triumph. On the afternoon she arrived, thousands of people braved a rainstorm to stand in a park near the University to catch a glimpse of her. Many women collapsed in tears after she stopped to say hello. Lucky teenager David Studnitzer asked for a hug and was rewarded with a kiss and a cuddle from the smiling Princess. 'I felt like a prince,' he said later.

Her relationship with Hasnat Khan had made Diana feel more secure and confident than ever before. A new serenity seemed to envelop her. At last, she had found a new meaning to life. Supporting the man she loved had given her what seemed like a brand-new existence. He was a man from a different world, a different culture, which in Diana's eyes meant he was untainted by any links with the British Establishment.

No longer troubled by the pain of her unhappy marriage, the Princess had become a calmer, more contented woman. Her divorce from Prince Charles was imminent but Diana's anxiety about this seemed to vanish once her decree nisi was granted on 15 July.

Friends remember that a transformation seemed to come over the Princess. 'She seemed to put all her old problems behind her and develop a more positive outlook on life,' one said. 'She looked on top of the world. I think a great deal of this new happiness stemmed from her love for Hasnat Khan.'

The Pakistani surgeon had turned her life around, healing the scars left by her unhappy past. He also helped her to forgive Prince Charles for his betrayal. Her devotion to the dark-eyed doctor taught her at last to understand why Charles was so obsessed with Camilla. For the first time in her life, she understood how overwhelming a great and true love could be.

'She no longer blamed them for what they had done,' Natalie says. 'She had found love again herself and had no enmity for anyone.'

Despite the clash of cultures in their different backgrounds, Diana was convinced that she and Dr Khan would prove to be a sensational team with their shared aim to help the sick and dying. She talked constantly about their compatibility. 'He's insecure and I'm insecure, so we have a lot in common,' she sighed.

Once she was legally free to marry again, Diana had only one aim in life — to become the wife of the man she admired so much. But there was someone who had other plans for the world's most admired princess.

6

On 5 May 1996, Princess Diana slipped away to the Costa Blanca for what the press reported was an assignation with a mystery man. It was later revealed that this was no romantic rendezvous. She had arranged to meet her former lover James Hewitt, who had promised to hand over the passionate love letters she had written to him during their five-year affair.

She had begged Hewitt to destroy her letters but he had not. Now, deeply in love with Hasnat Khan, she could not take a chance that Hewitt might one day make their contents public. She was prepared to go to great lengths to regain possession of the correspondence.

When reporters learned about her secret trip to Spain, although not the reason for it, she abandoned the attempt and flew home the following day without succeeding in her mission. Her desperation was increased by the fear that the letters could jeopardise her divorce negotiations if they fell into the wrong hands.

In January, Diana and Charles had been ordered by the Queen to bring an end to their chaotic situation and legally end their relationship. By this time, it was the last thing she wanted. Diana was depressed and apprehensive as she held meetings with lawyers to decide what she should do.

Each year seemed more stressful than the last. Each month brought a new sensation and every week she would encounter a clash with a cameraman in the street or some embarrassing revelation in a newspaper.

Since 1980, she had been living under unrelenting pressure. As well as the world's fierce scutiny, she had endured the pain of her broken marriage, her secret, half-hearted suicide attempts, debilitating illness and disastrous love affairs with unsuitable men. Any one of these problems could have destroyed a weaker woman. Yet Diana refused to allow the cumulative effect of her difficulties to crush her spirit.

Although newspapers and television reported her activities almost daily, not one of them ever added up the astounding number of problems she had encountered in her 16 years in the spotlight, or considered the heavy toll taken by them all. In retrospect, this oversight now seems quite extraordinary. How could sharp-eyed newsmen and women have missed what was happening to the world's most adored woman? The media focussed on the story of the day, never stepped back and took a long look at a Princess under pressure, and never really understood what she was going through or why she behaved as she did.

When she complained, 'My life is torture,' many journalists simply believed it was yet another bid for attention by drama queen Diana.

No one could fully comprehend the enormity of her predicament because it was so far removed from normal life. Perhaps only a handful of other twentieth-century women like Marilyn Monroe or Jacqueline Kennedy Onassis, who also lived under the searing heat of the media, could have had any conception of the fear and despair she experienced. At the height of her film fame, Brigitte Bardot, hounded beyond all endurance, was driven to attempt suicide. Peace came only when her acting career ended and her beauty faded.

Diana often behaved erratically and sometimes stupidly, but considering the life she was forced to lead, this should come as no surprise. She could be bitchy, wilful and had a tenuous hold on the truth. In her position, who wouldn't? Most of the time, she had her back to the wall, fighting to survive.

From the time she rebelled against the system and helped Andrew Morton to tell her shocking story, she became a royal outcast. Charles's family turned on her, not in public, of course, but behind palace walls, where they regarded her and her sister-in-law, Sarah York, as the source of all their problems. Diana had betrayed them and they could not wait to be rid of her.

In February 1996, after weeks of coercion, the Princess finally agreed to a divorce, and now all her efforts were devoted to obtaining a fair settlement. The House of Windsor was about to make Diana pay the penalty for her betrayal but she would not give up without a fight. A legal battle began to whittle away her rights and privileges.

For some months, she had been harassed by a

stalker. Dr Klaus Wagner was eventually committed to a mental asylum in March, but not before she had become alarmed by his deranged attention. And then there were the other stalkers, the paparazzi, who tracked her day and night, but could not be dealt with by the authorities because they claimed they were 'just doing a job'.

It was at this difficult time in her life that a call from Australia came into her office at St James's Palace. A charity fund-raiser named Marie Sutton had rung to invite the Princess of Wales to attend a grand dinner in Sydney. It would raise money for a medical research institute, set up in memory of heart surgeon Victor Chang, who had been murdered in a bungled extortion racket.

When Victor Chang was murdered in 1991, Marie became a great support to his widow Ann, spending a great deal of time helping her and her children come to terms with their loss. She also devoted a great deal of time to supporting their efforts to raise money for their Young At Heart charity. Marie felt the best way to commemorate the life of a great surgeon was to carry on his work. That is how she began fund-raising for the Victor Chang Institute, set up to continue Chang's research into heart disease.

In 1996, the charity's directors decided to plan a big fund-raising event in Sydney. Ann Chang asked Marie if she could think of anyone suitable to be guest of honour at a million-dollar dinner. She mentioned several she had in mind, but Marie remarked that they had appeared too often on the charity circuit. 'I'll start at the top and go for the biggest celebrity in the entire world,' she decided. 'I've got nothing to lose. Would you like me to try to get Princess Diana?' Marie asked.

Ann Chang laughed and replied, 'You're kidding!'

That was all Marie needed to spur her on. She was advised by James Pegum, who had helped to organise all the major royal tours of Australia over the past 15 years, to speak to a woman in the Princess's office called Angela Hordern. 'She was extremely helpful and professional,' Marie remembers. 'She suggested that I should write a letter outlining details of the proposed visit.'

Marie immediately sent off a letter along with one she had received from Dr Wayne Clarke, the General Manager of the Victor Chang Research Institute, asking Marie to extend a formal invitation to the Princess. A few weeks later, Angela telephoned to say that Diana was very interested and that her letter had been very well received.

Marie Sutton had no idea about the Princess's new-found interest in heart surgery. She simply believed that no one would attract more publicity for a good cause than Diana. But the name Victor Chang was well known to England's adored charity champion. Hasnat Khan had spent four years in Sydney training with the eminent surgeon and, devastated by his untimely death, had left Australia to continue his studies in Britain.

Soon afterwards, the Princess herself phoned Marie. She said she was very keen to go to Australia but explained, 'My life is in turmoil and I can't give you an answer immediately. But please don't forget about me. Please give me some time to sort out my life.'

Marie readily agreed and waited to hear more. It soon became clear that the Queen's approval would be needed before the Princess could agree to come. Diana was by then in the final stages of her divorce but was feeling bitter because negotiations were not going her way. She had demanded a £40 million settlement but was being forced to settle for less than half that sum.

From now on, her freedom would be even more heavily curtailed. She could go nowhere and do nothing without checking first with the Queen's advisers.

For weeks, her divorce negotiations had been deadlocked. Diana was refusing to sign an agreement to divorce until she received an acceptable financial settlement. Meanwhile, Prince Charles's lawyers were refusing to make a financial offer until his wife signed the divorce petition.

The Queen, dismayed by the slow progress of the negotiations, indicated that Diana should serve a period of 'probation' before being allowed to continue her charity work abroad. She did not trust her daughter-in-law, having been told that the Princess had ruined her 70th birthday celebrations by leaking the venue for the family party planned by Prince Edward. Diana denied this, but courtiers put pressure on the Queen to withhold approval of her projects.

A statement issued by Buckingham Palace clearly spelled out this attempt to clip Diana's wings. It said, 'Any visits by the Princess overseas (other than private holidays) will be undertaken in consultation with the Foreign and Commonwealth Office and with the permission of the Sovereign.'

The Palace was anxious to tie down its 'loose cannon' and, under the terms of her divorce settlement, from now on the Princess could undertake charity work abroad only after gaining official consent. This took some time to obtain. Two years earlier, the Queen had been asked by the Foreign Office in London to carry out a tour of Thailand which would coincide with Diana's Australian visit at the end of October. Her advisers were reluctant to sanction a trip by the Princess which would completely eclipse her mother-in-law's tour.

Faxes and letters flew between Australia and London. Diana also telephoned Marie to explain the delay in replying to her invitation. 'I do want to come, but you must understand, I need my mother-in-law's permission,' she said.

This was not the only problem. The Prime Minister of Australia, John Howard, also had to be consulted. No present or past member of the Royal Family could enter Australia without his say-so. Therefore, Diana's visit needed clearance from Canberra as well as Buckingham Palace. As a result, James Pegum set off for London to smooth the arrangements. As Canberra officials had explained to him, Diana's trip was not an *official* visit. She was not a guest of the Australian Government, so her arrival created a rather tricky situation, which needed delicate handling.

James Pegum's experience organising so many previous royal tours was considered invaluable, and officials in the Federal capital breathed a sigh of relief when he volunteered to take charge of logistics for the Princess's trip. This involved every move Diana made, air and ground transport, as well as security.

In London, he liaised with Palace officials and explained exactly what the Princess would be doing. All of these discussions had to be reported back to Canberra.

What Marie Sutton did not know, because no one at the Victor Chang charity had told her, was that Prime Minister John Howard and his wife had already been invited to be guests of honour at the fund-raising dinner to which she had invited the Princess.

Marie had at first imagined it would be a simple matter to gain the Princess's agreement to fly to Australia. She would say either 'Yes' or 'No'. But it was fast turning out to be a diplomatic nightmare. As the divorce, which would be finalised with a decree absolute on 28 August, drew nearer, Prince Charles's lawyers were insisting that Diana should be stripped of the title Her Royal Highness, and give up her office at St James's Palace, despite the fact that she was the mother of the future King William.

On top of this, with Diana's BBC TV *Panorama* programme fresh in their minds, they were demanding that she should sign a legally binding secrecy order promising never to reveal details of life within the Royal Family. The angry Princess said she would only agree to this if her husband did the same but he refused, claiming his word was as good as any bond.

These squabbles over major and minor sections of the divorce deal led to a stalemate in negotiations. Although Diana had once made up her mind to escape from royal circles and end her marriage, she began to realise that the divorce would not bring her the freedom she longed for. With new limits on her life, she would be more of a prisoner in a palace than she had been before. It was becoming clear that as a divorcée she would experience a dramatic drop in status and the loss of many royal privileges.

Slowly, she came to realise that some sort of concocted reconciliation would be preferable. However, Prince Charles would not consider a reunion under any circumstances.

The endless wrangling began to take its toll and, while leaving the office of her doctor, Mary Loveday, in Harley Street, she broke down in tears. 'No one in the world knows how I feel,' she sobbed to a sympathetic photographer waiting outside the surgery.

Downgraded and depressed, she began searching for some way to prove that she would not be

THE TRUTH

diminished by her divorce. The trip to Australia seemed the perfect solution. She had never before failed to win an ecstatic welcome from the Aussies and this charity visit was a chance to show her enemies at Court that she was still the greatest royal crowd-pleaser of them all.

Australia was the country that Prince Charles had always regarded as a 'second home'. He described his stay in Australia when he was 16 as one of the happiest periods of his life. If Diana on her own could win a big reception in the place regarded as Charles's territory, what a triumph that would be!

Diana was very keen to go, but insisted that she would not fly to Australia for just one charity. 'You'll have to add some other organisations to the schedule,' Diana told Marie. 'I'd like to visit a hospice — that's a must — and a charity connected with children.' Marie told her that would be no problem.

As arrangements progressed, protocol was forgotten. In the beginning, she had called the Princess 'Ma'am', as all female members of the Royal Family are addressed, and throughout her first phone call Diana called Marie 'Mrs Sutton'. But very soon, the relationship reached a stage when it was simply 'Marie'.

Late one evening, Marie received a phone call from the Princess's office. 'She has got some very good news for you,' she was told. 'Stand by for a call. She wants to tell you herself.'

Soon afterwards, Diana was on the line. 'I've got approval for the trip at last,' she said, her voice full of excitement. 'Tell your husband to start practising some dance steps and he can be my partner at the dinner.'

It was 14 July, just 24 hours before Diana was given a decree nisi in a London divorce court. If she felt down-hearted, it didn't show. She was bubbling over with happiness at the thought of flying out to Sydney.

After months of letter-writing and high-level diplomacy, it seemed Diana had got her way. The Queen had caved in and agreed to her Australian trip. As far as Diana was concerned, that was all there was to it. She did not realise that the situation was far more complex than she could ever have guessed.

The Queen and her advisers did not wish to approve Diana's visit down under, but felt they had no alternative. Since her separation from Prince Charles, the Princess had developed the habit of leaking her side of every dispute to the press.

One courtier explained, 'We could imagine the headlines — QUEEN BANS DIANA'S TRIP DOWN UNDER. We would look like the villains, so we simply had to approve the Australian visit.'

Unaware of this, Diana blithely continued to plan her journey. From then on, she phoned Marie regularly at all hours of the day and night. She was anxious that every little detail of her trip would be perfect.

Once the Queen's permission had been granted, Marie then had to go to the Governor General's office and tell them that the Princess wanted to come to Australia.

'Why didn't you go through the proper channels first?' Marie was asked.

With characteristic directness, she told Sir Douglas Starkey, 'I have a habit of going to the horse's head and not it's you-know-what!'

He laughed and said that final approval for the trip would have to come from the Prime Minister. John Howard quickly rubber-stamped the plan and generously bowed out as guest of honour at the Victor Chang dinner, explaining that the Princess could do more for the charity than he would.

THE TRUTH

'Marie has put so much work into this, let her have the Princess here,' he told his staff.

Meanwhile, Diana called constantly to check what was happening in Australia. Once she phoned sounding hoarse and coughed repeatedly. 'Sorry, I've got a cold,' she explained. 'I get a lot of infections because I spend so much time with sick people.' Diana was desperately run-down and suffering from the stress that accompanied the final weeks of negotiation over her divorce. She said she felt in need of a long, peaceful holiday.

Marie, too, was under pressure. She had been recovering from a severe bout of shingles when she launched her bid to bring the Princess to Australia. Victor Chang's widow, Ann, was also anxious about the event and telephoned regularly to ask how Marie's arrangements were working out.

At times, Marie wished she had never become involved. The endless meetings in Sydney 200 miles from her home in Singleton, New South Wales, constant telephone calls to London and the worry of organising such a vast undertaking began to take their toll.

Situated on the edge of the Hunter Valley winemaking district, Singleton is a relatively small town where everyone knows everyone else. Marie could not step outside her front door without curious friends and neighbours asking for details about the forthcoming royal visit.

There was so much to arrange, from security to airline tickets and ground transport, as well as accommodation for the Princess and her party.

'I couldn't have done it all without the incredible help of Logistics Officer James Pegum,' Marie says. 'He had organised so many royal visits before and his help was invaluable.'

While all this was under way, an official in Canberra, whom Marie knew well, contacted her to ask how she was getting on. 'Let me know how many knives you have stuck in your back, Marie,' the caller told her.

Marie said, 'That's a funny thing to say.'

The man replied, 'Just you wait.'

Marie hung up and thought no more about it. Now she recalls the conversation bitterly. 'How naïve I was,' she says. 'The knives turned out to be machetes.'

When the press learned of the planned royal visit, reporters and photographers began bombarding Marie's country home with telephone calls. Her number had been passed on to the media by the Princess's office, who no longer had the benefit of a Buckingham Palace press officer to sort out arrangements for photographers and reporters. The British Royal Rat Pack, ignoring the 11-hour time difference between Britain and Australia, often called from London at extremely unsocial hours with endless enquiries about details for coverage of Diana's movements by the media.

Everyone wanted something different and, with no previous experience of the press, Marie was almost overwhelmed. She had no secretarial help and no public relations officer to give her advice, so she carried on as best she could.

To add to her problems, everyone involved with the Victor Chang Institute had a different idea about what sort of hospitality should be extended to the Princess. Many of the arrangements Marie had so painstakingly made were tossed out as other people attempted to take control. She had managed to arrange for three free limousines to be at the Princess's disposal, but committee members decided they would use some from a different company. Constant wrangling over dozens of tiny details occurred and Marie began to regret becoming involved. Every decision she made was overturned.

Through all the months of preparation, she was cheered by her regular chats with Diana, whose excitement was contagious. 'What are you wearing to the ball — long or short?' the Princess asked Marie one night.

'Well, what are you going to wear?' Marie replied.

'Oh, I've got a long dress — Versace,' Diana told her.

Marie sighed. 'I don't own a long dress, but I'll buy one.'

Diana sounded horrified. 'Oh no, you mustn't. I'll feel awful if you do that for me. If you bought a long dress would you ever wear it again?'

Marie thought for a minute then said, 'No, I don't think I would.'

Diana had no idea of the Sutton family's comfortable financial circumstances, but she was insistent. 'I'll feel terrible if you buy a dress just for me. Please don't.'

On another evening, the Princess chatted about the BBC-TV *Panorama* programme she had made in November 1995, which had caused a worldwide sensation. 'What did you think of it?' she asked Marie.

'To be honest, I couldn't understand why you talked about mutilating yourself,' Marie replied.

Diana had a ready answer. 'I did it to help other people,' she explained. 'There are so many people with the same problem and I thought making it public would make them feel they are not alone.'

Intimate conversations like this became a regular feature of their growing relationship. 'What are they saying about me out there?' the Princess asked one day.

'Well, people are wondering why you still wear your engagement ring now that you're divorced,' Marie told her.

'Hummph! They're not going to take that away from me as well as everything else,' Diana said furiously. 'I'll wear it if I want to!'

Marie reported the growing interest in Diana's visit and suggested places she might like to see during her free time in Sydney. 'Maybe we could have a party,' the Princess said wistfully.

On another occasion, as they excitedly discussed Diana's imminent arrival in Sydney, she said to Marie, 'You know, your life will never be the same because of your association with me.'

Marie simply laughed. 'You obviously don't know me,' she protested.

She looks back now and cannot believe she made that foolish comment. 'How wrong I was,' she says. 'My life was changed utterly the day I made that first phone call to Kensington Palace.

'Since then, people have never stopped asking me questions about Diana. They phone me at home at all hours of the day and night. They stop me in the streets, at the hairdresser's, when I'm having dinner in a restaurant or travelling in a lift.

'Australian newspapers constantly contact me to ask my view on something that has happened involving Diana, her death or her life. Television stations send news helicopters to my home. Sometimes, it seems the whole world is obsessed with the Princess. Diana knew what she was talking about. After all, she had seen it happen a million times before.'

On 18 October 1996, Diana sent a hand-written letter to Marie. 'It is exactly two weeks until I arrive in Sydney and I did so want to write to say how much I am looking forward to meeting you!! With love from, Diana. X.'

As the notes and telephone calls continued, they steadily grew closer. Then one day Diana decided that she knew Marie well enough to trust her discretion. It was to prove a watershed in their friendship.

Choosing her words carefully, Diana confided her greatest secret. Marie sat back stunned as she listened to what she had to say.

7

After all the months of negotiation and preparation, Marie Sutton finally greeted Princess Diana at Sydney Airport early on Thursday, 31 October 1996. The divorced Princess was technically no longer royal, but she was treated like a queen nonetheless. After her Qantas jet touched down, she was whisked away in a white limousine without the formalities of Customs and passport control endured by ordinary visitors.

Marie had arrived at the airport so early that she briefly fell asleep while waiting for Diana's plane to taxi round to the terminal. Suddenly, the tall figure of the Princess dressed in a cream tailored suit appeared in the doorway and introductions were made as coffee was served.

'At last! It's lovely to meet you,' Diana said as she shook hands.

Next, Marie was introduced to Diana's Lady-in-Waiting, Viscountess Campden, who smiled and said, 'Call me Sarah and treat me like family.' But this pleasant atmosphere did not last long.

Although Marie Sutton had issued the invitation to visit Sydney, she was pushed aside and almost excluded from Diana's entourage by a few charity officials who disagreed with the way she had arranged things. As a result, Neville Ireland, the Special Branch officer in charge of security, acting on advice he had received, had ordered his assistant Scott Dennis to make sure that Marie would not travel in the motorcade with Diana on the short journey to her hotel in Double Bay.

When informed of this, the Princess put her foot down.

'Oh yes, she is!' Diana declared firmly and tucked her arm into Marie's. Then she turned to James Pegum, who was in charge of Logistics, and said, 'Where is that man?'

Scott Dennis had disappeared to check the motorcade arrangements outside. But Diana was not deterred.

'Come with me,' she told Marie and led her out towards the lift taking them from the VIP lounge down to the ground floor where the official cars were waiting.

As they stepped into the lift Marie stood there in a state of shock. Diana could see at once that she was upset. 'You're only a little thing, come and stand over here, near me,' she said. Once outside, a compromise of sorts was reached. Marie travelled behind Diana in a second car with the Princess's Private Secretary Victoria Mendham and Professor Bob Graham, head of the

THE TRUTH

Victor Chang Cardiac Institute.

Marie had no idea that the professor would be there, but guessed that this was the result of the confusing late change of arrangements. Then the motorcade swept out of the airport gates and headed for the eastern suburbs with an escort of police outriders to speed their way through the early morning traffic.

When they arrived at the Ritz Carlton Hotel, overlooking Sydney Harbour in Double Bay, Diana quickly disappeared inside, met the hotel management then went up to her top-floor suite to rest before the first big engagement of her visit — a banquet in aid of the Victor Chang Cardiac Research Institute at the Sydney Entertainment Centre.

Meanwhile, Marie, still suffering from shock at the appalling way she had been treated, was on the point of collapse. She went straight back to the Ritz Carlton Hotel and slept until a phone call from Sarah Campden woke her up. The Lady-in-Waiting wanted to go out for a get-to-know-you lunch while the Princess slept.

Marie felt so tired she could not face a trek across town and suggested they lunch in the hotel to avoid the press camped outside. Later, she regretted this decision. Sarah Campden worked so hard throughout Diana's visit that she never really enjoyed another spare minute. Marie wished she had braved the paparazzi and seized the chance to show the Viscountess around Sydney.

But she pulled herself together to have lunch with Sarah and was soon charmed by her informal and friendly manner as they finalised details for the tour.

'Right throughout the visit, Sarah and Diana's secretary Victoria worked non-stop,' Marie remembers. 'They used every spare minute to write hundreds of thank-you letters on the Princess's behalf. She had received so many bouquets and gifts from well-wishers on her arrival and Diana insisted that everyone should receive a letter expressing her thanks which she personally signed.' So while Diana tried to rest after her long flight from London, her staff had to shake off their own jet-lag and keep working.

It was the Princess's first appearance in Australia for eight years and she did not want to disappoint the hundreds of spectators that night who screamed with delight when she stepped out of her car and walked along a red carpet which led her past a greasy hamburger bar to where her hosts were waiting at the main entrance.

Friday, 31 October was Hallowe'en and the Princess certainly looked bewitching in an electric-blue Versace gown that clung to her slinky shape and left one shoulder beautifully bare.

The evening of spooks and witches was no doubt the reason why the interior of the Entertainment Centre seemed to have been transformed into a dark and gloomy dungeon with black tablecloths and miles of black drapes concealing its usual concert hall function. Flashing stars made a rather tacky decoration on the ceiling. Perhaps the sombre background was also designed to remind the 1,000 guests that the evening commemorated the work of the late Victor Chang, Australia's leading heart transplant surgeon, who had died in 1991.

At the top table, Diana sat with Professor Bob Graham and his wife, and Victor Chang's widow Ann, while Marie was relegated to another table nearby with her husband Bill Sutton and their son Timothy. At the last minute, she had been asked if she wanted to join the receiving line, but was unsure if she should after the bitter disagreements that had occurred.

Then Marie remembered that she had already

refused to accompany the Princess on a tour of the cardiac ward at St Vincent's Hospital next day because she was so upset about the changes in the schedule she had so carefully arranged. Unwilling to seem petty, she agreed to welcome the royal guest in the foyer.

Significantly, when officials made speeches of thanks to those who had arranged the event, Marie Sutton did not even rate a mention. Puzzled friends stopped to ask why Marie was not sitting with the Princess.

'Diana wouldn't be here tonight if you hadn't fixed it,' was a repeated comment.

And British pressmen, recalling the glittering dinner arranged for Diana in Chicago just months earlier, wondered why the room looked so shabby.

'Is this the best Sydney can lay on for our Princess?' one man enquired.

Marie shrugged her shoulders. 'Don't ask me,' she said. 'This wasn't my idea.'

Instead of a dinner held in the back streets of Chinatown, Marie had suggested to Mrs Chang, when asked about an ideal venue, that it might be better to hold the event in a vast marquee erected in the grounds of Vaucluse House against the glorious backdrop of Sydney Harbour. She was certain it would have been a far more stylish event.

But all arrangements for Diana's visit had been hijacked by people who felt they knew best. Marie's plans were ditched and new ones replaced them. From then on, it seemed everything turned out in a most peculiar way.

Rock star Sting provided the cabaret before, not after, dinner, so that he could dash across town and perform at another venue later in the evening. He serenaded a delighted Diana with two of his greatest hits — 'Fields of Gold' and 'Every Breath You Take'. As he finished his act and walked towards her, the Princess stood up to thank him.

Every member of the British press corps present was desperate to get a photograph of the Princess and the famous English pop star together. But a local magazine had obtained exclusive rights to take photographs at the dinner and the Brits were not at all happy.

So when Diana shook hands with Sting, James Whitaker, a rather portly reporter from the *Daily Mirror*, dashed forward to snatch a photograph of the Princess with Sting, using a Sure Shot camera. He was promptly seized by security men, his camera was confiscated and he was unceremoniously hustled out of the building.

This mini-drama was soon forgotten when Diana, whose commitment to cardio-thoracic surgery in Britain was by then well known, made a heartfelt speech praising the work of the Victor Chang Institute. She said: 'Just over five years ago, a doctor tragically died. But no — this man was no ordinary cardiac surgeon. He was a visionary, he was an original thinker and a great team leader. His mind was not fixed on the traditional way of doing things. Ladies and gentlemen, that, as all of you will know, was Dr Victor Chang.

'The Institute helps us to remember Dr Chang's great talent and service as he established Australia's national heart transplant programme back in 1984. It helps us to draw inspiration from his leadership. It has been said that for evil to triumph good men must do nothing. Tonight, we give heartfelt thanks that a good man, Dr Victor Chang, did a great deal and of that we can all be thankful as we look forward to the future.'

Despite having slept for several hours during the

THE TRUTH

day, Diana was still quite tired and from then on the evening seemed to go steadily downhill. Only a month earlier, she had attended a fund-raising ball in Washington and was annoyed to find herself blitzed by camera-carrying guests. In Sydney, she was surprised to find even less regard for the niceties of protocol.

A never-ending stream of total strangers stopped by her table to badger her with questions. One woman presented her with a flower then returned five minutes later to ask for it back.

'Now you've touched it I want to keep it for ever,' she gushed.

Other guests asked for autographs and brusquely interrupted her conversation with her companions.

Some over-familiar women even began to stroke Diana's arms and back in a bid to be noticed. The Princess later sarcastically told Marie that she called such people 'new-found friends'. Although annoyed by such appalling behaviour, she understood it. Most people she met felt they knew her well, simply because they had seen her on TV and in the newspapers almost daily for 15 years.

Normally, a Scotland Yard bodyguard would have prevented such intrusion and protected the Princess from this unwanted attention. But now no longer royal, she no longer rated such protection. Diana had become philosophical about it all. This was just one change in her life among so many.

Finally, the moment came that she had been dreading ever since she had arrived at the dinner. When the Australian Brandenburg Orchestra began to play, Diana was obliged to get up and dance. Her request that Bill Sutton should be her partner seemed to have been forgotten by the event's organisers. It seemed that security had been forgotten, too.

As soon as she stepped on to the dance floor with a charity official, other dancers crowded around them and Diana began to look increasingly uncomfortable as she fox-trotted around surrounded by a sea of staring eyes.

Singer Doug Parkinson pleaded with the guests to leave the overcrowded floor but no one took any notice. Hordes of couples swarmed around her, many knocking into her.

Irritated and exhausted, she was in no mood to tolerate this scrutiny and managed to mouth to her Lady-in-Waiting, 'Get me out of here!' Then she spotted the perfect excuse to escape. Noticing a British journalist she knew well, she made an excuse to walk over and talk to him.

Robert Jobson, Royal and Diplomatic Editor of the *Daily Express*, was standing on the edge of the dance floor when Diana walked up to him. She had read a report he had written earlier in the week from Bangkok where he was covering the Queen's tour of Thailand.

In it, Jobson claimed that senior courtiers were angry because Diana's visit to Australia clashed with the Queen's trip. Most of the journalists travelling with the Queen had abandoned her half-way through her tour so that they could be in Sydney for the Princess's arrival.

'It is an unwritten royal rule that one never upstages a foreign tour by the Queen,' he had explained. And that is exactly what Diana had done, he added, 'in what some people called a fit of pique because she had been stripped of her HRH title. Among the Palace Old Guard many now think Diana is out of control,' he wrote. 'They hate the fact that they can no longer manipulate her.'

Normally, Diana had a good relationship with the

suave, Armani-suited reporter who made her laugh with jokes about the job whenever they met. But she had read his story filed from Bangkok and hit the roof. As far as she was concerned, the Queen had given her approval of the Australian trip. That was the end of the matter.

She did not realise that some officials in the Queen's tour party had briefed Jobson along with several other pressmen that Her Majesty was not at all happy about the divorced Princess staging a rival roadshow.

It was a classic example of the Machiavellian way the British Establishment works. Publicly, it seemed the Queen was happy to allow her former daughter-in-law to travel to Australia. Privately, she was extremely annoyed, aware that her Thai trip would be overshadowed by Diana dazzling the Aussies. But they had reluctantly sanctioned the Princess's tour, worried that if they did not, she would tell the world that they had blocked her very first big trip after her divorce.

'She is holding a gun to the Queen's head,' one angry courtier had complained. 'Why couldn't she have gone to Australia a week later? There was no need for this clash,' he argued.

Foreign Office officials also pointed out that the Queen was working hard for Britain selling Rolls-Royce cars and other British goods abroad.

'What is Diana doing for the country?' they asked. 'She is only selling Versace gowns and dancing with a load of Republicans who want to abolish the monarchy.'

With a system of leaks and off-the-record briefings that has served courtiers well for centuries, the Queen's men let it be known that their boss was far from pleased. Naturally, Diana remained in the dark about this and simply believed that Robert Jobson had written a story which was wildly inaccurate. She strode over to him and waved a finger in his face.

'You got it wrong!' she hissed. 'I did get the Queen's permission for this trip!'

Jobson was surprised by her outburst but stood his ground.

'With great respect, Ma'am, ' he said. 'I had a Foreign Office briefing which explained there is more to it than that.'

Diana's blue eyes blazed and veins stood out in her neck as she stared him down. 'I don't care. You were wrong.'

With a shrug of his shoulders, Jobson retaliated, 'I'm sorry, but a briefing is a briefing. I have to be guided by what I'm told.'

On hearing this, Diana turned on her heel and headed straight for the door. The row with Robert Jobson gave her the perfect excuse to leave an event that she had not enjoyed from the beginning. As charity officials scrambled to catch up, Diana forced a path through the crowd with the help of a security man and walked straight out of the door three-quarters of an hour before she was scheduled to leave.

The next morning, she was worried what people might think of her sudden departure from the dinner. 'What happened after I left? What did people say?' she asked Marie Sutton.

'I have no idea,' Marie replied. 'I was too busy trying to stop my husband, who is not a violent man, from breaking a few legs. I was just glad to get out of there early.'

Bill Sutton had grown increasingly angry throughout the evening when his wife's months of hard work had not been acknowledged or given even the briefest mention. He could not believe that people involved in charity work could be so uncharitable.

In retrospect, Marie looks back and thinks perhaps she should have cancelled the whole trip. The Princess's office had been growing increasingly concerned about disagreements in Sydney over arrangements for the visit and asked Marie if it should go ahead. Marie promised to think about it. But later she decided that she would use any influence she had so that the people of Sydney would not be disappointed. She was also concerned that huge sums of money for charity, which would be raised by Diana's presence, would be lost if the Princess's visit was cancelled.

From the low point of the Entertainment Centre dinner, things could only get better and they did next day when Diana attended the Commonwealth Day Council lunch at Darling Harbour. An enormous crowd, at least ten times greater than the number who had turned up the previous evening, had gathered to see the Princess.

This time, Marie was sitting with Diana at the top table and made certain that she enjoyed every moment of the luncheon. As they finished their meal, the Princess whispered to Marie that she would like to go to the loo.

The two women walked outside and headed for the nearest ladies' lavatory. But when they pushed open the door they were greeted by a queue of astonished women who began to scream, 'It's her! It's her!'

Diana and Marie quickly turned on their heels and ran out of the door, with half the women trailing in their wake. In what quickly became a kind of Keystone Cops chase, they dashed around the vast building until they chanced upon a second ladies' toilet.

There were more than 1,100 guests at the lunch and, not surprisingly, this toilet block also turned out to be packed with women who began shrieking at the sight of the Princess.

With a groan, Marie turned away and sought the help of a policewoman who quickly guided them both to a lavatory which had been specially reserved for Diana's sole use. They rushed inside and breathed a sigh of relief to be alone at last, while the policewoman mounted guard outside.

'God Almighty!' the exasperated Princess said as she stood watching Marie wash her hands at a basin. 'I thought we'd never escape. It's unbelievable.' Then she added, 'Did your father ever tell you not to talk to strangers?'

Marie replied, 'Yes, he did.'

Diana let out a long sigh. 'My father always told me never to talk to strangers. And I've spent the last 15 years doing nothing but talk to strangers!'

As she talked, the Princess became increasingly agitated. For the first time, Marie began to realise that normal life was impossible for someone so fantastically famous. Diana could not find the privacy she craved even when she went to the loo.

'Someone is always following me,' she complained. 'Usually in London it's the paparazzi. They are always on my tail everywhere I go. It is getting to the point where no human being should have to endure what happens to me. I have got to put a stop to it somehow, and I am determined to do it. They (the paparazzi) are sick, aren't they? It's not me, is it, Marie?' Diana asked. 'They're definitely the sick ones.'

Marie was sympathetic. 'I couldn't stand to live your life,' she told Diana. 'Why don't you get out?'

Diana shook her head. 'There is no way out,' she

said sadly. 'I am William's mother and I have to look after him.'

As they stood enjoying a brief moment of peace, the Princess tried to explain how trapped she felt in a life she loathed. 'I have to go on, no matter how awful my life has become.

'I have to stick with it for the sake of my boys. Perhaps their lives will be better than mine. That's the only thing that keeps me going.'

Marie could easily understand the distress Diana felt with no end to her prisoner-like existence in sight. But why didn't the Princess seek help earlier? And couldn't the Queen have done something?

At the mention of her former mother-in-law, Diana's face twisted into a bitter smile. 'I only ever asked for help once from the Queen. I asked her to speak to my husband and persuade him to end his affair with Camilla — not just for my sake, but for the family, for all our sakes. But she refused to help me. She said she couldn't intervene. After that, I never asked for anything ever again.'

By the time they had slowly walked back to their table, Diana was composed and beaming at the crowd once again. Her momentary lapse into despondency was over. She was back on duty, sitting down to applaud as the entertainment began. Youngsters, who had been helped by the Commonwealth Day Council, got up on stage to display their impressive talents. Marie whispered to Diana that it was a shame she was not scheduled to make a speech. 'A few words from you would really thrill everybody here,' she suggested.

Diana smiled and reached for a menu and turned it over. Then she took a pen from her handbag and began to scribble down a few notes. A roar went up from the crowd when the Princess got up and approached the podium. In a brief but well-worded speech, she talked of the importance of the Commonwealth, the way it unites peoples around the globe, and hoped the Commonwealth Day Council's work in helping children would always prosper.

Diana's mood could not have been more different from the evening before. Clearly enjoying herself, she then went on a surprise walkabout among the guests, stopping at each table to collect hugs from many young people. This was the Queen of Hearts at her best, comforting sick children, encouraging their parents and taking the time to circle the room completely, delighting everyone she met.

Marie was thrilled. The lunch had been a total success and everything had gone just the way she had planned. If only the rest of the Princess's trip had been left in her hands.

A visit to the Victor Chang Cardiac Research Institute had also been scheduled and Diana went through with it with good grace, although she was not interested in looking down microscopes or learning the finer points of experimental studies. Her love for Hasnat Khan had focussed her interest on cardiac surgery and she was much happier when she spent two hours meeting cardiac patients at St Vincent's Hospital. She went around every bed and spoke to everyone in the wards. No one was left out as the Princess learned as much as she could about the unit's work.

The following morning on her third day in Sydney, Diana's main duty was a visit to a hospice in Darlinghurst run by the Sisters of Charity. To protect the privacy of the patients no press were permitted to enter the building and the Princess strolled around with Sister Maria Cunningham along with Marie, the Lady-in-Waiting and the Princess's secretary free from the

THE TRUTH

attention of the media. When they reached the most critically ill patients, Diana was left alone with them, while the other women went off with Sister Maria for a cup of coffee.

The Princess spoke softly to each patient, gently drawing out information about their condition as she sat at the bedside making real contact, not just by holding a frail hand in hers, but also with real understanding of each person's plight. The Sisters of Charity were amazed as they watched people who, just hours earlier, had seemed on the brink of death, rally in the warmth and cheer of Diana's presence. She had insisted that a visit to a hospice be included in her four-day schedule and left thanking the nuns for allowing her to come.

Outside in the Darlinghurst Street several colourful local characters were waiting to lay on a very special 'Darlo' welcome. They were transvestites from nearby King's Cross who greeted Diana with jokes that she was only a princess while they were queens.

Diana giggled and stopped to chat with them, laughing as they boldly invited her to join them later that night if she wanted a good time. Surprising encounters like the meeting with the 'Ladies' of Darlinghurst always delighted Diana.

On this occasion, it provided a bit of fun after the sombre visit to the hospice. She was feeling particularly cheerful on that Saturday in Sydney because the highlight of her trip was about to happen. It wasn't on any official schedule but, for Diana, it was the main reason she had travelled to Australia.

8

Princess Diana was looking as inconspicuous as she possibly could in a pair of black jeans and a T-shirt with a sweater tied loosely around her neck. Despite her dressed-down appearance, her tall, slender figure still drew every eye as she stood in the foyer of the Ritz Carlton Hotel in Double Bay, Sydney.

Passing through on her way out for dinner on Saturday night, Marie Sutton was surprised when Diana waved at her.

'Are you going out?' Marie asked.

'Oh no, I'm just waiting for some friends to arrive,' the Princess said with a big smile. 'They're friends of a very special friend of mine — you know who I mean.'

Marie nodded slowly. She knew exactly who Diana

was referring to. Her 'special friend' could only be one person — the tall and darkly-handsome Pakistani doctor Hasnat Khan.

Diana's devotion to the surgeon, who had trained for three years in Sydney, had been known to Marie for many months. She had talked about him on the telephone from London when she confided her biggest secret.

She wanted her doctor lover to join her in Australia. What was behind this bizarre plan Marie never knew. Was Diana determined to 'go public' with the man she loved? Or did she hope his arrival would go unnoticed?

Marie realised how much Hasnat Khan meant to Diana when she revealed that she had bought a plane ticket to Sydney for him. He would, she explained, fly out on another airline at a different time. Could Marie possibly arrange a ticket for him to attend the gala dinner held in aid of the Victor Chang Institute?

Marie was amazed by the Princess's request and said she would think about it overnight. Diana's plan worried her a great deal. She doubted that the eagle-eyed pressmen at the party would fail to notice the presence of the tall, imposing stranger from London and realise why he was there. She had told Diana so in a very diplomatic way.

'If he comes, no one will pay any attention to the charity we're trying to help,' she pointed out. 'The only story the media will be interested in will be you and your doctor friend.'

She was also concerned about other arrangements for Dr Khan's arrival. 'Where will he be staying in Sydney?' she asked.

Diana said simply that he would stay with friends.

There had been so many stories about his

friendship with Diana in newspapers and magazines that Marie predicted his arrival would create a sensation.

The Princess listened but continued to insist that she wanted the man she loved by her side. Marie rang off with a sense of foreboding. She could not believe Diana would be so foolhardly. At the same time, she realised that love has a way of destroying common sense and sympathised with the Princess's yearning to share her trip with the surgeon who had trained in Sydney.

A few days later, she was rather relieved when the Princess's secretary rang to inform her that Dr Khan was not coming to Australia after all. The Princess had changed her mind after considering the idea again and had decided that it would be better if he didn't come. Marie suspected that the busy doctor had simply declined Diana's invitation, but she was told that Diana had said, 'He is bound to steal the spotlight from the work I'm trying to do in Sydney.'

Marie did not bother to say, 'I told you so.' She simply replied, 'I'm sure that's very wise. The Princess has made the right decision.'

When she could not enjoy Sydney with the doctor she adored, Diana did the next best thing — she decided to arrange a meeting with his closest friends; Paul, a surgeon with whom Hasnat had trained in Sydney; his brother Frank, a lawyer; and Paul's pregnant wife, Erin Mander, a slender brunette with a luminously lovely face.

By the time she arrived in Sydney, Diana already felt she knew the trio very well. As Erin explains, 'About a year earlier, Paul and I had phoned Hasnat in London to invite him to our wedding. He was thrilled and accepted at once but asked if he could bring someone with him. As he was flying all that way to attend our wedding, we naturally said we would be delighted. He could bring anyone he wanted.

'Then he sprang the big surprise on us. He laughed and said very slowly, "... Well, the girl I want to bring is very pretty ... and very famous ... and her name is Diana!"'

Erin's first thought was that Hasnat must be dating a supermodel. When he told them he actually meant Princess Diana, Erin and Paul did not believe him. He could not possibly mean the world's most famous princess, could he? When Hasnat insisted that he really did mean the Princess of Wales, they were stunned.

To prove that he was not lying, Hasnat then said, 'Well, if you don't believe me, I'll put her on the phone. She's here with me now!'

Then a light, high Sloaney voice came on the line. 'Hello, it's Diana here.'

Erin strained to listen hard, trying to detect the faintest hint of someone at the other end playing a joke. When she heard the cut-glass accent of the Princess, she was still doubtful. How could Hasnat Khan possibly be involved with the woman every other woman envied for her elegance, beauty and charm?

Still uncertain that she was actually speaking to the Princess, Erin cannily decided to give the woman claiming to be Diana a small test. She tried to catch her off guard with a jokey request.

'I'll invite you to my wedding on one condition,' she declared.

At the other end, she heard the Princess say, 'Yes, what is it?'

Erin went on with mock seriousness, 'When you arrive, I want you to wear a paper bag over your head. I don't want you upstaging me at my wedding. I'm the bride and I want to be the centre of attention, not you!'

Diana burst out laughing and readily agreed.

'Or, you could wear a balaclava, if you like,' Erin added, keeping up the pretence. The Princess told her that a paper bag would be 'just fine'. Although she wasn't positive, Erin slowly began to believe that just maybe it *was* the Princess of Wales on the other end of the telephone.

Sadly, by the time the wedding drew near, the Princess realised it would be risky to accompany her doctor lover to Australia. Her divorce negotiations were at a tricky stage and she knew it would be impossible to avoid publicity if they went abroad together. Reluctantly, she made her apologies and explained that she would not be turning up in a paper bag after all.

So Hasnat Khan flew out to Sydney alone and stayed with Paul and Erin until the ceremony. One night, they all went out for dinner near their home in Narrabeen, a beachside suburb north of Sydney. Hasnat tried to telephone Diana from the restaurant but she was unavailable. After their meal, they went back to Paul and Erin's home and sat enjoying a cold beer in the back garden.

Just then, Diana returned Hasnat's phone call. By then, Erin had spoken to the Princess many times on the phone but she could never really believe she was not dreaming. As she explained to the author of this book, 'It seemed unbelievable that the person calling our little house in Narrabeen was a princess in a palace. I just couldn't take it in.'

Disappointed that she had not been able to attend their wedding, Diana determined that she would see Erin and Paul when she came to Sydney in 1996, and also meet Paul's brother Frank. They were Hasnat Khan's closest friends in the world and she wanted them to be her friends, too.

Unwilling to expose them to harassment by the media, she decided not to go out anywhere with them. To risk being seen at a fashionable restaurant would expose them all to unwanted publicity and ruin their evening together. Instead, she invited them to have dinner with her in her suite.

Erin remembers it as the greatest dinner party she has ever been to.

'It was wonderful to meet her in the flesh after speaking to her so often on the telephone. I asked her if anyone else had ever demanded that she should wear a bag over her head. She laughed and said, "No, you're the first."'

Within minutes of their arrival, Diana's guests felt they had known her for decades.

'She was very welcoming and very relaxed,' Erin says. 'Diana had chosen the menu for us and it was superb, the very best that the hotel had to offer. It was all set out waiting for us when we walked into her suite. We had a wonderful dinner with the best steaks, delicious vegetables and salad. As I was pregnant, I just wanted something healthy. So did Diana, but the boys decided to share a creamy trifle. Diana urged us not to hold back. She said, "Go on, have one each. It doesn't matter what it costs."'

The Princess was a generous hostess and also ordered several bottles of very expensive wine which Paul and Frank enjoyed immensely. 'Diana and I didn't touch alcohol,' Erin remembers. 'So we sat talking quietly while the boys sampled the wine.'

Naturally, all four talked mostly about their mutual friend. Diana made them all laugh as she told how, when she first set eyes on Hasnat Khan while visiting the Royal Brompton Hospital in London, he didn't know who she was.

Diana said, 'I thought he was drop-dead gorgeous, and when he walked away I saw the name KHAN on the back of the shoes he wore in the operating theatre. I made a mental note to remember it.'

She asked about his years in Australia and the life Paul and Hasnat had all led while training to become cardiac surgeons. She wanted to know as much as possible about the man she loved. Erin recalls that the Princess also told her that she had hoped Dr Khan could join her on the trip.

'She told me she had bought an airline ticket for Hasnat so that he could be with her in Sydney, but at the last minute she had decided it wasn't a very good idea. I know it would have created a huge fuss in the press if they had both come out from London.'

Erin could see why the Princess was so smitten.

'Hasnat is a very lovable man. He's a real teddy bear,' she says. 'There's something about him that is very warm and kind and good. He is so easy to get to know. People feel relaxed and at ease with him immediately.'

Diana also talked at length to Erin about childbirth and babies. She said, 'The births of both my sons were specially induced to fit in with my husband's polo games.'

Erin remembers, 'She seemed rather bitter about that, which I could understand.'

The Princess also asked Erin how her pregnancy was progressing and compared notes on the physical changes each had experienced. While Erin explained she had enjoyed a trouble-free time and stuck to a vitamin-rich diet of healthy, fresh food, especially raw, organic fruits and vegetables, the Princess, suffering from an eating disorder, had been ill throughout most of her pregnancies.

Diana laughingly told Erin, 'It wasn't so bad when I was expecting William, but I was sick all the time with Harry. At one point, I was throwing up so often I didn't know whether it was morning sickness or bulimia.'

The Princess and her new friends talked late into the night. Erin says, 'By the time the evening drew to an end, the boys were half asleep, but Diana and I were still talking. I could have talked to her all night.'

It was sad to say goodbye, but they all hoped to meet again one day. Diana was anxious to stay in touch and to receive reports on the progress of Paul and Erin's baby. When a healthy and hefty girl weighing 8lb 10oz arrived four months later, the Princess telephoned as soon as she got the news.

By chance, her call came through to the home of the happy new parents when Erin was sound asleep and her mother Stephanie answered the telephone. 'Can I speak to Erin?' Diana asked.

'No, she's sleeping,' said her protective mother, unaware that she was speaking to the Princess.

'Is Paul there? Can I speak to him, please,' Diana suggested.

'Well, he's busy upstairs with the baby,' she was told. 'Would you like to leave a message?'

Diana hesitated then said, 'It's a bit difficult.'

Something about the voice on the other end of the phone made Erin's mother change her mind.

'Just hold on, I think you had better speak to Paul,' she said hastily.

The Princess was thrilled about the new arrival and wanted to hear all about the little girl she hoped to meet one day. Sadly, she was never to see blue-eyed, blonde little Lucy, who is now Hasnat Khan's goddaughter. A year after Diana's death, he finally met the little girl he now calls 'my other little princess'.

'It is a sign of Hassy's kind heart and lovely nature that he is extremely good with children,' Lucy's mother says. 'We all enjoyed a holiday together in Spain in 1998 and he was so good with Lucy and she adored him.'

Looking back, Erin could tell as she listened that night to Diana talking about Hasnat and recalling the way Hasnat had raved about Diana, that they were both mad about each other. 'I think they would have got married eventually if the Princess had lived,' she says. 'They were a couple who were really in love.'

Hasnat Khan told his friends that he had been away on holiday when the Princess lost her life and he had returned home to find a birthday card from Diana sent in time to arrive at the end of August. His star sign is Virgo. This is undeniable proof that the Princess and the Pakistani surgeon were still in close touch. By a heart-rending coincidence, he also found on his doormat an invitation to her funeral.

Hasnat Khan firmly believes that Diana's death was nothing more than a horrifying accident and refuses to give any credence to reports of conspiracies to murder her. But in his mind there is always the thought, If only ...'

The dinner with Erin, Paul and Frank was to prove the high point of four disappointing days in Sydney. Late the following afternoon, Diana was back at Sydney's Kingsford Smith Airport waiting for a flight to London.

The dazzling smile that had captivated Australia during her brief visit had disappeared as she paced up and down the VIP suite. This was a different Diana, a tense, edgy woman who seemed troubled by some unexplained problem.

She had regarded the trip as the perfect opportunity to reinvent herself as an independent woman after her divorce. To the people of the world's largest island continent, she was more admired and respected than any other member of her ex-husband's family. When she left London for Sydney, she was convinced that she was set for another triumph.

Sadly, the 12,000-mile journey had not worked out the way she had hoped. As the divorced wife of the heir to the throne, Diana no longer received the unstinting support of Buckingham Palace. Inexperienced local charity workers could not equal the smooth professionalism of palace courtiers, as she soon discovered. Her itinerary had not been very well publicised and, as a result, the crowds waiting to greet her had sometimes been embarrassingly small. Diana was fast learning what life was really like in the cold world outside the royal Court.

It was also the first time she had travelled abroad on an official trip without a Scotland Yard bodyguard at her side. At her own request, she had dispensed with police protection at the end of 1993. Accompanying her in Sydney were just two women, a Lady-in-Waiting and a secretary. On previous visits to Australia, she and Charles had travelled with an entourage of up to 27 people including a maid, a hairstylist, a doctor and four protection officers.

Such extravagant style was consigned to the past. Her hosts on this humanitarian trip could not afford to pay for dozens of royal aides, and it was clear that was how life would be from now on.

It wasn't surprising, therefore, that Diana was in no mood for pleasant chit-chat at the airport. She snapped at Viscountess Campden, her Lady-in-Waiting, when offered a cup of coffee and continued her restless pacing around the lounge.

As the minutes ticked by to departure, Marie Sutton tried to cheer her up. 'I suppose you can't wait to get home,' she suggested.

Diana frowned. 'No, I don't want to go back to London. I hate going home.'

Marie tried again. 'Well, why don't you get on a plane and go somewhere else?'

Diana sighed. 'No, I've got my boys and they are my first priority. I have to go home to them.'

It was not hard for Marie to understand why Diana was reluctant to return to the difficulties she faced back in Britain. Over the past six months, she had gained an amazing insight into the unhappy life of the world's most glamorous woman.

The harassment the Princess endured daily from the paparazzi had reached such a point that she had been forced to take legal action against a man she accused of 'stalking' her. As the bitter realisation of all she had lost and the full implications of her new solo life sank in, Diana had come close to a break-down.

Marie Sutton understood better than most how the Princess's life had been affected by her exit from the Royal Family. Diana was slowly building a new life, but the old constraints still surrounded her.

For all these reasons, the newly-single Princess had looked on her trip down under as a great opportunity. Diana had invested a great deal of hope and energy into the journey. She had believed that Australia would be a new beginning.

When royal aides Sarah and Victoria left the VIP lounge to do some duty-free shopping, Marie sat down beside Diana to say a final goodbye.

'Thank you for coming,' she said. 'I'm sorry it

didn't work out the way we had planned.'

There had been a scheduled trip on the harbour, a cocktail party in a six-star hotel, a suite with her own private gym and swimming pool, all of which had been cancelled by charity officials. Diana's luxury hotel in the centre of Sydney had been switched at the last minute to the Ritz Carlton Hotel in Double Bay, allegedly because news of where she had planned to stay had leaked out.

This explanation surprised royal observers and the travelling press who had flown out from London with the Princess. They knew that details of hotels the Princess had stayed in on other tours had always been announced well in advance. Changing hotels seemed even more incomprehensible when the President of the United States, Bill Clinton, and his wife Hillary arrived in Sydney and the whole country knew where they would be staying. The most important man in the world had managed to walk the streets, stop and talk to crowds of well-wishers, go shopping and act normally. He and the First Lady of America had had a wonderful time.

Diana's visit to Australia had been quite different. In between charity engagements, she had spent four days with the curtains drawn in her suite, blocking out the sunshine and the harbour breezes. Like a virtual prisoner, she had been trapped in her hotel, just as she had always been imprisoned in Kensington Palace.

Sydney had turned out to be no different from London.

As she later told friends, one day she was surprised to hear a loud knocking on her hotel bedroom door. She opened it to find that a man, who had somehow evaded the hotel's security, wanted a chat. Diana was thoroughly unnerved. Not even her bedroom seemed to be safe.

This was not what she had envisaged when she first agreed to visit Sydney. She had asked Marie to plan several outings and parties.

'Do you know any nice men we could invite?' she had asked with a giggle.

'I'll put my thinking cap on,' Marie had promised.

Diana said she definitely wanted to take her hostess out to lunch to repay her for organising the trip. Marie had booked a table for 12 at the world-famous Doyle's fish restaurant right on the beach at Watson's Bay. She had asked for an upstairs room so that her royal guest would have a wonderful view of the harbour.

The lunch party was later cancelled. One by one, the fun outings she had hoped to enjoy became impossible as the press laid seige to her harbourside hotel.

Diana's next trip, she hoped, would take her to Malaysia in March 1997, a journey which was later postponed until the autumn.

'I just love leaving Britain,' she explained.

She was heading back to London aware that her old adversaries at Buckingham Palace would already know that her Sydney visit had been far from a success. Slowly, she was being forced to realise that, from now on, she was truly out on her own. Had her long, fierce struggle to start a new life ended on the other side of the world, in disillusion and failure?

9

No longer a Royal Highness, yet far from a private citizen, Diana found herself trapped between two worlds — the Court she had left and the carefree life she craved. Following her divorce, she existed in a kind of post-marital limbo, expelled from the Royal Family but more popular than any of its other members.

Stripping away her royal title had failed to reduce public interest in Prince Charles's ex-wife. Her fame could not be withdrawn from her as many of her royal privileges had been. She was the mother of a future king, and this alone granted her a special status. The media also continued to regard her as the most intriguing and attractive woman on the planet, so her quest for a normal life seemed doomed to fail.

For 15 years, the press had been obsessed with her, and although she loathed their constant scrutiny, she needed publicity to maintain her celebrity and prove that divorce had not reduced her popularity. At the same time, she did not want her critics, especially those at Buckingham Palace, to believe that she was co-operating with journalists. As a result, she constantly confronted photographers in the street, shouting, screaming and begging to be left alone.

It is surprising that a woman who had coped so magnificently with the paparazzi before her engagement to Prince Charles failed so miserably to deal with them later. If she had ignored them, their pictures would generally have been worthless. It was only when she broke down in tears, sobbing in the street, or arrived at her fitness club in a revealing outfit, that they made money out of her.

Perhaps the long years of being hunted like an animal had destroyed her judgement or the insults some of the cameramen hurled at her pushed her beyond endurance.

She attempted to take control by cosying up to editors, but this sometimes failed. After reneging on several arrangements she had made with the *News of the World*, she once invited its then editor Phil Hall to lunch. He declined to accept.

Other editors were often more willing to collaborate with her. In May 1997, she visited young women suffering from eating disorders at the Roehampton Clinic, a private hospital in South London. She talked in graphic detail about her own battle with bulimia, which began, she said, because she was trying to copy her adored anorexic sister Sarah.

The following morning, the *Mirror* ran the 'world exclusive' story over three pages, explaining how the tension of living with the Royal Family at Balmoral and Sandringham had increased the agonies of her illness.

Diana immediately released a statement in which she deplored the fact that one of the patients or hospital staff had betrayed her confidence by speaking to the newspaper. In fact, Diana herself had ordered an assistant to phone the *Mirror*'s editor Piers Morgan and give him the exclusive. As she stood listening nearby, Diana felt the young woman was not reporting the story correctly, so she grabbed the phone and continued to give Morgan a lengthy account of her visit to the hospital.

Why did she feel the need to arrange such self-glorification? Was she simply desperate to retain her hold on the nation's heart strings? Or was she trying to counter-balance the disparaging publicity she had received?

In the last 18 months of her life, Diana was subjected to unprecedented criticism. It began when a newspaper revealed that the Princess had been spreading a malicious rumour about Tiggy Legge-Bourke that she was romantically involved with Prince Charles. At the 1995 staff Christmas party at the Lanesborough Hotel in London, Diana had approached Tiggy and said, 'Sorry to hear you lost the baby.'

Tiggy was so shocked by this unfounded allegation that she burst into tears and had to be comforted by her colleagues. Her parents decided it was time to stop the Princess's appalling slurs on their daughter's character and intructed the lawyer Peter Carter-Ruck. He contacted Diana's lawyer, Anthony Julius, asking his client to stop spreading spiteful stories.

A Palace source explained, 'Tiggy had no intention of forcing the Princess to admit her mistake in court, she simply wanted to stop her spreading lies.' Diana quickly backed down and the litigation was resolved.

There were other unexplained outbursts against her staff, many of whom suddenly departed. Just days after the attack on Tiggy was made public in January 1996, Diana's Private Secretary Patrick Jephson stormed out after she subjected him to a tirade of abuse. The speed of the former naval officer's exit indicated that a serious bust-up had occurred.

The following day his assistant Nicki Cockell left Diana's employment, and her devoted chef Mervyn Wycherly, who had faithfully served the Royal Family for 22 years, was made redundant the same day. Chauffeur Steve Davis's contract was not renewed after the Princess learned he was romantically involved with her dresser Helen Walsh. Enraged that they had enjoyed assignations at Kensington Palace, Diana insisted that Steve should be banned from the building. Palace officials thereupon informed Diana that the dresser was quite entitled to entertain friends at her quarters until midnight.

Seizing on this knowledge, the Princess waited outside Helen's flat until the witching hour then began beating on her door, shouting, 'I know you're in there.' Helen was soon looking for employment elsewhere.

Senior aide Angela Hordern, who had worked as diary secretary to Prime Ministers John Major and Margaret Thatcher, had left Diana's office in mid-November. Around the same time, Press Officer Geoff Crawford had also resigned from her staff, believing he could no longer work with the Princess after she had failed to inform him of her sensational *Panorama* interview. She eventually replaced him in January 1996 with publicity adviser Jane Atkinson who lasted just six months. She resigned because Diana plagued her with non-stop phone calls which almost wrecked her marriage, starting at dawn and continuing until after midnight.

In January 1997, her most trusted aide Victoria Mendham resigned and was replaced by Louise Reid-Carr, who lasted just six weeks in the job. The following month, Diana personally sacked cleaner Sylvia McDermott, who had worked for her since 1987. Determined to get her job back, Sylvia sued for unfair dismissal at an industrial tribunal. The Princess's lawyers claimed she was dissatisfied with Sylvia's work, while the cleaner said she had never before received a complaint.

The case was settled out of court when, according to unsubstantiated allegations, Diana heard that Sylvia proposed to tell the court she was often unable to clean her bedroom because Hasnat Khan was asleep in the Princess's bed. To preserve her secret, Diana agreed to a settlement. Sylvia received an undisclosed sum which, she claimed was 'better than winning the lottery'.

The same month it was learned that Diana had also forced Highgrove groom Marion Cox to stop working with William and Harry and ordered her to work in the gardens. Newspapers speculated that jealous Diana thought Marion had become too close to her sons.

What prompted Diana's wild and erratic conduct? TV personality Clive James perhaps came closest to an explanation in an article he wrote for the *New Yorker* after Diana's death.

'Clearly on hair-trigger, she was unstable at best,' he wrote. 'And when the squeeze was on, she was a fruitcake on the rampage.' Yet he loved her to distraction, as he freely admitted. Even when she looked him in the eye and lied, and ignored his advice while pretending to consider it, he never wavered in his affection for her.

Most people who came close to the Princess, even those who were damaged by her in some way, felt the same. She had the seductive power of the sirens in Greek mythology, able to enchant men while luring them to destruction.

Most of those who became involved with her suffered for it in some way. James Gilbey will forever be remembered for the embarrassing Squidgygate tape. James Hewitt was branded a 'love rat' for publishing the story of his affair with Diana. As married men, Oliver Hoare and Will Carling both had to face an ordeal by media as well as their furious wives.

Hasnat Khan, an intelligent and thoughtful man, was no doubt well aware of the Princess's turbulent romantic past. He had no intention of being consumed by the Diana inferno, yet he was irresistibly drawn to her.

Most of all, he did not want to become prey to the paparazzi, having to look over his shoulder every time he went anywhere and make elaborate arrangements to throw them off the scent.

A small band of freelance cameramen devoted their entire time to chasing Diana. They were prepared to follow her to the ends of the earth, and frequently did, turning up in Spain, Switzerland and the United States when she was on holiday. Whenever she stepped outside the front door of Kensington Palace, they were snapping at her heels.

Kensington Palace sits half-way up a private road, which connects two of West London's main thoroughfares — Bayswater Road to the north and Kensington High Street to the south. The paparazzi, usually on motorbikes or in fast sports cars, would split up into two groups waiting at the north and south exits of the palace, then feed one another news of her

THE TRUTH

movements on their mobile phones.

Occasionally, Diana hid on the floor of a taxi to escape their attention. One evening, a cab driver was called to the palace to pick up a Miss Mendham. As he boasted to pals afterwards, 'The door of my cab opened and Princess Diana scuttled into the back and sat on the floor. I was so surprised I almost stalled the engine.'

More often than not, she drove at high speed out of the palace gates hoping to get lost in traffic before the photographers could follow her.

One morning in early April, she drove down to the Harvey Nichols department store in Knightsbridge, pursued by a pack of cameramen. To their surprise, she parked her Audi in the store's basement, dashed through the ground floor, dodging astonished customers standing at the beauty counters, then ran out through the front door and jumped into a taxi. One of the photographers said later, 'She raced through the store like an Olympic runner, desperately trying to shake us off, and she succeeded.'

Such small triumphs were rare. Diana had no country home, no bolt-hole where she could retreat from the scrutiny she endured in London.

Her brother Charles had refused her request to use a small house on his Northamptonshire estate, Althorp, allegedly claiming that he did not want 'paparazzi hanging out of the trees' and frightening his children.

Diana could have bought a house outside London with money from her £17 million divorce settlement, but such a move would have been controversial. Any local police force would find the cost of protecting her property a financial strain, and taxpayers would prefer their money spent on catching criminals rather than patrolling a royal residence. Without round-the-clock security, her sons would be unable to stay with her, so the cost of a country haven hardly seemed worthwhile.

Diana had another reason for remaining in London. She wanted to stay close to Hasnat Khan. The hardworking surgeon and the Princess were closer than ever in the spring of 1997. Diana cherished the hope that they would share a lifetime of working together to relieve poverty and suffering. She talked of these plans endlessly to friends and confided to her hairstylist Natalie Symons, 'We're made for each other. I'll raise the funds so he can carry out his life-saving work.' In her mind, they were a dream team who would conquer the world.

For years, she had been searching for a way to make her life more meaningful. Supporting this dedicated doctor in his pioneering work seemed the finest way she could gain fulfilment. The men she had fallen for in the past seemed shallow in comparison. Never before had she known someone so unimpressed by her rank and her regal lifestyle. Hasnat Khan loved Diana the woman, not the Princess, of that she was sure. He loved her for herself alone, and this was a new and heady experience. In fact, Dr Khan made it clear that he was totally uninterested in her luxurious existence. He regarded her worldwide fame as an appalling obstacle blocking any hope of living an ordinary life.

It was, in part perhaps, a bid to make him realise that her notoriety could be beneficial that Diana had embarked on a new crusade in January 1997. She flew to Angola to support the Red Cross's campaign to ban landmines. The trip was to prove the most satisfying and high-profile mission she had undertaken since she began lending her support to AIDS patients.

On landing in the Angolan capital Luanda, Diana made a speech stressing the need to draw the world's attention to the devastation caused by landmines.

'The international community must work together for an end to the use of these weapons,' she declared.

Predictably, some members of the Establishment tried to belittle Diana's efforts. A political row broke out when Earl Howe, a government minister, accused her of meddling in politics. Describing her as 'a loose cannon', he complained that her request for a ban on all anti-personnel mines differed from official government policy. Another minister sniped, 'The parallel that comes to mind is Brigitte Bardot and cats.'

Britain had made a commitment to a future worldwide ban while insisting that, in the meantime, it would continue to use 'smart mines' which became harmless after a period of around six months

Political pundits warned that a stockpile of landmines could be 'strategically useful'. Furthermore, 360,000 people were employed in the British defence industry, producing sales of weapons worth £7.6 billion.

Diana's intervention raised questions about her new, post-divorce position. Was she a free agent who could give her support to whatever or whomever she chose? Or, as the mother of a future king, should she steer clear of politically sensitive areas? The Royal Family had hoped that Charles and Diana's divorce would draw a line under the public relations nightmare for which they believed the 'out-of-control' Princess was responsible. The Angolan trip proved that the divorce had solved nothing. As London *Evening Standard* columnist William Oddie wrote, 'What it did was make clear that the bottomless public fascination with Diana was irreversible. Her identity as someone with almost magical powers to understand and articulate the world's sufferings was now unassailable.'

The Princess was amazed when informed of the headlines at home and stoutly defended herself.

'I was only trying to highlight a problem going on all around the world,' she explained to journalists. 'I am not a political figure. I am a humanitarian figure — always was, always will be.'

Mike Whitlam, then Director General of the British Red Cross, travelled with Diana and kept a detailed diary of the trip.

'I was mystified by the fuss,' he noted, 'because nothing the Princess had said differed in any way from British Government policy, which the Foreign Secretary Malcolm Rifkind later pointed out.'

Back in London, photographs of Diana walking through a newly-cleared minefield sent out a message that was picked up around the world. As she so often said, 'The cost of landmines in limbs, lives and land far outweighs any military advantage they might bring.'

She would take her crusade against landmines to Washington six months later, making the keynote speech at a Red Cross fund-raising dinner, and later, just three weeks before her death, to Bosnia on visits with people injured or bereaved by mines. There were those who claimed she made these trips as part of her quest for recognition.

'They would be wrong,' said *Daily Telegraph* columnist WF Deedes, a long-time campaigner against landmines who was invited to accompany the Princess. 'Her visit to Angola unquestionably put landmines higher on the agenda and indirectly quickened the movement towards a universal ban.'

Diana's mission elevated her to new heights in the public's regard, and also seemed to win approval from the only person whose respect she really craved — Hasnat Khan. They were so close after her return from

Angola that she began telling confidantes, 'I am going to marry him.'

By this time, Hasnat Khan was regularly spending nights with Diana at Kensington Palace. Hairstylist Natalie Symons recalls: 'I always knew when he was there. When I arrived early in the morning, I normally styled the Princess's hair in her dressing room. When Hasnat had stayed over, she would stop me at the top of the stairs and direct me into her sitting room. She used to explain that the electric socket where I plugged in my hairdryer in her room wasn't working. I had to smile because that socket used to break down at least three times a week.' She adds, 'Sometimes, when I passed her bedroom door I could see his jacket or other clothes hung on the back of a chair.'

Dr Khan was undoubtedly the only man Diana had loved and revered since she had become infatuated with Prince Charles. Now that she had found the first real love of her adult life, she did not intend to lose him. If there were obstacles blocking their marriage, then she was determined to overcome them — somehow. The main problem they faced, Diana believed, was Hasnat's parents, who had always expected that their son would marry a respectable Muslim girl from the Pathan tribe to which they belonged. Realising that Hasnat would never disobey them and marry without their approval, Diana decided to win them over.

It was not difficult to find an excuse to return to Pakistan. She had made two trips to Hasnat's hometown Lahore in the past. First, she had toured the country on an official visit arranged by the Foreign Office in 1991. Later, she had made a private visit to raise funds for the cancer hospital founded by Pakistan's former cricket star Imran Khan (no relation to Hasnat).

She had a standing invitation to return at any time, and in May 1997 she agreed to make a third, secret trip, ostensibly to help Imran and his English heiress wife Jemima Goldsmith with their charity work.

Her plan leaked out and planeloads of press were soon winging their way to Lahore. Despite this, within hours of her arrival in the steamy city, she slipped away from her security guards for a clandestine visit with Hasnat Khan's relatives. The Princess met his mother, father, grandmother and several other relations at 36G Model Town, a rather run-down, colonial-style mansion. This is the home of Hasnat's uncle, Professor Jawad Sajd Khan, a leading heart surgeon in Pakistan.

Her disappearance with Imran Khan's sisters Aleema and Noreen immediately caused a security alert. The Pakistani bodyguards hired to protect her did not know where she had gone.

It was so hot when the Princess greeted Hasnat's family that they did not linger inside the humid rooms of the house, but sat out in the garden where the temperature of the evening air was somewhat cooler. Mr and Mrs Khan Senior had driven 140km south to Lahore from their home in the small town of Jhelum especially to meet the Princess and, from the moment they met her, they were totally captivated.

Diana wore a pale blue and white *salwar kameez*, the traditional Pakistani dress consisting of a long, loose gown over loose-fitting, matching trousers. Her choice of outfit was carefully calculated. Pastel colours indicate a mark of respect in that country.

While Diana sat drinking tea with Hasnat's father Rasheed, his wife Naheed and around ten of their relatives, a number of small children played around their feet. But for more than an hour the old, colonial house had no lights or electricity for fans as a

THE TRUTH

thunderstorm had caused a power cut.

Pressmen covering her visit soon discovered that she was missing and suspected that she might have gone to the Khans' family home. But by the time they found the right address, Diana was long gone.

The following morning, Rasheed Khan, then 65, told newsmen that the Princess's visit was a social call.

'She is a family friend,' he explained.

'Diana wanted to meet us, we invited her and she was kind enough to come here,' he added. 'We just chatted, nothing else, for about one-and-a-half hours.

'I had not met her before, but some of the others had. My wife's mother Nanny Appa, as we call her, had met the Princess before at Kensington Palace. She (Nanny Appa) says, "Diana is my daughter." She likes her endlessly because Diana does social work.'

He went on to say that Hasnat would have to seek the blessing of his parents if he wanted to marry. He said that there was no religious reason why Hasnat, a Muslim, could not marry a divorced Christian woman with children, but he added discreetly, 'I don't think they will marry. Neither of them has expressed this thing to us at any time. If they asked us, then we would consider it. We can think over it — this is only speculation.'

When Diana's secret visit to her lover's family was made public in Britain, reporters turned up on Hasnat Khan's West London doorstep to seek his reaction. He expressed amazement and claimed he did not know why the Princess would want to visit his family.

A very private man who did not like to discuss personal matters with the press, he said as little as possible before returning to his work. But when Diana returned to London, he was extremely angry with her. He had assumed that she would not risk visiting his relatives with dozens of media men hot on her trail. He was wrong.

In a stormy scene at Kensington Palace, the irate doctor accused Diana of being 'stupid' and shouted that she must have been crazy to go to his family's home when journalists were watching her every move. He also accused her of deliberately arranging the visit to give the media a clue to the seriousness of their relationship. Diana had broken their agreement to keep the romance a secret, he raged. Her only response was to burst into tears and deny everything.

A palace worker who overheard the row later revealed, 'He was incredibly angry, got very personal and was extremely sarcastic.'

Diana was distraught when the doctor walked out saying that he could not put up with her any longer. 'Let's cool it for a while,' he said.

Within a few hours, he was on the telephone to apologise and sent Diana a huge bouquet of red roses.

Confused by his contradictory behaviour, Diana asked her friend Natalie Symons, 'What does it mean when a man says he doesn't want to see you any more, then sends flowers and phones every hour?'

Throughout the summer of 1997, their love affair continued to be turbulent. Natalie arrived on several mornings to find the Princess red-eyed and distraught after yet another bust-up with the surgeon. Whenever a story appeared in the press about them, he suspected Diana had leaked it. Diana denied this and claimed that an astrologer she knew was leaking information to newspapers. Dr Khan did not appear to believe her.

It was certainly true that she talked openly about how much she loved him to a great many people.

'We're definitely going to get married. Spread it around,' she told Natalie. 'His parents loved me and they have given us their blessing.'

But the surgeon was apprehensive about becoming linked with such a high-profile woman. He knew that his private life would be destroyed if the world knew the true state of their relationship. He was also becoming increasingly worried about its effect on his medical career. Hasnat Khan worked with the team of world-famous cardiac transplant surgeon Sir Magdi Yacoub, whom film star Omar Sharif credits with saving his life. How could an ordinary surgeon progress up the career ladder if he became Diana's husband? He could not abandon his critically-ill patients to accompany her to film premières and charity fund-raisers, or take time off to follow her around the world on tours. Besides, he had no interest in the glitzy world she inhabited. His work was his life.

In a way, this lack of interest in the glamorous life Diana led was to her one of his most appealing traits. He had come from a world where material things did not matter.

But a great cause of friction was his reluctance to make his private life public. As a high-caste Pathan, he considered it unseemly to court publicity. He felt his work should speak for itself and did not seek to promote his career through his relationship with a famous woman.

His Pakistani background also meant that he was neither part of, nor influenced by, the British Establishment. He did not live by their rules, something Diana found extremely attractive, although she constantly complained about his refusal to 'go public'.

Hasnat Khan was the first man who had not immediately fallen at her feet. And his initial refusal to capitulate to all her demands had made him all the more attractive in her eyes. So Diana continued to do all the running, trying to keep their romance on track, while constantly rowing then passionately making up again.

After one really blistering fight, Diana caved in and begged him to come back to her. Then, in June, she made him wildly jealous by going out on a date with another eminent Pakistani, wealthy Gulu Lalvani, then 54, the Asian head of the Binatone Electronics company.

Lalvani, a businessman from Karachi, who had been married and divorced twice, took her to London's most exclusive restaurant, Harry's Bar, then on to dance at Annabel's, the Berkeley Square nightclub. When he drove her home to Kensington Palace, paparazzi cameramen were lying in wait, but instead of trying to avoid them, the Princess gave them a dazzling smile. It was her way of sending Hasnat a very pointed message — if you don't want me, other men do.

The photographs of Diana and her date published the following day in British newspapers made Dr Khan upset, but he angrily told Diana that he didn't care who she saw or where she went.

This constant conflict was slowly undermining the love they shared. It seemed the happiness that once appeared to be within her grasp was as elusive as ever.

But Diana was determined to make the relationship work. She refused to give up on the future she envisioned would be theirs one day. He was the man she wanted and nothing and no one, she believed, could come between them.

10

Just when Diana despaired of ever resolving her differences with Dr Khan, a new man entered her life.

The Harrods tycoon Mohamed Al Fayed had frequently offered her the use of a villa he owned in St Tropez for a holiday. Over dinner on 3 June 1997, he repeated his invitation. They were idly chatting after watching a performance of the English National Ballet at the Royal Albert Hall. The evening ended with a black-tie dinner at the Inter Continental Hotel. As they finished their meal, they began to discuss their plans for the summer. One guest recalls that Diana was in a strange mood, behaving in an off-hand manner, speaking very curtly to the people at her table as if sitting there under sufferance.

Then the wealthy Egyptian suggested that she and her sons William and Harry might like to spend some time at the compound he owned in an exclusive hilltop area overlooking the sea. Diana brightened as he explained that it had a large guest house with its own pool which would be hers to enjoy.

In the weeks that followed, Diana began to consider Al Fayed's offer seriously. It was always difficult to find a suitable place where her sons could have a good time in the sunshine yet be guaranteed privacy. They had spent several holidays at the K Club on the Caribbean island of Barbuda, an ultra-exclusive resort where the local constabulary protected them from prying eyes. But they were beginning to grow bored with all it had to offer. Diana was on the lookout for something new. St Tropez, the haunt of millionaires and movie stars, sounded far more exciting than a Caribbean island. William and Harry were scheduled to finish school in early July and join her for a month. Mohamed's invitation seemed the ideal solution. St Tropez was only a two-hour flight away and her host would lay on his own private jet to take them there.

It just so happened that Diana was desperate to escape from London that month. Prince Charles had arranged a lavish party to celebrate the 50th birthday of his mistress Camilla Parker Bowles in the middle of the month. When it happened, his former wife wanted to be far, far away, preferably somewhere exotic. So she gratefully accepted Mohamed Al Fayed's offer.

If she realised that St Tropez was the very worst place she could have chosen, she did not appear to care. It was the scene of the Duchess of York's downfall in 1992 when the notorious Daniel Angeli, known as the King of the French paparazzi, had photographed her in compromising circumstances with her financial adviser John Bryan.

Surely, the Princess, one of Sarah Ferguson's closest friends, had not forgotten this?

It is well known in media circles that the South of France attracts celebrities from around the world during the summer months. And where the stars of stage, screen and television go, cameramen are sure to follow. The French paparazzi are the most professional and the most dogged in Europe and as strictly-enforced privacy laws often prevent them from pursuing wary, local celebrities, they focus their long lenses on foreigners instead. Diana was their dream target.

Within hours of the Princess's arrival with her sons, news desks in London were alerted as to her whereabouts, and teams of reporters and photographers rushed down to the Côte d'Azur.

When the first pictures of Diana sunning herself with Mohamed Al Fayed arrived in London, the tabloids had a field day. It was well known that the tycoon was not romantically interested in the Princess, and he was accompanied by his wife Heini and their young children.

What astonished and dismayed Establishment figures in London was Diana's lack of discretion in associating with a man who had such a questionable past. The Egyptian's rapid rise to become a well-known public figure was as mysterious as his background. First, he had taken over the House of Fraser stores, including its flagship, the world famous Harrods department store in Knightsbridge, in a way that surprised and mystified the British business world. Everyone wanted to know — where did he get that kind of money?

Al Fayed was also the man who had helped to wreck the last Tory government's chances of being re-elected just two months earlier in a row about sleaze in politics. Critics were astounded that the Princess would permit her sons to accept the hospitality of such a controversial figure.

No one had ever been able to discover how he had risen to such wealth and eminence. A Department of Trade and Industry enquiry into the business affairs of the Al Fayed family had concluded that Mohamed and his brother had 'dishonestly represented their origins, their wealth, their business interests and their resources'. He had twice applied to become a British citizen and had twice been refused.

At first, Diana was not really bothered by this. She had received the permission of both Prince Charles and the Queen to take the boys to St Tropez and, through friends, she leaked this information to confound her attackers.

But this minor drama was soon forgotten when the Princess began to behave in an extraordinary way. She paraded around the shoreline in a leopard print bathing suit, providing the preying packs of paparazzi with the sensational pictures they sought. Earlier the same day, she had coyly hidden beneath a beach towel as if determined not to be seen.

With Al Fayed's high-powered yacht *Jonikal* at her disposal, she could have disappeared over the horizon to sunbathe on a private beach miles away. Yet, much of the time, she chose to stay where the cameramen were and to subject her children to their constant scrutiny.

Then, suddenly, Diana decided to complain about the invasion of her privacy in a surprising manner. She boarded a launch and zoomed across the water to where several British pressmen were observing her antics from a hired cabin cruiser.

Confronting the man she knew best, the *Sun*'s photographer Arthur Edwards, she asked him how long they intended to stay. The reply she received was, 'As long as you're here, we'll be here.'

She went on to complain that 'William can get freaked out' by the photographers who pursued her and revealed that her sons were urging her to leave Britain and live abroad.

Then James Whitaker of the *Mirror* decided to ask her why she had chosen to holiday in the paparazzi's favourite hunting ground.

'Where else can I go?' Diana replied lamely.

'Well, not here,' her inquisitor declared. He made it plain he thought her choice had been ill-advised.

Close to tears, Diana retaliated with a cryptic remark she knew would keep her tormentors guessing.

'You will have a big surprise coming soon, with the next thing I do.' Refusing to explain what she meant, she then roared back to the shore in her launch.

The following morning, when her comments were reported in the British press, the Princess denied that she had said them, claiming that the reporters had misquoted her. The journalists were adamant that they had accurately written down exactly what she had told them.

Some commentators suspected it was another example of the Princess's totally irrational behaviour.

'She may be a few diamonds short of a full tiara,' Robert Hardman speculated in the *Daily Telegraph*. 'Even her most ardent admirers are running out of excuses, tentatively suggesting that the Princess might seek some sort of political or even psychiatric advice.'

Since then, journalists have debated exactly what Diana meant by those intriguing few words. Was she planning to live abroad, or to abandon all charity work?

Most veteran royal watchers believed that the real reason Diana had approached the newsmen had been a bid to steal the spotlight from Camilla Parker Bowles, whose 50th birthday party was attracting a great deal of publicity back in Britain.

The cat-and-mouse game continued. One morning, British and French press boats followed *Jonikal* as it left port, hoping that Diana and her boys were aboard. Some miles off shore they began circling the stationary yacht, jostling for position. The only familiar figure who appeared on deck was Mohamed Al Fayed, who wanted to go swimming.

Unfortunately, the wake from the press boats bashed him against the hull of his yacht. Refusing to endure this treatment, he summoned the coastguard who ordered the British pressmen to return to the shore.

Just as the furious Fleet Street men were sailing out of camera range, the Princess began to put on a tantalising performance. Swinging out from the deck of the yacht on a rope like Tarzan's Jane, she twisted and turned displaying her voluptuous figure to great advantage before dropping into the water.

The French photographers, who had not been ordered away from the yacht, gleefully fired off roll after roll of film. The angry Brits could only seethe as their rivals got the pictures they desperately wanted.

At the end of the week, the downbeat Englishmen returned to London. Their only consolation was that their picture editors had refused to pay the extortionate sums demanded by the Frenchmen for their exclusive pictures of Diana's display so they did not get wide coverage in Britain.

Meanwhile, a better story was taking shape which the newspapermen would not discover for a few more weeks. At his father's request, Dodi Al Fayed had joined the happy family party in St Tropez. He had arrived on 15 July, leaving his girlfriend Kelly Fisher behind in Paris. Although he had met Diana twice before, they were not really well acquainted.

Their first meeting had come five years earlier when the Princess had attended the London première of the film *Hook* starring Robin Williams, which Dodi had co-produced. They had shaken hands when introduced in a receiving line and exchanged only a few words.

But in spring 1997, Diana's stepmother Raine, Countess de Chambrun, had invited her to a dinner party at which Dodi was one of the guests. As the Princess later recalled, 'It was sort of like a blind date.' She had a pleasant evening and enjoyed Dodi's company but, at the time, she was wildly in love with Hasnat Khan and soon forgot about the pleasant Egyptian who was struggling to continue his career as a film producer in Los Angeles.

Then he came back into her life in July when her romance with the hard-working doctor was rather rocky. Dodi was fun. He was also very, very charming. Everyone who knew him described him as a really gentle man, kind-hearted and great company. What's more, he had a reputation as a lady-killer who had romanced some of the world's most gorgeous women. His former dates included actresses Brooke Shields and Joanne Whalley, models Marie Helvin and Denice Lewis.

If he had a flaw, it was a minor obsession with his health. One friend called him 'germ-phobic' and claimed he was in the habit of using paper tissues to turn light switches on and off.

For Diana, he was at first an amusing companion. He organised outings in St Tropez for the Princess and her sons. He knew just where to go and what they would enjoy most. He was considerate and nothing was ever too much trouble.

The night before she and her boys left London, Diana had had another big bust-up with Hasnat Khan and Dodi Fayed was the ideal person to make her forget about her broken heart. Although she was due to return to London on 18 July, she postponed her departure for a few more days.

Whether this was a ploy to make her doctor lover jealous or simply that she was enjoying her time with the Al Fayeds is impossible to say. The Al Fayed family were thrilled to extend their hospitality a little longer.

Back in London, Diana received a huge box of exotic tropical fruit from Harrods and telephoned her host to thank him. 'If we eat all this we won't stop running to the loo,' she joked. She also received a roomful of pink roses from Dodi. Soon afterwards, he also sent her a Cartier Panther watch.

Still, no one outside the Princess's household knew of their flourishing friendship. When Dodi whisked Diana away by helicopter the following weekend, the press did not realise she had left London until she was spotted returning on Sunday night.

Even she had not known where Dodi was taking her when they set off. She confided to her hairstylist, 'I don't know where he's taking me. It's a big surprise.'

Her new suitor had reserved the plushest suite at the Ritz Hotel in Paris, which happens to be owned by his father. Diana was relaxed and happy when she returned, telling staff that she had had a wonderful time.

Just four days later, they left London once again to cruise around the Mediterranean aboard the *Jonikal*.

Debbie Gribble, a member of the crew on the

THE TRUTH

Jonikal, recalled in an interview for American television that, 'It was very romantic. Dodi was very attentive towards the Princess. He would send me off on errands to get chocolates and flowers for her. They were very happy and they laughed a lot. They were always constantly talking.'

Debbie added that Diana adored the romantic film *The English Patient* and watched it on video repeatedly, often with Dodi. Their days were spent lazing in the sun and their nights dining under a star-filled sky on deck. Sometimes, they went ashore to stroll around picturesque ports. Still, their romance remained their secret.

One wealthy yachtsman who anchored next to the *Jonikal* did notice Diana and Dodi but, typical of his kind, he was not in the habit of contacting the press. Only later did it occur to him to pass on the information to a journalist, who simply did not believe it.

For once Diana was not trying to hide her new love. Perhaps she wanted to be photographed frolicking with Dodi to make Hasnat Khan pay for their recent row. She may also have thought it was a superb way to wipe Camilla Parker Bowles out of the headlines. Camilla's star was in the ascendant as Charles felt free at last to acknowledge her role in his life more openly.

An Italian paparazzo named Mario Brenna, who haunts the Italian Riviera in summer, finally revealed her secret to the world. He had seen Diana and Dodi together and managed to get close enough to take pictures of the Princess in the arms of her playboy lover. It wasn't so very difficult as the Princess was hardly hiding from view.

If Diana and Dodi did not spot him as Brenna closed in for the shots which would make him a very rich man, the Al Fayed bodyguards should have done so. It remains a mystery why Trevor Rees-Jones and Kez Wingfield, two very professional security men, failed to notice the presence of the photographer.

But the cat was well and truly out of the Gucci bag. Brenna's exclusive photographs were soon on the Picture Desks of London newspapers who began frantically bidding for the right to publish them.

Back in London, Diana was constantly on the phone to Dodi.

'I love his exotic accent,' she told hairstylist Tess Rock. 'I love the way he says "Di-yana, you're so naughty!"'

They were now the biggest news story of the summer and photographers followed them everywhere. When Diana visited Dodi's apartment for dinner on 7 August the press camped on his Park Lane doorstep. But with the help of his bodyguards who devised an elaborate number of decoy cars, the Princess managed to leave unseen.

Dodi was due to return to Los Angeles and Diana had work to do in Bosnia. Their hot new romance guaranteed that the press corps who normally followed her on trips abroad had more than doubled by the time she arrived in Sarajevo.

Throughout the trip, she studiously ignored questions about Dodi shouted at her by reporters. But she could not have failed to realise that the media circus would benefit her landmines campaign.

Meanwhile, Dodi's life in Hollywood had proved irresistible to Fleet Street's investigative reporters. Ex-girlfriends, and even his ex-wife Suzanne Gregard, were all beseiged to tell their stories.

Generally, the stories were not very complimentary. One report wrongly claimed that Dodi had left a trail of bad debts in Los Angeles. The biggest bombshell that emerged in this scuffle for scandal came from the woman Dodi had ditched for Diana. Kelly Fisher tearfully appeared at a press conference to claim that she had been engaged to marry Dodi and now intended to sue him for breach of promise. She explained that she had accompanied Dodi to St Tropez but he had left her on a boat in the harbour each day to entertain the Princess and her sons. She complained that Dodi had been two-timing her with Diana and was eager to tell the world of his shortcomings.

When Diana picked up a newspaper in London and read about this, she anxiously asked a friend if Dodi was deceiving her. 'He said he would never lie to me, but people always lie to me,' she sighed.

It wasn't a great surprise when Kelly Fisher sold the story of her romance with Dodi to a newspaper, in which she claimed that he was a disappointing lover. 'He doesn't know how to pleasure a woman,' she declared.

Whether Kelly Fisher's allegations influenced the Princess is now impossible to work out. But, while still in close contact with Dodi who was on a short trip to the USA, Diana remained involved with Hasnat Khan. Staff later reported that he was still seeing her up until two weeks before her death. Their claim is backed up by Hasnat's Australian friend Erin who recalls, 'I know they were still together until a short time before the Princess's death — about two weeks.'

But she doubts that Dodi had replaced Hasnat in Diana's heart. 'I think they would have got back together again if she had lived,' Erin says. 'They were so in love.'

On 15 August, Diana left for Greece to enjoy a long-arranged break with her closest female friend Rosa Monckton. With the help of the Al Fayed family's aircraft, jokily called 'Air Dodi' by the media, they managed to evade pursuit and enjoy a relaxing holiday on the Greek island of Hydra.

Only one cameraman managed to snatch a picture of the two women together, and he was a 'civilian', just a sharp-eyed tourist who knew a lucky break when he spotted one. His picture ended up on the front page of the *Sun*.

Diana and Rosa flew back to London on 20 August. The next day, the Princess was due to embark on yet another holiday in the Mediterranean with Dodi. As she walked through the door of Kensington Palace, she yelled to Paul Burrell, 'Get my doctor.' Her monthly cycle had gone haywire over the past few months and she was concerned because she was menstruating twice a month.

Within a short time the doctor appeared, to Diana's surprise. She had only wished to speak to him on the telephone. When she explained her problem, he seemed annoyed at being summoned for such a trivial matter and informed her that he had no magic pills which would instantly provide a solution. It is clear from this incident that there was absolutely no chance that Princess Diana could have been pregnant, as some wild rumours have suggested.

As she prepared to leave once more, there was only one topic of conversation among Diana's staff — was she preparing to marry Dodi and leave Britain? If so, what would happen to them all? Stylist Tess Rock did not believe it and bet Diana's dresser Angela Benjamin £50 that she would still have a job with the Princess in six months' time.

To cover herself, she joked as she said goodbye to the Princess, 'Don't do anything stupid!'

Diana reassured her with a laugh and replied,

'Don't worry, I won't.'

Angela Benjamin was not convinced. As Tess left, she said, 'You could be seeing the Princess for the very last time.'

11

As they drove away from Le Bourget Airport a few minutes after their private jet touched down in Paris at the end of their Mediterranean holiday, Diana and Dodi had a violent disagreement.

Dodi had ordered their driver Philippe Dorneau to speed up so that they could shake off the pursuit of the paparazzi. Soon, the speedometer was touching 100mph as their Mercedes car weaved through heavy traffic.

Diana began screaming in terror and begged Dodi to slow down. Ignoring her fears, Dodi once again urged the driver to go even faster.

In what now seems a chilling portent of the tragedy which occurred minutes after midnight the same day,

Dodi acted recklessly, disregarding any natural concern for his own or others' safety. He was trying to make a big impression on the woman who had changed his life, the Princess who had transformed him from a very minor film producer in Los Angeles to a man who had captured the world's greatest prize.

Emad 'Dodi' Al Fayed, still dependent on his millionaire father for his luxurious lifestyle, was attempting to show Diana that, for once, he was totally in control.

They were accompanied by Dodi's bodyguard Trevor Rees-Jones, a former soldier who had served in Northern Ireland and the Gulf War. His best friend and colleague Ben Murrell, then 33, was also with the couple on their last day in Paris. He remembers, 'Dodi was definitely trying to impress the Princess, but Diana was angry and scared. By the time they arrived at the location, the luxury villa where the Duke and Duchess of Windsor once lived, she was flustered and red-faced.'

Tall and powerfully-built with a military-style haircut, Ben joined the Al Fayed security team as a general bodyguard after leaving the Royal Marines in 1995. With typical serviceman's language, he explains, 'I would liaise directly with Mohamed and also with the Ritz Hotel in Paris, overseeing visits to the villa and co-ordinating movements in the area. Mr Al Fayed liked to have someone on hand at every one of his homes to deal with any problems that might arise. In my three years working for the Al Fayeds, I spent 18 months at the Windsor villa with my wife Rebecca looking after security procedures.'

On Saturday, 30 August 1997, he received a telephone call informing him that Diana and Dodi were on their way from Le Bourget Airport and opened up the main rooms of the mansion at 4 Route du Champs d'Entrainment.

When the couple arrived with Trevor Rees-Jones, Ben Murrell was standing at the front door to greet them. It was immediately obvious that the Princess was extremely upset. He says, 'I showed her into a small office where she sat down and tried to compose herself.'

As soon as he had a chance, he asked Dodi's chauffeur what had happened to make Diana so distressed. 'Philippe told me that the Princess had been genuinely frightened when Dodi ordered him to lose the photographers following them. He said she was crying out, afraid there would be a crash. She was worried about her own safety and also that the paparazzi racing alongside them might be injured. It was the first time he had driven the Princess and he was shocked at how distraught she became on the journey from the airport to the Windsors' home.'

Ben asked how Dodi had responded to Diana's pleas. 'The chauffeur said he did not react in any way to her input. He just sat back in the car.'

Following this terrifying drive to the villa, it is not difficult to imagine her panic just hours later as the Mercedes 280S in which she was a passenger hurtled into the Pont d'Alma tunnel. If she had ever regarded Dodi with affection, her feelings were beginning to change as their holiday drew to an end.

Inside the Windsors' former home, Diana spent some minutes trying to calm down, Ben says, before she rather reluctantly followed Dodi on a short tour of the house.

'They spent five minutes looking at exhibits of the Duchess of Windsor's clothes, which are kept in glass cases, then they spent another ten minutes walking past some of the furnishings and pictures.'

With his direct gaze and precise recollection, the bodyguard insists that Diana did not venture upstairs and looked around the mansion only briefly.

'She seemed as if she could not wait to get the visit out of the way and get back to the hotel,' Ben recalls. 'I thought she appeared to be quite uncomfortable, while Dodi also looked embarrassed.'

As he looks back, Ben Murrell particularly remembers that Dodi was not his normal self. Everything he said sounded stilted and unnatural, as if he was under pressure. Ben also doubts that the visit to the villa was Dodi's idea and thinks he may only have been carrying out his father's wishes.

He remembers that the couple's body language was significant as they walked around the house. 'I followed them at a distance and noticed that they did not hold hands or display any other kind of affection. In fact, they looked quite distant from each other. Anyone would have thought they were a thousand miles apart. They seemed like two acquaintances looking around a small museum,' he says. 'On her part, there was no enthusiasm at all.'

Ben stresses that Diana's visit to the Windsor villa lasted little more than 25 minutes, and *not* two hours, as Mohamed Al Fayed had claimed. 'The visit lasted less than half-an-hour; in fact, exactly 28 minutes, and that includes driving in and driving out of the property,' he asserts.

Dodi's father, perhaps anxious to prove that Diana intended to marry his son, is alleged to have told his staff that she was planning to set up home there with Dodi. Gregorio Martin, the 60-year-old butler who worked at the house, gave several interviews to the media in which he claimed Diana had twice visited the mansion, once with an interior designer.

'Shortly after the accident, a TV crew arrived,' Ben recalls. 'I was quite shocked when Gregorio went in front of the cameras and said he was butler of the day when the Princess visited the house. He said he had escorted them around the house for two hours. I was quite mystified because he was not even in the country that day — he was on holiday in Spain.'

Ben later asked the butler why he said this. 'Gregorio held his hands up and said, "I'm under pressure. Please go on television and say the same as me."'

The bodyguard refused. 'The way I see it, he was told by Mohamed Al Fayed to say this was going to be the marital home of the Princess and Dodi. Martin was near to retirement and he had a great deal to lose. He is an old man, so I understood.'

Ben Murrell is positive Diana did not make any other visit to the villa. 'That is simply not true,' he says. 'If they had, I would have known about it. I had lived there for more than a year with my wife. Her visit on 30 August was her one and only short visit.'

Ben's claims about the Princess's brief visit are supported by the evidence of a security video filmed by closed-circuit television cameras which recorded the time Diana and Dodi arrived at, and left, the Windsors' former home in the Bois de Boulogne. The time sequence on the film shows that Diana stepped from a car outside the house at 3.47pm. A later frame shows Diana leaving at 4.15pm.

Ben says, 'The whole thing was presented in a way so that people would think Diana and Dodi planned to live in the Windsor mansion after marrying.' Why would Mohamed Al Fayed wish to promote this idea? 'I can only surmise one reason would have been to strengthen his links with the Royal Family through Diana.'

Later, Dodi's butler Rene Delorm also turned up at the mansion with another television crew and gave an interview in which he claimed Diana had explored the whole house, looking at the staff quarters, opening cupboards and even going down to the basement to look at the central heating boiler.

He also declared that the Princess had looked around the grounds, and had even wanted to see the dog kennels.

'Rene was telling a fairytale which bore no relationship to the facts whatsoever,' Ben insists.

What made Rene Delorm give such an account? Ben says, 'The supposed two-and-a-half-hour visit to look at the house as a marital home was the best way he could prove Diana and Dodi were planning a future together. To my mind, that's not true. It was just a summer romance. They certainly didn't look in love to me.

'I felt sad that Diana's name had been tarnished and I was angry that the person giving the interview was saying those things. Rene didn't seem embarrassed. He was quite excited and having a good time. It was almost as if he was living out a fantasy. And I am sure Mohamed would not let him say anything unless it had been authorised.

'I was asked if I was in a position to back up his story by the television producer, but I declined. My main aim was not to be put into a position where I would be drawn into this distorted account.'

The bodyguard adds that Diana did not appear to be at all interested in the house as a future home.

'As I followed her around the place, I could see she just wanted to get out of there. If you were looking for somewhere to live, I think you would spend a lot

THE TRUTH

longer than 20 minutes looking around it,' he points out.

'I felt very uncomfortable about all the stories. But a year on, the story had got larger and grown out of all proportion. People were convinced Diana would marry Dodi, so I felt I had to speak out and tell the truth.'

Ben, who served as a Royal Marine in the Gulf War, saw no indication whatsoever that the Princess planned to marry Dodi Fayed, as his father has repeatedly claimed. In fact, he believes that Diana was not seriously involved with the playboy film producer at all.

Several of the Al Fayed security team, shocked that a Princess would bother with such a well-known playboy, asked Diana what she was doing with Dodi.

'She just shrugged her shoulders as if to say, "I don't know,"' Ben says.

She gave every indication that she had nothing better to do and Dodi was simply a way to fill in her empty weeks while her sons were with their father.

'They certainly did not look like a couple in love to me. They were quite cool towards one another. I got the impression they weren't enjoying each other, just the press attention,' Ben adds.

When their Mediterranean holiday ended in Sardinia with a brief stop-over in Paris, Ben had a chance to discuss security arrangements with Trevor Rees-Jones, the only survivor of the fatal car crash.

'Trevor was in a foul mood and was ready to quit his job. He told me that Dodi was ignoring all his advice.'

In later conversations with Trevor, he learned the full details of the lax security arrangements surrounding the Princess.

'Trevor was normally a bubbly guy, but on the day

he arrived at the villa he was very sombre and quiet. He told me he was having problems with Dodi who was overruling all his arrangements.

'The bottom line is, of course, that an employer makes all the decisions and a security officer makes suggestions. But we are employed because of our expertise and if our advice is ignored, there is not much point in our being there.

'Trevor was determined to have it out with Dodi when they got back to his apartment, but they never arrived there. It was not just one single day which made him angry, it was a combination of everything that had happened on the whole trip.

'Dodi had been overruling him on almost every security decision and Trevor was concerned that all his arrangements were being ignored.'

Working for Dodi was not as glamorous as it might seem, Ben adds. 'Dodi was generally polite, but to him we were just servants, very low on the pecking order as far as he was concerned.

'He would ask us to pick him up at 9.00pm and then he wouldn't appear until 2.00am. We spent a lot of time just waiting around for Dodi, but Diana was different. She was very considerate of everyone's needs. I think she was getting very irritated by Dodi's manner. I had hoped he would learn something from her and I think his attutude to us could well have annoyed Diana.'

Just minutes before Diana, Dodi and Trevor Rees-Jones set off on that last fatal drive through Paris, the bodyguard was becomingly increasingly angry. Ben remembers that Trevor told Dodi's other bodyguard Alexander 'Kez' Wingfield that things were coming to a head and he couldn't go on any longer. In fact, he was so furious that Kez suggested he should take Trevor's place in the Mercedes while he relaxed.

'Trevor remembers clearly that he was in a situation he was not happy about. Dodi's plan to leave the Ritz Hotel by the rear entrance had major flaws. He was not using the correct driver and he was not using a second back-up vehicle to protect the rear of the Mercedes.

Dodi Al Fayed had decided that the Mercedes in which he and Diana had arrived should leave the hotel's front entrance with a back-up car, hoping this decoy would draw the waiting paparazzi off on a futile chase. This seemed naïve to the bodyguards, who knew that the wily pressmen would also have colleagues checking the back door of the Ritz, just in case the couple tried to escape by this route.

'Dodi was out of his depth. He had no knowledge of security procedures, yet he overruled Trevor's advice,' Ben says. 'This was the final straw for Trevor, but he tried to make the best of the situation and he refused to let Kez Wingfield take his place. After that, he has an almost complete memory loss.'

Although he had to endure months of reconstructive surgery to rebuild his face, Trevor Rees-Jones was amazingly lucky to be the only survivor of a crash in which three other people died. As he states in his book *The Bodyguard's Story*, he cannot remember if he was wearing a seat-belt during the fatal drive through Paris. Normally, when driving through a city, he did not fasten his belt. The official Paris enquiry into the accident later decided he had not been wearing one. His life was saved by the airbag which protected his body, although his face was smashed beyond all recognition.

Ben Murrell says, 'Any bodyguard in a speeding car would turn and warn the back seat passengers to put on their seatbelts. But if they refuse point blank, there's not a lot you can do.'

Diana should have been aware of the necessity for seat-belts. In February 1993, she had been caught without one while sitting in the rear of her Jaguar when a police car, travelling too close behind, collided with it. Although her composure wasn't dented, her car was and it had to be hauled away for repairs.

Despite the introduction of a law in Britain requiring passengers to 'belt up in the back', official figures indicate that around 43 per cent of adults ignore it. Tragically, Diana seems to have been one of them.

In September 1999, the official French report into the Paris crash concluded that 'Emad (Dodi) Al Fayed and Lady Diana Spencer would have survived if they had fastened their safety belts.'

As Al Fayed's Paris security officer, Ben Murrell was ordered to look after Trevor Rees-Jones' anxious mother and stepfather, Jill and Ernie Rees-Jones, who kept a vigil at his bedside while he remained in a coma. Even when Trevor began drifting in and out of consciousness, he was unable to communicate. His jaw had been wired up as doctors painstakingly restored his shattered features.

Ben says, 'I was told to make sure his parents kept to Mohamed's way of thinking. And I had to stop Trevor giving any statement to the police until he had been debriefed in London by Mohamed and his security staff.

'I think they were concerned about what he might say. They didn't want to be held responsible for the accident, so Trevor had to give the right statement.

'Trevor is the sort of person who is extremely loyal and all he wanted to do was go back to work and put all this behind him. He felt in some way responsible for the crash. He has come a long way physically and is now playing rugby again, but the scars go deeper than the flesh. It's going to take him a long time to recover mentally from the accident.

'Anyone who had any involvement, even in the smallest way with the crash, is thinking, If only ... So human nature dictates that he feels pretty bad. I think hindsight is a wonderful thing. Part of the guilt Trevor feels are the factors contributing to the accident. One of those factors was that the driver Henri Paul was drunk. He was employed by Mohamed Al Fayed.'

When Diana and Dodi arrived at the Windsor mansion, Ben Murrell had met Henri Paul and noticed to his surprise that he had been drinking.

'He drove up in the second baggage car following the Princess and I could smell alcohol on his breath. He seemed like someone who had had a very good lunch with booze and food. Normally he was a very quiet, passive man, but on this occasion he wasn't himself. He was acting completely out of character. He leaned out of the window of the Range Rover and shook me by the shoulders. "Eh, Ben, are you having a good time?" he asked in his thick French accent.'

Later the same day, Dodi's driver Philippe also noticed that the balding chauffeur seemed to be drunk. Afterwards, he told Ben that he felt concerned about a man who had been drinking taking the wheel of a car in which the Princess was travelling.

But Henri Paul was the Ritz Hotel's Deputy Chief of Security while Philippe was just a lowly chauffeur. He did not dare to complain about the senior man's unprofessional behaviour.

Henri Paul was born in Lorient, a naval base in Southern Brittany, in July 1956. He went to a private school where he excelled at violin and piano playing. He gained his pilot's licence at the age of 17 and studied aeronautics. But poor eyesight wrecked his hopes of becoming a military pilot. In 1986, he heard about a vacancy at the Ritz Hotel and was soon employed as a member of the security team. At his death, he had risen to become Acting Head of Security with 20 employees under his command.

Unknown to his colleagues, Paul was also working for British Intelligence. As Richard Tomlinson, a former MI6 agent, later revealed, 'Henri Paul was an MI6 contact. He had been for years.' Working at the Ritz he was well placed to observe the comings and goings of wealthy and influential guests, and make reports on their activities to the British intelligence-gathering organisation.

Many of his colleagues informed the French investigation that Paul had a habit of drinking heavily. Just hours before the accident, Trevor Rees-Jones had spotted Henri with a yellow-coloured drink and asked what it was. Henri replied that it was a soft drink. Tests later proved he had been drinking *pastis*. Neither man knew then that Henri Paul was also taking anti-depressants.

The offical report of the inquiry into the Paris accident later revealed, 'The autopsy on the body of Henri Paul rapidly showed the presence of a level of pure alcohol per litre of blood between 1.73 and 1.75 grams which is higher in all cases than the legal level,' (three-and-a-half times the French legal limit of 0.5 grams and more than double the English limit of 0.8 grams).

'Analyses revealed that he regularly consumed Prozac and Tiapridal, both medicines which are not recommended for drivers, as they provoke a change in the ability to be vigilant, particularly when they are taken in combination with alcohol.'

It was also noted that Paul, who normally drove a Mini, did not have the special limousine licence required under French law to drive high-powered motor vehicles. As a result, a drunken driver was in control of a car with faulty brakes, which he was not qualified to drive, leading with a terrifying inevitability to tragedy in the Pont d'Alma tunnel.

'As a bodyguard, Trevor did all he could,' Ben declares. 'But if your advice is ignored, there is little you can do about it.'

Ben Murrell decided to quit his job as a security guard for the Al Fayed family in 1998 because he was disgusted with the conspiracy claims made by Mohamed Al Fayed. He was interviewed in May 1998 in London.

'I just couldn't take it any more,' he says. 'I thought it was time to make a stand and tell the true story.'

Trevor Rees-Jones resigned from Al Fayed's employ in April 1998, and his colleague, Yorkshire-born Kez Wingfield, left his job in June 1998, after seven years with the Al Fayed family. Ben reveals that Kez was also asked to back up Al Fayed's fantastic claims in a television interview.

'He knew that he could not refuse to do this unless he was prepared to quit. There was a row which got quite heated and Kes decided that his position was untenable so he left his job.

'Kez was called into an office and he was told to go on a TV programme and perpetuate the story that Diana and Dodi were going to get married,' Ben explains.

He has tried to understand why the Harrods tycoon wants to conceal the truth. 'I could understand that he has lost his son which is terrible. But I can see there is a big smoke-screen surrounding the crash. Mohamed Al Fayed is a very powerful man. He seems to have been ambitious to gain British citizenship, which has been refused. This supposed romance would have gone a long way to attach himself to Diana, Princess of Wales.'

Al Fayed staff continue to encourage the belief that Diana's relationship with Dodi was far more serious than it actually was. On 27 August 2000, Karen MacKenzie, the housekeeper at Dodi's London apartment in Park Lane, gave an interview to the *Sunday People* in which she talked about 'Dodi's three months of happiness with Diana'. She said, 'I remember Diana's first visit to the flat in June 1997.' This is decidedly odd, because the Princess did not really get to know Dodi until her holiday with the Al Fayed family in July 1997. As a result, their relationship lasted a mere six weeks, not three months.

The housekeeper recalled that when Diana was in London, she would usually stay overnight, as often as four nights a week. In his autobiography, Trevor Rees-Jones describes the elaborate arrangements needed to take the Princess safely back to Kensington Palace after evenings with Dodi. Karen MacKenzie may have been genuinely mistaken or influenced by the fact that she still works for the Al Fayed family, while Trevor Rees-Jones does not.

The conclusions reached by Ben Murrell are echoed by Diana's close friend Rosa Monckton who shared a holiday with Diana in the Greek islands just ten days before she died. After months of refusing to talk about her late friend, Rosa finally broke her silence in February 1998 with an article in the *Sunday Telegraph*. She said that 'morbid fantasising' in the media had forced her to set the record straight about rumours that Diana could have been pregnant and had planned to marry Dodi Al Fayed.

'I know that it would have been biologically impossible for her to have been pregnant at the time of the crash,' Rosa asserted. 'As for marriage, there was no question of it. She had only known Dodi for six weeks.

Rosa, the Chief Executive of Asprey & Garrard, added that the Princess was emotionally very insecure and demanded constant reassurance in her relationships. For those who knew her well this was not unusual because it had happened before. Rosa asserted, 'Neither on her holiday with me, nor when I spoke to her last, on the Wednesday before her death, did she show any indication of a desire to marry Dodi.'

To support her claims, Rosa spoke to another close friend of the Princess, Annabel Goldsmith, who told her that Diana had expressed similar feelings to her. When Annabel asked her to be careful with Dodi, she was told, 'Don't worry, Annabel. I'm having a wonderful time, but the last thing I need is a new marriage. I need it like a bad rash on my face.'

The Princess had made a very similar comment to the Greek millionaire Taki Theodoracopolous when he called Diana to ask if she was seriously involved with the Egyptian film producer.

It is not difficult to understand why the world wished to believe that, in the last weeks of her life, the sad Princess had found someone who would love and cherish her at last.

The myth of a great but doomed love affair began almost immediately. DIANA DIED WEARING DODI'S RING screamed a headline in the *Daily Mail*, a story which later proved to be totally untrue. A caption under a photograph of the couple on holiday in the Mediterranean read: 'So in love'. The *Daily Mirror* gushed, 'Diana's romance with Dodi Fayed will be remembered as one of the most tragic affairs of the century.'

This romantic fantasy was encouraged by Dodi's

father Mohamed Al Fayed who claimed repeatedly that the couple were hoping to marry. In an interview with the *Daily Mirror* in February 1998, he said his son had told him on the night of the crash that he had proposed marriage and that the Princess had accepted. Four months later, Mr Al Fayed suddenly remembered that he had also spoken to the Princess that night. 'She was completely full of happiness, full of joy,' he stated.

How surprising, then, that Dodi's butler Rene Delorm, writing in his book *Diana and Dodi, A Love Story*, seems to contradict the Egyptian tycoon.

In it, he claims that Dodi was planning to propose but had not actually asked the Princess. He says that his employer had been preparing to offer Diana a ring at the end of their last evening in Paris.

Mohamed Al Fayed was among the first to trot out the theory that the Princess and his son had been assassinated. Essential to a conspiracy was proof that Dodi and Diana were planning to marry. Many other outlandish allegations were made, particularly in the Arab world, which suggested that the British Establishment did not want Diana to give her sons a Muslim brother or sister.

Intelligence operatives pour scorn on such claims, explaining that no sensible assassin would attempt to use a traffic accident to kill someone.

'The problem is you cannot guarantee the success of your mission,' one long-serving security officer says. 'As we know, Trevor Rees-Jones survived and both Dodi and Diana would have emerged relatively unscathed, too, if they had been wearing seat-belts.'

Mohamed Al Fayed's credibility appeared shaky when he made other claims which were decisively dismissed. On the eve of the Princess's funeral, Harrods spokesman Michael Cole announced that his employer had met a nurse who had passed on Diana's dying words. He added that her 'final words and bequests' had been conveyed to the appropriate person.

Members of the Spencer family immediately called this statement 'preposterous' and extremely distressing. At the same time, a senior executive at La Pitié-Salpêtrière hospital, where Diana died, accused Al Fayed of 'invention'. Thierry Meresse, Communication Director at the hospital, denied that the Princess had spoken any words at all. He said, 'The Princess was unconscious on arrival and then she had a heart attack. She was not capable of speech in her last hours. It is utterly untrue to suggest that she was.'

This unedifying debate went on for some weeks as the Al Fayed lawyers, Diana's family and friends, as well as a French priest who attended her in hospital, all made claims and counter-claims.

If Diana was hoping to marry Dodi, why did she not mention this good news to any of her close friends or her family? She had told her confidantes every detail of her new relationship right up until the day she died. If she had no intention of accepting Dodi's proposal, why would there be any need to kill her?

Perhaps for a short while, Diana did hope that Dodi would be someone worthy of her affection. But did she really plan a future with the Egyptian playboy?

The Princess's dearest friends, a tiny handful of people who spoke to her by telephone while she enjoyed her last holiday in the Mediterranean, know that this is simply not true.

As she headed for home on the last day of her life, Diana was disillusioned and depressed about the time she had spent with the millionaire playboy. Whether he was aware of her change of heart is unclear, but there is some evidence that he was.

Weeks earlier, well-meaning friends had tried to warn her not to get involved with Dodi Al Fayed. They pointed out that just two years earlier he owed £80,000 in unpaid taxes and had gained a reputation as a man who reneged on deals, but she had refused to listen. By the end of August 1997, her attitude had changed. She had noted that Dodi constantly left her side to visit the bathroom. During dinner or a quiet evening watching videos on the *Jonikal*, he disappeared so often that she began to wonder what was going on.

A long-time campaigner against drug abuse, the Princess was quite knowledgeable about the signs of drug addiction. She detested and pitied people who wasted their lives using illegal substances.

Perhaps her suspicions were misplaced. Perhaps she had tired of the affair and was simply looking for a way out. Interestingly, many of Dodi's Los Angeles acquaintances later claimed that he had a serious cocaine habit. Three months after his death, former friend Nona Summers told *Vanity Fair* magazine, 'He was into cocaine.' Another unnamed acquaintance revealed that the Egyptian playboy would buy a kilo of cocaine a week. Another well-known Hollywood producer revealed, 'Dodi had not had a hit movie for many years. No one wanted to do deals with him because everyone knew he had a serious coke habit.'

It matters not now whether this was true or false. The fact is that Diana gradually began to grow concerned about Dodi's strange behaviour.

One of the last people to speak to her was Colin Tebbutt, the chauffeur she asked to meet her at London airport.

'Make sure you are there on time,' she told him. 'I just can't wait to get home.'

This hardly sounds like a woman enjoying a dream

holiday with a new love. It is also intriguing that she clearly did not wish to drive home with Dodi.

Six weeks was too short a time for a woman with Diana's past experience to decide if she should commit herself to another man. After all, the most important men of all in her life were her sons, and she would have wanted their approval before giving them a stepfather, no matter how charming or kind. Dodi did not appear to share her dedication to the sick and dying. He had never shown the slightest interest in charity work or helping others. His life was totally hedonistic and self-centred. Diana may have been fond of him for a time, but did she ever respect him?

In the six weeks of their acquaintance, Diana went to Bosnia, enjoyed a week-long holiday with Rosa Monckton and Dodi went on a business trip to Hollywood. Their relationship therefore lasted little more than one month. Was this long enough to erase from her heart her two-year love affair with Hasnat Khan?

12

Paul Burrell walked out of the La Pitié-Salpêtrière hospital with misery written all over his face. Close behind him came Diana's chauffeur Colin Tebbutt.

'We've just been in to see the boss,' the butler said to a journalist he knew well, who reached him on his mobile phone. 'We've lost the captain of our ship. It's so sad to see her in there. I can't tell you how sad.'

Both men had rushed over to Paris on the first flight leaving London early on that late summer Sunday in the hope that they could somehow still be of service to the Princess even though they already knew they would be too late.

In just a few hours, Colin had been scheduled to pick up the Princess at the airport in London and drive her home to Kensington Palace, where Paul would have been waiting to greet her. Now their years of royal service were over.

In the darkest hour of the night, just before daybreak in Paris, doctors at the hospital had finally given up the fight to save Diana, Princess of Wales at 4.05am on 31 August 1997. By a bitter twist of fate, in the last weeks of her life, Diana had been on the brink of a new dawn.

After the pain and upheaval of her divorce, she had at last reached a state of calm and stability. Britain's new Prime Minister Tony Blair had been encouraging and had promised her his backing for her work overseas.

Her campaign to rid the world of landmines was gaining increasing support and she was planning to embark on a major new crusade in the early months of 1998. For two years, she had been planning to team up with Canadian psychologist Peggy Claude-Pierre to help sufferers of eating disorders like anorexia and bulimia, which had blighted her own life for so long.

After watching an American documentary on Peggy's pioneering work at her clinic, the Montreux Centre in British Columbia, she asked to meet her and together they had arranged to launch a fund-raising benefit for people with eating disorders in New York. Diana was very excited about it and, shortly before her death, she talked about it constantly to her hairstylist Natalie Symons.

'It's going to be my next big campaign and I can't wait to get started,' she said. 'Peggy Claude-Pierre has a whole new approach to this problem which really works.'

The Princess was looking forward to a whole new life opening up for her outside the confines of the royal Court.

Then, with a squeal of tyres followed by the shattering sound of metal grinding into concrete, all this was swept away. A high-speed car crash had extinguished the life of Diana and her companion Dodi Al Fayed in the most brutal way. She was exactly 36 years and 2 months old.

Prolonged efforts to resuscitate the Princess had failed because her injuries were too severe. For more than an hour, she had been bleeding internally, flooding the thoracic cavity, and had suffered a cardiac arrest. A priest on duty at the hospital gave her the last rights according to the Catholic faith. Father Yves Clochard-Bossuet later told the *Mirror* newspaper, 'She was already dead. They had taken her to a private room upstairs. I prayed for her soul. I was alone with her for four hours.'

All he could think of, he recalled, was the sad fact that Diana had had everything to live for. He added, 'I thought of the sadness she had endured in her short life. I am a priest, but I am also a human being. It touched me very much.' Later, an Anglican vicar took over the vigil beside the Princess until Prince Charles was ready to take her home to England.

The Prince of Wales had been awoken from a deep sleep at Balmoral in Scotland and was informed that his former wife had been involved in an accident in Paris. It was at first believed that the Princess had not suffered any serious injury. Radio stations were reporting that she had sustained only a deep gash to one thigh. So the decision was taken to let his sons sleep until more information could be gained.

A later phone call to the British embassy in Paris brought the shocking news that the Princess was dead. At once, the whole royal household was plunged into turmoil. No one was quite sure what to do. Charles and the Queen's first thoughts were for Diana's boys William and Harry. Telling them of the accident which claimed the life of their mother was the hardest thing the Prince had ever had to do. Early on the Sunday morning of 31 August, a brief statement was hurriedly issued from Balmoral which said simply, 'The Queen and Prince of Wales are deeply shocked and distressed by this terrible news.'

At 11.00am, the family went to nearby Crathie parish church, as they usually did on a Sunday morning, but there was no mention of the late Princess during the service. Perhaps this was designed to avoid upsetting Diana's grim-faced sons, sitting in a front pew, but it appeared difficult to understand.

Later that day, Charles flew to Paris with Diana's sisters Sarah and Jane to bring home the body of his ex-wife. President Chirac was waiting with two of his cabinet ministers to greet him at the hospital. Still in shock and dazed by grief, the Prince had to go through the formalities expected of a future king. He made a point of thanking the medical staff who had tried so valiantly to save his former wife — anaesthetist Bruno Riou, and Alan Parvie, the cardio-thoracic surgeon, as well as other hospital officials.

The coffin was carried to the military airport at Villacoublay in a hearse with blinds drawn. The motorcade drove off with Prince Charles in a Jaguar directly behind the hearse. Diana's last journey home had begun.

When the plane touched down at RAF Northolt on the edge of London, a huge contingent of media was waiting behind barriers. Among the journalists was Jayne Fincher, the royal photographer who had been invited by the Princess to do many private photo sessions for her. Diana had even acted as Jayne's assistant on one shoot at Highgrove, carrying her equipment and crawling around the floor plugging lights into power points in the sitting room.

Jayne stood stunned as the coffin bearing the woman she knew so well was carried out of the aircraft. She remembered waiting on the same spot nine years earlier when the body of Hugh Lindsay, who died in the Klosters avalanche, had been brought home in exactly the same way to the same place. On that other sad day, Diana had been standing on the tarmac beside Hugh's widow Sarah.

To Jayne, it seemed she was reliving that earlier event and, at any moment, she expected to see Diana's tall figure beside Prince Charles.

'The eeriest moment that day came when the glass-sided hearse drove past and stopped briefly in front of the press barriers,' Jayne recalls. 'I stared at the coffin and could not believe that the Princess, who had been so full of life, could be lying inside it. It was simply inconceivable. I could not accept that I would never see her laughing face again.'

In August, London is virtually deserted. Parliament is in recess for the summer holidays, and the Royal Family abandons its official residence Buckingham Palace to the tourists. Suddenly, an unprepared Establishment had to return to the capital and hurriedly prepare the funeral of a Princess. The Queen was at first reluctant to fly back to the capital, aware of the inconvenience this would cause because the palace staff were all on holiday. Both she and Prince Charles felt that Balmoral was the best place for the boys to be. On this vast, secluded estate, William and Harry could begin to come to terms with their loss in seclusion.

In the first, agonising days after the car crash in the

Pont d'Alma tunnel, shock and disbelief turned to a sense of intense loss, even among people who had never met Diana. Searching for someone to blame, the public turned on the Royal Family who, far off in Aberdeenshire, seemed to be distancing themselves from the nation's grief.

Indecision and confusion reigned at Balmoral among royal advisers. Tense talks between the Queen and her family centred around arranging a funeral fit for a woman once destined to be a queen. Back in London, heated debate concerned the empty flagpole high above Buckingham Palace. All over the country, flags were flown from public buildings at half-mast, the traditional sign of public mourning.

The public expected the royal residences to follow suit, while the Queen insisted that it would be best to follow protocol, which rules that no flag can be flown at Buckingham Palace unless she is there. This created an impression of an uncaring monarchy and a growing gulf opened up between the angry mood of the general public and a Royal Family which remained closeted in a Scottish castle.

The green of Kensington Gardens outside Diana's London home became a swelling sea of flowers as hordes of mourners were drawn there to pay tribute to the People's Princess. Britons' stiff upper lips crumpled in an unprecedented display of emotion. The overwhelming tide of sorrow which swept over Britain was for a young life cruelly cut short, but it was also for a people who felt robbed of her shining spirit. People patiently queued for up to ten hours to sign books of condolence at St James's Palace. They waited without complaint despite the fact that they had to stand for the entire time and no refreshments were available. Rudimentary lavatories were installed in The Mall and

THE TRUTH

St James's Park but police described them as 'woefully inadequate'. The St John Ambulance Brigade reported treating 20 people in a single day who had collapsed in the queues for lack of food.

Buckingham Palace had asked the Salvation Army and the Women's Royal Voluntary Service to help, but they could supply only two small mobile canteens. It was left to Mohamed Al Fayed, the grieving father of Dodi Al Fayed, to come to the rescue of the thousands waiting in pouring rain. He dispatched four vans with 20 volunteer staff to dispense tea, coffee and sandwiches.

No temporary cover had been organised to protect people from the wet weather, yet still they came, keeping a vigil outside Buckingham Palace, St James's and Kensington Palaces all night in many cases. The authorities still had not realised the enormity of what was happening and were not able to make proper provision for it.

The public's hostility steadily grew as the Royal Family remained at Balmoral, 550 miles from London, showing no public sign of sorrow. SHOW US YOU CARE screamed one newspaper headline. Constitutional historian Dr David Starkey declared that 'outrage' was sweeping the country.

'The Royal Family are at a cross-roads,' he said. 'They are facing a huge wave of public resentment.'

Stung by criticism that the monarchy had appeared aloof while the nation mourned, the Queen's press officer Geoff Crawford, hastily summoned back from a holiday in Australia, issued a statement. He said, 'The Royal Family have been hurt by suggestions that they are indifferent to the country's sorrow at the tragic death of the Princess of Wales.' Continuing this extraordinary response to public pressure, he went on, 'The Princess was a much-loved national figure, but she was also a mother whose sons miss her deeply. Prince William and Prince Harry themselves want to be with their father and grandparents at this time in the quiet haven of Balmoral.'

Finally bowing to pressure, the Royal Family appeared at the gates of Balmoral Castle late on Thursday, 4 September to examine the hundreds of bouquets left there in Diana's memory. Dressed in suits and black ties, William and Harry, holding his father's hand, bent down to gaze at the messages attached to the flowers. One card read: 'William and Harry, live your lives in her spirit.'

Along with their cousin Peter Phillips, the Queen and the Duke of Edinburgh, the young princes stopped to inspect the floral tributes on the way back from a special service at Crathie Church. A Palace spokeswoman denied that it had been laid on following censure from the public, explaining instead that it had been arranged to help William and Harry prepare for their mother's funeral.

'This is not in answer to the public criticism, this is a family going to church to private prayers in view of what has happened,' said the Prince of Wales' press secretary Sandy Henney.

The entire Royal Family came back to London the following day, and Diana's boys, in a move that surprised many, acknowledged the strength of public feeling for their mother as they moved among mourners outside her home Kensington Palace. Just days earlier, they had expected to be going back to the Princess's apartment to spend a week with her before returning to school. Now, with heart-rending dignity, they were accepting words of condolence and encouragement from thousands of well-wishers who shared their loss.

THE TRUTH

At times, both William and Harry appeared close to tears, but generally they displayed a maturity and composure beyond their years. In an atmosphere charged with emotion, they managed to offer their gratitude for the kindess and comfort of strangers. 'Thank you for coming,' each repeated time and time again.

Later that day, in a televised speech delivered to the nation on the eve of the funeral, the Queen managed to defuse much of the people's animosity. In an inspired move, she sat facing the television cameras with her back to the open palace windows, revealing crowds of mourners flocking down the Mall to lay floral tributes at the gates. Here was the sovereign with the public symbolically behind her.

Her words were astonishingly personal and touching coming from a woman who is famously not given to outbursts of emotion.

'What I say to you now, as your Queen and as a grandmother, I say from my heart,' she said. 'First, I want to pay tribute to Diana myself. She was an exceptional and gifted human being. In good times and in bad, she never lost her capacity to smile and laugh, nor to inspire others with her warmth and kindness.

'I admired and respected her for her energy and commitment to others, and especially for her devotion to her two boys. This week at Balmoral we have all been trying to help William and Harry come to terms with the devastating loss that they and the rest of us have suffered. No one who knew Diana will ever forget her. Millions of others who never met her, but felt they knew her, will remember her. I, for one, believe that there are lessons to be drawn from her life and from the extraordinary and moving reaction to her death. I share in your determination to cherish her memory.'

The death of the world's favourite Princess still did not seem real. It was not until the gun carriage bearing her coffin emerged from the gates of Kensington Palace that the full realisation of what Britain had lost was appreciated. Atop the coffin was a wreath of white roses bearing a note addressed simply 'Mummy'. It was a reminder that no matter how great our loss, her sons were even more heartbroken.

More than a million grief-stricken people wept and threw flowers when Diana's coffin was drawn on a gun carriage through the streets of London to her funeral service in Westminster Abbey. One of the eeriest moments of the service was the reading of a poem by Diana's sister Lady Jane Fellowes.

> *Time is too slow for those who wait,*
> *Too swift for those who fear,*
> *Too long for those who grieve,*
> *Too short for those who rejoice,*
> *But for those who love, time is eternity.*

For those who knew Diana, had heard her laugh and chatted idly to her, the similarity between her voice and her sister's was a heart-rending shock. It was as if Diana herself was speaking, repeating once again, as she had done so often, that love was life's greatest gift.

After Prime Minister Tony Blair read the lessons from I Corinthians, 13, Diana's friend Elton John sat down at a grand piano and sang 'Candle in the Wind', the song he had first written in tribute to Marilyn Monroe, re-created with new lyrics by his collaborator Bernie Taupin. When it was first announced that the pop star would perform one of his best-known hits in between hymns in this historic setting, the idea had seemed vulgar and unappealing to many. In reality, the

Diana in St Tropez in August 1997. *Above:* Relaxing with Dodi Al Fayed and, *below*, enjoying spending time with Prince Harry.

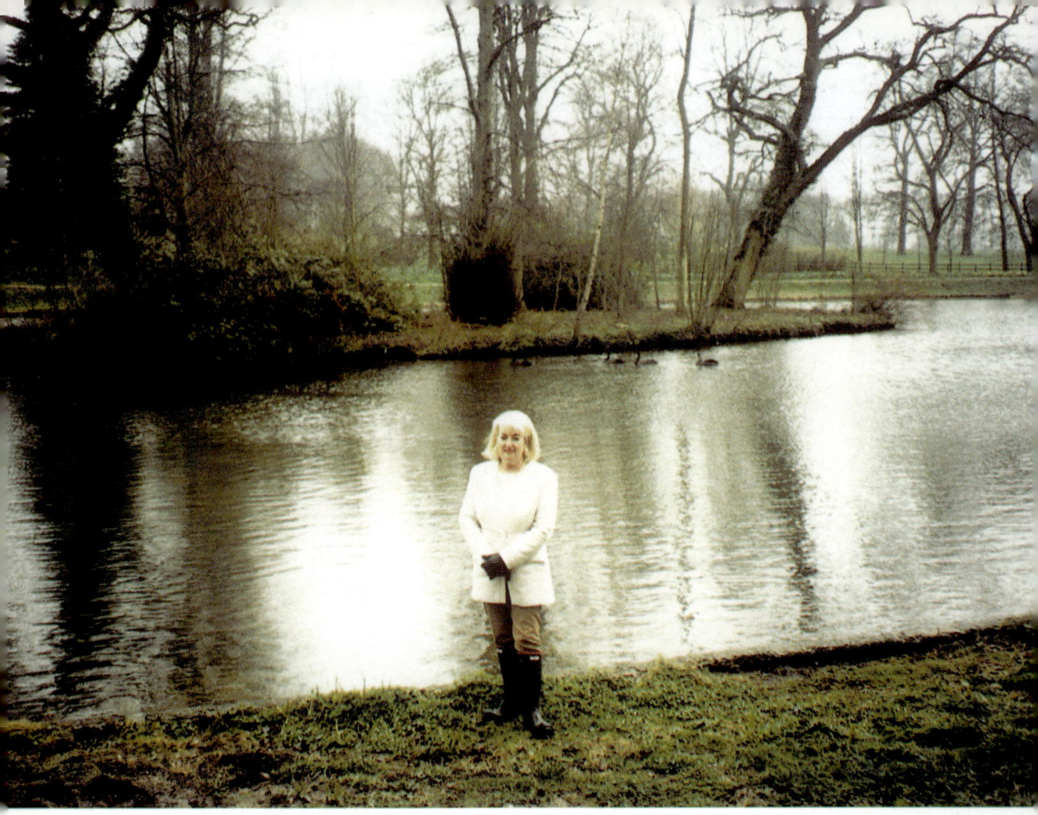

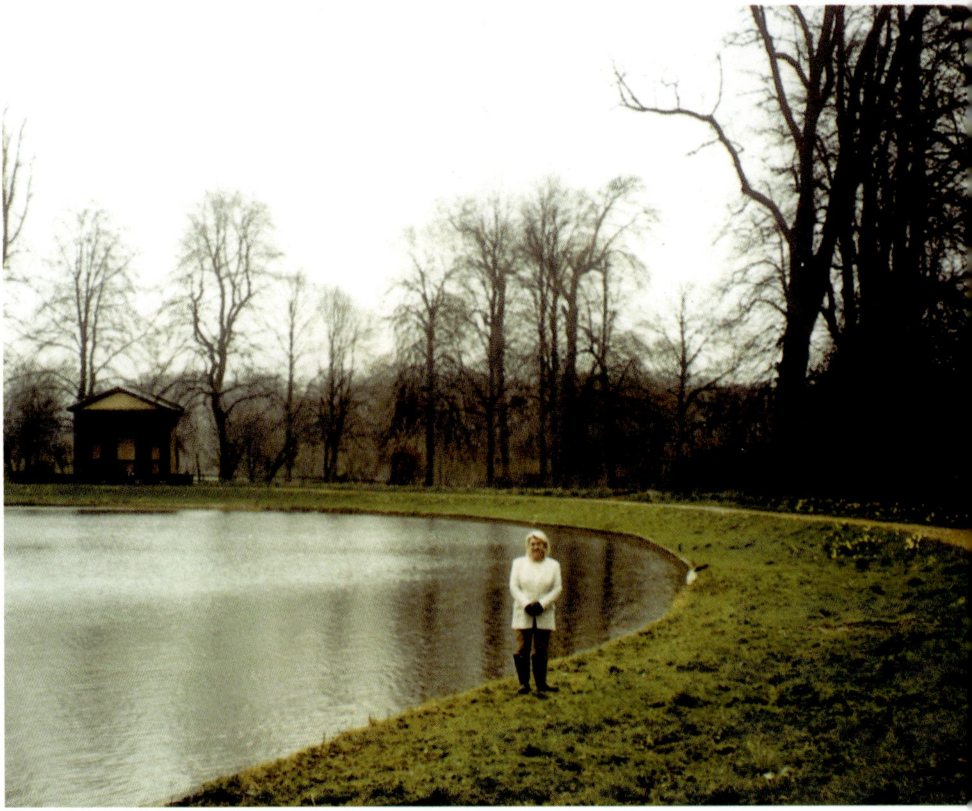

Marie at Althorp in April 1998.
Top left: Diana's grave can be glimpsed behind Marie's right shoulder, where some small white flowers are just visible. Althorp has planted metal all over the island to confuse those trying to locate the grave with metal detectors.

KENSINGTON PALACE

16th August, 1996

Dear Marie,

I just wanted to send you my <u>heartfelt</u> thanks for your invaluable assistance during the past week. I know from my office that your telephone has not stopped ringing!

More seriously, I am greatly looking forward to my visit to Sydney and in particular to meeting you on 31st October ...

With my best wishes.
Yours sincerely,

Diana

Mrs. Marie Sutton

A heartfelt thanks from Diana to Marie Sutton and, *inset*, the two pictured together.

A rare public display of affection between Charles and Diana at a Polo match in 1987.

James Hewitt. Hewitt became Diana's riding instructor in 1986, and they had a passionate, and subsequently much-publicised, affair over the course of five years.

a as a mother. *Above:* with Charles and the new-born Prince William and, *below*, with
am at Wimbledon in 1991.

September 1997. The nation mourns the loss of its Princess. *Main picture:* The coffin is carried to Westminster Abbey. *Inset:* Charles, William and Harry look at the floral tributes to Diana.

song and the composer's impassioned rendition, had an extraordinary power which left many in tears. Not just in the abbey, but around the globe, as millions watched the funeral service on television. The star later told the *Daily Mirror* that he was fairly composed until the beginning of the last verse 'when my voice cracked and I was really chock full of emotion. I just had to close my eyes and grit my teeth and get through it.'

Then Diana's brother Charles, Earl Spencer, stepped up to the pulpit to deliver his tribute.

'I stand before you today the representative of a family in grief, in a country in mourning, before a world in shock,' he began.

'Diana was the very essence of compassion, of duty, of style, of beauty. All over the world she was a symbol of selfless humanity, a standard-bearer for the rights of the truly down-trodden, a very British girl who transcended nationality; someone with a natural nobility, who was classless and who proved in the last year that she needed no royal title to continue to generate her particular brand of magic.'

His words seemed to have been aimed straight at the Queen and her family, sitting just yards away, who had stripped Diana of the title Her Royal Highness 12 months earlier.

'There is a temptation to rush to canonise your memory,' he added. 'There is no need to do so. You stand tall enough as a human being of unique qualities not to need to be seen as a saint. Indeed to sanctify your memory would be to miss out on the very core of your being, your wonderfully mischievous sense of humour with a laugh that bent you double; your joy for life transmitted where you took your smile, and the sparkle in those unforgettable eyes; your boundless energy which you could barely contain.'

Then came his most controversial comment, his promise to protect Diana's boys.

'On behalf of your mother and your sisters, I pledge that we, your blood family, will do all we can to continue the imaginative and loving way in which you were steering these two exceptional young men so that their souls are not simply immersed by duty and tradition, but can sing openly as you planned.

'We fully respect the heritage into which they have both been born and will always respect and encourage them in their royal role, but we, like you, recognise the need for them to experience as many different aspects of life as possible to arm them spiritually and emotionally for the years ahead. I know you would have expected nothing less from us.'

After this barbed attack on the family which had discarded its greatest treasure, he ended his tribute with the most moving words ever written by a brother to his sister.

'Above all, we give thanks for the life of a woman I am so proud to be able to call my sister, the unique, the complex, the extraordinary and irreplaceable Diana, whose beauty, both internal and external, will never be extinguished from our minds.'

An eerie sound, like rain tapping at the windows, softly at first then growing steadily louder, poured into the abbey. It was the sound of the thousands outside, listening to the funeral service relayed on loudspeakers, breaking into applause. Two billion people watching via TV satellite links witnessed this extraordinary event.

Soon, critics condemned this verbal strike against the monarchy in the place where its sovereigns have been crowned for 1,000 years. It may have seemed inappropriate to a few, but the public disagreed. On the day he buried his sister, Charles Spencer was the most admired man in Britain.

The last glimpse the world saw of the Princess was when her hearse disappeared through the iron gates of Althorp. Later that day, in a private service attended only by her immediate family and her faithful butler Paul Burrell, Diana was laid to rest on an island in the Pool, an ornamental lake in the grounds of Althorp, her family's Northamptonshire home for 400 years.

Until April 1998, no one outside the Spencer family had visited the grave until Marie Sutton was invited to Althorp while on a visit to England. Marie had been invited to discuss the commemorative tour she was bringing to Althorp from Australia in August 1998. At the time, rumours were circulating that Diana had not been buried on an island grave on her family's estate, but had been interred with many of her ancestors in the parish church of St Mary the Virgin in the nearby village of Great Brington.

Many believed that Diana's coffin should have rested in this 800-year-old church, but the Spencer crypt at one side of the nave had long ago been filled. As a result, her father Johnnie Spencer, the eighth Earl, had been cremated and his ashes scattered over the churchyard. Even if the tomb had greater capacity, it would not have been a suitable place for the Princess's burial. The small village would have been unable to cope with the heavy traffic drawn to visit the church. There were fears that normal life in Great Brington would have become impossible.

This was one of the main considerations when the Spencer family, headed by Charles, the ninth Earl, discussed where to bury Diana. Despite this, the rumours persisted, even spreading as far afield as Australia where Marie Sutton was accosted in the streets of Sydney by people informing her of this wild theory. It is believed that speculation started when villagers learned that the Spencer family crypt had been opened within days of Diana's death. In fact, this had been done as a precaution in case permission was not granted to consecrate the island as a Christian burial ground. The site was consecrated by the Bishop of Peterborough, the Right Reverend Ian Cundy, in a private ceremony on the Thursday evening before the funeral on the following Saturday.

Finally, to quash all the rumours, the Bishop released Diana's burial certificate. It stated that on 6 September 1997 'Diana, Princess of Wales was buried in an extra-parochial place, namely at Althorp Park in the County of Northamptonshire in the grave previously consecrated by the Bishop of Peterborough on the island in the Oval Lake.' It was signed by Victor Christian de Roubaix Malan, vicar of Hunston, West Sussex, who had officiated at the burial. The Bishop explained, 'Once somebody starts with a conspiracy theory there is no stopping it. We had had that certificate for the last four months and we decided it was time to release it.'

Diana's mother Frances Shand Kydd confirmed this information when she opened her heart at a memorial mass for her daughter in the Scottish cathedral where she worships. She described how she rowed across to the island where her daughter was buried on the Althorp estate. She told the congregation, 'I felt certain that my beloved Diana was at peace and I was at peace, too.'

Just months later, as she drove up to the imposing gates of the estate, Marie Sutton could see the posies and bouquets left day after day on the iron railings to honour Diana's memory.

Seven months after her death, flowers were still

being left with messages of love by people who had come from the four corners of the world. Even a steady downpour did not deter a dozen or so people standing quietly by the roadside.

Marie later recalled, 'We were met by Peter the gatekeeper who was obviously expecting my car. He told the driver to carry on up the long drive to the mansion. My first impression was that the magnificent grounds were very well kept. Diana had come home to a very beautiful place.'

Althorp has been home to the Spencers since the late fifteenth century, although it was originally only used for a few months each year. The family then spent most of their time in Warwickshire. It was John Spencer who, in 1486, leased the property from the Abbot of Evesham. Twelve years later, the family bought the then moated red-brick building.

John's grandson, Sir John Spencer, added two long wings jutting out into the forecourt from the original building. More than a century later, the open courtyard at the centre of the building was given a roof beneath which a very wide wooden staircase led to a picture gallery above, both of which remain to this day.

In 1786, George, the second Earl Spencer, ordered an architect to cover the house's brick exterior with the white tiles, which give it a strangely modern look.

As her car swept past the old stable block, then being transformed into the Diana Museum, and across the gravelled courtyard in front of the house, Ian the butler was waiting to greet Marie.

'Come in out of the rain and let me get you something warm to drink,' he said as she walked through the vast main door into the grand entrance hall.

It was in Wooton Hall, this square, pillared foyer, that the young Diana once practised tap-dancing, making her steps echo around its lofty ceiling. And every Christmas from the mid-1980s until his death, her father, the eighth Earl Spencer, used to have an estate worker dressed as Santa Claus ride in through the front door on a pony cart loaded with presents to the delight of the little princes William and Harry.

Despite its grandeur, Althorp has a homely feel which Marie immediately sensed. A fire was blazing in the sitting room where Ian introduced Celia Deely, private secretary to David Horton-Hawkes, Althorp's estate manager. They sat down to enjoy a delicious morning tea while they discussed the opening of the estate to tourists in July and August.

Marie had brought along an album containing photographs of Diana with her in Australia as well as letters she had received from the Princess, which Celia avidly studied. Surprisingly, she and the butler admitted that they had never met Diana.

Celia then took Marie on a tour of the great house. She was surprised to discover that as well as its priceless collections of porcelain, its great portraits and valuable antique furniture, Althorp was very much a family home. Toys belonging to Earl Spencer's three little daughters Kitty, Eliza and Katya and his son Louis were piled up in one of the rooms. And everywhere there were family photos. More than a dozen in silver frames stood on the grand piano.

Then the butler returned to announce that he had turned off the electronic security system in the grounds in case Marie wished to visit the Pool and see the Princess's resting place.

'I took a deep breath as I was not expecting to be granted such a privilege,' Marie later remembered. 'Then I said I would very much like to visit it.'

As the steady rain had left the grounds muddy,

THE TRUTH

Celia and Marie donned two pairs of Wellington boots belonging to the family and trudged around the back of the house through dripping trees down to the edge of the oval Pool.

It had been a very dry winter and Marie noticed that the water level was quite low. It seemed almost as if she could take just a few steps across the shallow lake and reach Diana's island grave.

Black swans glided serenely across the Pool with white geese on their way back north after wintering in a warmer climate down south. They seemed like graceful guardians of the Princess's burial place, spreading their wings and stirring up the calm surface of the lake at the approach of a stranger.

The carpet of flowers which had covered the island last summer had disappeared over the preceding harsh winter. A monument in the shape of a tall plinth topped by an urn, both designed by Edward Bulmer and carved by Dick Reid, was planned to stand among the greenery at the north end, but had not yet been erected. The grave was lying a few feet from the shore on the south side, almost in the centre of the island.

On the then still visible mound of earth, beneath which Diana lay, was a simple bouquet of her favourite flowers, white lilies. Their fresh perfection was proof that her resting place was carefully tended.

Dan Pearson, a gold-medal winner at the Chelsea Flower Show, had landscaped the gardens in a bid to create an effect that was peaceful and serene.

'On the island itself we planted 100 white rambling roses to drip their flowers from the trees,' he explained. The variety he chose was Bobbie James which can reach a height of 30ft and has magnificent, scented blooms. In addition, he added 100 water lilies to float on the surface of the lake.

Spring daffodils were the only other blooms on the island beneath trees just beginning to turn green once again with new leaf. It was a peaceful scene, yet Marie found it moved her in a way she had never before experienced.

'In the days, weeks and months after Diana died I never once cried,' she recalled. 'I couldn't quite believe that she had gone. It seemed impossible, so unreal. But when I actually saw her grave, at last the tears came.

'I was overwhelmed with mixed emotions. At first, I cried for a girl whose life had brutally ended too soon. At just 36 she should have had years ahead of her to mother her sons and watch them grow up. But the atmosphere of peace and solitude gradually made me believe that Diana would be safe in this serene place where no one could touch her or trouble her any longer.'

Diana's brother had been under attack many times for incidents in his private life, yet these flaws pale into insignificance beside the great tribute he has paid his dead sister. He brought her home to Althorp where she will be shielded from the outside world for ever. No location could be more perfect for a princess. While it is true that Diana lies alone on her island grave, 20 generations of her ancestors are buried little more than a mile away in Great Brington's village church.

Diana did not belong with her former husband's ancestors, interred in their cold marble tombs at Frogmore. Although she became a princess, she clung on to her Spencer roots throughout her life and rejected the chilly formality of the Windsors. And neither should any corner of Westminster Abbey have been chosen for her lasting resting place. There she could not have been protected from the crowds who wished to pay

THE TRUTH

tribute, and no doubt she would have laughed at the thought of lying among the exalted figures honoured there. No, Althorp was the ideal, the only fitting burial ground for a unique woman who had, in the truest sense, always gone her own way.

Marie walked across the grounds to the Greek-style temple overlooking the Pool, and sat down to say a short prayer for her friend. Her strong faith in God convinced her that Diana had been taken so that she could find everlasting peace.

Sitting in the temple, which seemed a fitting place to remember a woman many people regarded as almost a goddess, she thought of her very down-to-earth friend. Marie smiled as flashes of the Diana she knew came flooding back.

She recalled the Princess being driven past St Mary's Cathedral in Sydney as a bride and her attendants were entering the church. Leaning from the window of her car Diana yelled, 'Don't do it!' then sank back into her seat giggling at her prank. She remembered her asking Marie to arrange a party with plenty of good-looking men. All her memories were happy ones.

The sad times had been buried with Diana and now she could only think of the fun-loving girl she had known.

Celia explained that the temple would soon be converted into a monument to Althorp's most famous daughter. A black-bordered plaque bearing Diana's silhouetted head on white marble would be its main feature. Beside it would be a touching message in words Diana herself used just weeks before her death: 'Whoever is in distress can call on me; I will come running, wherever they are.' Opposite, another plaque was planned bearing the lyrics of Elton John's song

'Goodbye, England's Rose'.

All the anger Marie had felt when she first heard of the Princess's death on the August Sunday morning in Sydney suddenly melted away. Instead, she experienced a sense of perfection in the beautiful surroundings. Diana was at home with her own people for ever.

In the ensuing summer, many thousands of people would follow in Marie's footsteps to visit the estate and walk sadly around the Pool and visit the temple. Most would be in groups. None would, like Marie, have the chance to be alone with Diana one last time. And none would see the site of Diana's grave, which, by 1 July 1998, when Althorp was opened to the public, was hidden by dense foliage.

Most may feel that despite her title, her fame and her fortune, the Princess was cheated of something far more important — lasting love. But who can say that a short but passionate affair is not better than a lifetime of comfortable affection?

Diana was not robbed of real love. She had the love of millions around the world, a devoted following of admirers who had watched her grow from a naïve teenager into a global icon. They shared her lows and her highs, applauding when she confessed her own failings, her eating disorder, depression and self-mutilation so that she could help others.

Marie is also convinced that Diana experienced a true and great love, which in its way surpassed her youthful crush on Prince Charles. She was a mature woman of 34 when she met and fell in love with Dr Hasnat Khan.

From her personal knowledge of the Princess, the confidences they exchanged in Sydney and in long, late-night chats on the telephone, Marie believes that

Diana would have been reconciled with the dedicated doctor.

'Dodi Al Fayed was just a summer romance, at first just a way to make Dr Khan come back to her,' she claims.

The reason why most people feel that Diana and Dodi had a future together is the photographs of them on holiday together in the Mediterranean. No similarly affectionate pictures were ever taken of the Princess with Hasnat Khan, none with James Gilbey, only a few with Will Carling and a handful in public with James Hewitt.

With her experience of handling the media, and the awful example of Fergie's tabloid exposure, Diana was careful never to be caught in compromising circumstances with a man who really mattered to her. That is why the only time a photographer came close to catching her with Dr Khan was when one snapped him leaning in through the window of her car to chat to her in a London street.

If Dodi had really been important, would Diana have flung her arms around him while sunning herself in the Mediterranean, where she was surrounded by dozens of other holidaymakers?

In fact, by openly associating with Dodi Al Fayed, she moved media scrutiny away from the man she had loved for more than two years — the Pakistani heart surgeon Hasnat Khan.

It is now known that the Princess was still seeing Hasnat secretly while also dating Dodi. Up until two weeks before her death, the doctor was still visiting her at Kensington Palace.

His Australian friends Erin and her husband Paul are convinced that the couple would have been reunited and that their love was too strong to end abruptly. Diana needed not just a man to dance attendance on her and drive away her demons, she wanted someone she could respect, a man who gave meaning and purpose to her life.

The only man she knew who could do this was the tall, quiet surgeon who loved her passionately but was also devoted to his life-saving work. It was unlikely that a Hollywood playboy like Dodi Al Fayed, despite his famous charm, would have held her interest for long.

Dr Khan could not lavish expensive gifts on his Princess but he cared deeply for her reputation as much as he was concerned for her welfare. In fact, he cared so much for Diana that he did not wish to wreck her divorce negotiations and create more gossip by being seen in London with her. He carefully kept their romance under wraps, unwilling to become part of a media circus.

The lack of visible proof of their affair has left many people ignorant of the depth and seriousness of their relationship. But there is no doubt that it was perhaps the greatest love of her life.

When Diana died, Hasnat Khan was one of the first invited to her funeral. His friends say that, at first, he was reluctant to go, afraid that it would prove too upsetting. He was finally persuaded that he would later regret it if he did not attend the service at Westminster Abbey.

He walked in alone, a poignant figure, hiding his sad eyes behind dark glasses as he found his seat in the great church. But his heart was broken and those close to him believe he will never really recover from the tragedy.

'I took such great care of her,' Hasnat told them. 'If she had still been with me, she would be alive today. I would never have allowed this to happen because I

THE TRUTH

always protected her.'

If their affair had ended in marriage, as Diana had hoped for so long, it might have been a tempestuous partnership, but one that could have helped a great many people around the world.

Their East–West romance could have been an example to everyone, bridging creeds, cultures and continents. Their joint dedication to aid the suffering and their determination to overcome prejudice, ignorance and poverty should have shone a bright light in our dark world.

It was not to be, but Diana's secret love at least deserves after her death the recognition it did not widely receive during her life.

13

Diana, Princess of Wales was not a great beauty in the true sense. Her nose was too prominent and her chin rather small and pointed. A shade too tall, she towered over most people she met and, at first, she had a rather ungainly, duck-like walk.

None of this mattered when you gazed into those enormous, ocean-blue eyes. They could stop even die-hard Republicans dead in their tracks. Men and women alike were mesmerised by the directness of those unforgettable eyes. Fringed with long, silky lashes, they dominated her face and became her trademark. Many of the Royal Rat Pack photographers used 'Blue Eyes' as their code-name for the Princess.

Her complexion was peachy with a naturally high

colour in her cheeks and, unusually, her fair skin never freckled, just tanned easily.

'I love going brown and never worry about getting wrinkles from too much sun,' she once told me on a trip to Nigeria where we had both been coping with temperatures hovering around 110°C.

Most people looked up to Diana, literally, because she was a long-stemmed English rose, more than 6ft tall in her highest heels. Her fantastic legs looked even more shapely when she sashayed around in stiletto heels. She called them her 'tart's trotters', knowing just how seductive they looked.

No, Diana was not a true beauty in the classic style, but she was simply gorgeous in her own traffic-stopping, jaw-dropping, heart-leaping way. The whole package from the top of her glossy blonde head right down to her painted toes was so incredibly alluring that she rivalled supermodels and movie actresses as the foremost beauty of the late twentieth century.

Why, then, did her husband not appreciate what he had? When a man abandons his wife for a younger woman, it's considered sad but not really surprising. But trading in a glamorous young wife for an older, less attractive model is generally regarded as total madness. Camilla Parker Bowles, with her country woman's weathered face and unfashionable hairstyle, is the type men forsake, not fall for.

To risk the Crown for a woman who is past her best years, is disdained by millions and who has no very obvious appeal is perplexing, to say the least, and perhaps foolish at worst.

Most men who ditch their first wives for a 'trophy' second wife want someone who reflects their newly-acquired status, who proves that they really have arrived at the top.

The Prince of Wales doesn't need to prove anything. He was born at the top. Therefore, he has no need of a woman to add to his grandeur. But why choose a woman who threatens it?

Repeated opinion polls indicate that the majority of Britons would not countenance Camilla as Queen, although a large percentage also confusingly believe that Charles and his long-time love should be allowed to marry. Under British law, a wife takes on the rights and titles of her husband, which would mean that once married, Camilla would be our next Queen. The Prince insists that he has no plans to wed, but if he should change his mind, there is still a very real risk that he might have to choose between Camilla and the Crown.

Apart from public opinion, there is considerable opposition to a marriage between Charles and Camilla from certain sections of the Church of England, which still does not sanction the remarriage of divorced people. As the future Supreme Governor of the Anglican Church and Defender of the Faith, the Prince can hardly flout its laws.

His sister Anne, the Princess Royal, found a way around the Church's stance by arranging her second wedding over the border in Crathie, Aberdeenshire, where the Church of Scotland takes a more lenient view. This caused no problems because Anne, once second but now eighth in the line of succession to the throne, will have no role to play in the Church of England.

The Reverend David Streeter, former director of the Church Society, believes the Prince should put duty to the throne before his own personal happiness.

'If he wants to be King, he has got to grit his teeth and do the job as constituted,' he says firmly. 'The trouble is, I think he wants the job but he doesn't want the job description.'

He disapproves of relaxing the rules to allow people who promised to stay together for better or worse, make the same vows with someone else. He is also scathing about Charles's ecumenical views.

'He talks about being a defender of faiths, instead of the Defender of the Faith — a position which is non-existent.'

No matter what the cost, Charles will never give up Camilla. He is a man accustomed to getting what he wants and flies into a rage when he is thwarted. He lives like a Renaissance prince in far greater style than the Queen and accepts gifts and favours from wealthy friends that no politician would be permitted to receive.

In return for his prison-like existence and a life that is so programmed it fills him with gloom, he enjoys a great many rights and privileges as well as an annual income running into millions after tax from the Duchy of Cornwall. He also dares to meddle in politics, most notably when he declined to attend a dinner for the Chinese leader as he disapproves of China's human rights record.

He obviously sees himself akin to the Dutch boy who put his finger in the dyke and saved the Netherlands. He wages a one-man war against barbarism in architecture, the destruction of the environment and falling standards in education.

As he once explained, 'I happen to be one of those people who minds about the way in which this country goes. I happen to feel since the Sixties a great deal of destructiveness has taken place in terms of throwing the baby out with the bath water in many of the things that matter to me and, I think, to a lot of other people. What I want to try and do is to bring the baby back.'

The lack of appreciation for his work has always

frustrated him, especially when his efforts were constantly eclipsed by his former wife's far more popular campaigns. He has no such problems with Camilla, who does not relish a public role.

Members of the Camilla camp explain that she is warm and witty, unstuffy and totally without affectation. All of which may mean she is a woman with many fine qualities, but it hardly makes her exceptional or equips her to be a queen.

There is no doubt that Camilla was fairly attractive once. In her youth, she was popular and pretty in the restrained style of the average debutante. The great-granddaughter of Alice Keppel, mistress of Edward VII, she allegedly propositioned the Prince on their first meeting.

'My great-grandmother and your great-great-grandfather were lovers, so how about it?'

This was the amusing young woman the Prince fell in love with. Unfortunately, he was not ready to settle down and, with the arrogance of his position, he believed every eligible girl in London, and a few who were not quite so eligible, were his for the taking.

As that great observer of the monarchy, Walter Bagehot, once wrote, 'All the world and the glory of it, whatever is most attractive, whatever is most seductive, has always been offered to the Prince of Wales of the day, and always will be.'

In his twenties, Charles had the world at his feet, little realising that one day a woman would have the world at his throat.

Perhaps it was not only a desire to sow wild oats that prevented the Prince from marrying Camilla when he had the chance. The hypocrisy that still persisted in Court circles ordained that he should choose a virginal wife. It was well known that Camilla had been involved with more than one man before she met Charles. In Seventies Britain, this made her unsuitable to be a king's consort. Well aware of this, Camilla seems to have cherished no dreams of becoming a Princess. While Charles was on an eight-month stint serving with the Royal Navy aboard *HMS Minerva*, Camilla did not sit around waiting for him to come home. She announced her engagement to his friend Andrew Parker Bowles.

Almost 30 years later, the world has moved on, attitudes are more relaxed and Camilla, now a divorcée, is the Prince's wife in all but name. They live together. She shares his private life and increasingly shares more and more of his official life.

They have a great deal in common. Both are happiest in the countryside, both love hunting, polo and gardening. Camilla has even taken up watercolour painting because it is one of Charles's favourite hobbies.

It's obvious that he loves her, and has always loved her. Part of her appeal may be that she prefers to stay in the background and is never likely to outshine him. From the day he was married, he was constantly upstaged by his gorgeous wife. Accustomed to being the star, Charles did not enjoy being downgraded to the role of supporting act. Gradually, he came to resent Diana's popularity. After all, he was born royal while she had been a commoner until he married her.

Her fame and status all came from him and were not hers by right. Apparently, he could not understand why people did not seem to recognise this. He failed to appreciate that Diana's title may have made her a public figure but it did not inspire the affection the public felt for her. She earned her place in the hearts of the nation with her compassion for the sick, the homeless and the forgotten members of society.

By comparison, Camilla is not noted for her charity work. Apart from a little private support for the Osteoporosis Society, she does not excel at helping others. In fact, when she was involved in an accident in which another woman motorist was injured, instead of calling for assistance she fled from the scene.

A St James's Palace source quickly explained that Camilla was not heartless, merely worried that she might be the victim of a terrorist trap and that her mobile phone did not work as the area was in a cellphone black spot. It still appeared rather strange that Camilla did not even check to see if the other woman was severely injured.

No one would regard Camilla as a sister of mercy, but she possesses one quality which makes her indispensable to the Prince. This is her total, unwavering support which props up an often indecisive and weak man. The most compelling proof of Camilla's ability to bolster Charles came in the notorious 'Camillagate' tape. In the recording of their late night telephone conversation, she constantly reassures the Prince in a submissive and almost sycophantic way. She tells him that she not only adores him but that other women do, too. Referring to a friend called Nancy, Camilla observes, 'I think she's so in love with you.'

The Prince does not argue but merely agrees. 'Mmmnh.'

Then Camilla adds, 'She'd do anything you asked ... You've got a great hold over her.'

Later in the recording, she asks to read his latest speech, making her admiration obvious. She also piles on the flattery, telling him, 'You're a clever old thing. An awfully good brain lurking there, isn't there?'

At times, she sounds just like a devoted nanny

speaking to an insecure little boy. 'I do love you and I'm so proud of you,' she sighs.

Charles recognises the difficulties she was then enduring by saying, 'You suffer all these indignities and tortures and calumnies.'

Camilla's reply is unequivocal. 'Oh, darling, don't be so silly. I'd suffer anything for you. That's love. That's the strength of love.'

All men enjoy honeyed words. Many would-be *femmes fatales* are convinced that a few blandishments can be amazingly effective. Butter a man up to the point at which you want to throw up, they say, and you will only just be starting to make an impression. The male ego soaks up compliments like a desert hit by a rainstorm. Of course, some subtlety is needed to sound thoroughly credible, and studying the Camillagate tape indicates that she is a mistress of male manipulation.

A photographer once bumped into her by accident on a London street as she was parking her car. He introduced himself and asked if he might take her photograph. Instead of rushing away, as Diana might have done, she agreed, telling him she knew of his work and was delighted to meet him. He was instantly charmed and ever since has been telling everyone he knows how lovely she is.

A man like Charles whose path through life is not of his choosing, who will carry the burden of the Crown until the day he dies, undoubtedly needs a supportive partner. He requires someone by his side who will make a life dominated by duty a little easier to bear. Camilla seems to be exactly what Charles needs.

Her protests of devotion sound utterly sincere although she has paid a high price for loving her prince. There is little doubt that she suffered more than he did when their adulterous relationship became public knowledge. Camilla, whom Diana dubbed 'The Rottweiler', was forced to disappear from society and hide out in her Wiltshire home until the furore died down.

After the Camillagate tape hit the headlines in 1993, Charles broke off the relationship for a while, convinced that it was too dangerous to continue their meetings, although he did not break off all contact with Camilla. He found he could not live without her and the relationship was soon resumed. After Diana died in 1997, Camilla became a hunted woman and fled to South America staying with Charles's old friend Lucia Santa Cruz to avoid the media back in Britain.

Once again, public attention soon switched to other scandals and Camilla could start to live a normal life once more. She was able to continue her campaign to remove all traces of Charles's wife from his homes.

First, she tackled Highgrove, moving in her own decorator a short time after Diana moved out in 1992, then she set about transforming his new apartment at St James's Palace.

She was soon mistress of his household, playing hostess at dinner parties and making suggestions about the way staff ran Charles's residences.

Diana had decorated Highgrove House with the help of her mother's decorator Dudley Poplak. Although fresh and airy, it reflected the taste of a young, inexperienced girl who had a fondness for florals and Laura Ashley-style prints. Ten years later, it was perhaps in real need of a make-over.

Camilla's personal style could not be more different from Diana's. The Princess was meticulous about every detail of her home and once redecorated a room at Kensington Palace seven times before she got it right. Camilla, by contrast, sticks to the traditional country house look, now rather dated. Dog hairs on sofas and crumbs on the carpet never seem to worry her, friends say. She is the type who likes piles of Wellingtons, walking sticks and dog baskets in the hall, creating a rather cluttered but cosy atmosphere.

While Diana came across as fragile but feisty, her rival has always appeared to be as tough as a Guardsman's old boots. She has ridden out every storm by lying low and remaining silent, which is a strategy that has worked well, says Christopher Wilson, author of *A Greater Love, Charles and Camilla*.

'One-to-one, Camilla is absolutely charming,' he says. 'But she can't mix and mingle with crowds the way Diana did — simply because she hasn't got the common touch. So she should just stay out of it.'

He also notes that Camilla's stocks have been slowly rising. 'At first, she had zero public acceptance, then by 1996 it had risen to 50 per cent plus. It was looking very good for Camilla, then Diana died. That's when Camilla's attempts to win public favour came to a sudden halt.'

Christopher Wilson believes that 'a significant proportion of people believe she is responsible for the break-up of Charles's marriage. An ingrained hatred of Camilla is still very much in evidence, especially among those who are a little less tolerant of human frailty.'

To transform Camilla into a popular figure would be a job which might defeat the most intelligent public relations people, he says. 'Camilla has never shown any love for her fellow human beings,' he points out. 'She has done some work for the Osteoporosis Society and that's all. So, she is in a bind. If she does nothing, people will never get to know her, and if she does something, it could equally destroy the little support she has got.'

While researching his book about Camilla, he says, 'I became convinced that she does not want to play the glad-handing lady, which is just as well. She does not have the warmth, the divine touch Diana had. She is not user-friendly.'

Camilla belongs to a fast-vanishing breed, the upper-class gel who has never had to work for a living. Of course, she toyed with office work for a short time before her marriage, but she has not been a part of the working world since then. She appears out of touch with the rest of us, especially with regard to her favourite winter sport, fox-hunting, which the majority of British people would like to see banned by law.

Mrs P-B, as Prince Charles's staff call her, has never shared Diana's passion for fashion and good grooming. In fact, until spin-doctors got to work recently to improve her shabby image, she appeared to look on the world of high fashion with disdain. It would not be surprising if she regarded prancing around in a designer bikini on a beach besieged by photographers, as Diana did more than once, as the sign of a vulgar exhibitionist. Such showiness is not well regarded in the shires and women like Camilla prefer to spend money on horse blankets rather than *haute couture*. Diana's compulsive shopping at one point in her life was not viewed as a substitute for emotional security by her rival's supporters, but as sheer extravagance.

Their contempt for the Princess's scrupulous attention to perfecting her appearance, thrice-weekly workouts in the gym, regular facials and daily hairdos, was apparent in the nickname Camilla's circle gave to Diana. They jokingly referred to her as 'Doris', implying that she was rather common and extremely vain.

The origin of this nickname is unknown, but it may

have been inspired by Doris Day, the American movie star so popular in the Sixties, who had a short blonde hairstyle and a permanent cheesy grin. 'Doris' is not a name favoured by the upper classes, who seem to prefer girls' names which end in the letter 'a', such as Camilla, Diana, Zara, Tara, Laura, and so on. 'Doris' is decidedly a downstairs name, often given to servant girls at the beginning of the last century. Camilla's girlfriends giggled every time they used it.

But was Diana 'common'? She certainly had the common touch which enabled her to communicate with people on every level. For a few years when she permed her hair, had a penchant for wearing leather jackets and skirts slit to the thigh, perhaps she appeared a little racy, but she never ever looked tarty. At times, she may have come perilously close to looking a little garish, especially in the early Nineties when *Tatler* magazine claimed she was dressing like an 'Essex girl'.

In March 1994, the glossy magazine observed, 'The Princess of Wales has dismissed her bodyguards, relinquished her public duties and, so it would appear, mislaid her style advisers.

'Left to her own devices, she shows a bewildering penchant for all things Chigwellian. Is Essex set to be the next royal county, or will the fashion police arrive in the nick of time to snatch Diana from the clutches of the white cowboy boot?'

It sniped at the frosted blonde highlights in her hair, a black leather blouson she had worn on an outing with her sons, and a blue-and-gold two-piece knitted outfit she wore to the Sticky Fingers restaurant. It proved, said *Tatler*, 'that if you dress five years out of date, you look "dead common".'

It compared the Princess with *EastEnders* star Gillian Taylforth, model Mandy Smith and Linda

Robson of the TV show *Birds of a Feather*, which is set in Essex.

The very week that the magazine hit the newsstands, Diana visited her new-born nephew in hospital wearing an ensemble from Escada — a £685 black jacket with gold elephants embroidered on the cuffs, a £71 tie dotted with gold elephants and a £165 belt whose buckle appeared to depict a pair of elephants mating. All this was teamed with black jeans bought from Banana Republic in New York and a pair of sneakers.

'You can't imagine Princess Caroline of Monaco ever getting it quite so wrong,' sneered the *Daily Mail*'s Fashion Editor Gail Rolfe.

Maybe the outfit was a trifle flashy but it made Diana appear more like a Jewish Princess from Golders Green than a Charmaine from Chigwell.

Heaping scorn on a superior something or someone is often the result of envy. This may have been the reason for Camilla and her chums disparaging Diana in this way. She was so tall, so terrifically glamorous, so different from almost every other woman. What is more, everyone adored her.

English upper-middle and upper-class women have never been noted for their elegance and sleek style. The understated chic that distinguishes Continental women has somehow never managed to cross the Channel. While French and Italian ladies believe that money spent on pampering themselves is a good investment, their English equivalents save any spare income for school fees and renovating the roof.

The more charitable ladies in the county set believed that Diana needed to dress to excess for her role as an ambassador for Britain. Those close to Charles and Camilla were less kind, regarding her wardrobe as rather glitzy, gaudy and distinctly down-market.

Ordinary English women looked upon Diana quite differently. After generations of dumpy, frumpy royal ladies, they welcomed the appearance of a shining new star in the royal ranks. Diana proved that the monarchy could be exciting and glamorous and every young woman wanted to look just like her.

Within weeks of her engagement, the rush by factories to copy her romantic, ruffled clothes was said to have saved thousands of jobs during Britain's economic depression. Even the then Prime Minister Margaret Thatcher praised her style, explaining, 'To have a fashion-setter like that is marvellous, just what we need at the time when we've got a number of superb designers.'

By 1984, a panel of 20 American fashion editors, the final arbiters in the international Best-Dressed Poll, had named Princess Diana as 'the world's most influential woman in fashion today'.

Throughout the Eighties, Diana experimented wildly with fashion and, in retrospect, many of the gowns she chose to wear now look gimmicky and overly elaborate. But by the mid-Nineties, she had pared down her look to a much sleeker, slinkier silhouette.

Three years after her death, America's celebrity magazine *People* declared that Diana was the best-dressed personality of all time, beating the suave, superbly tailored actor Cary Grant into second place. The Princess also totally outstripped the graceful Audrey Hepburn at number five, who is still influencing new generations of young fashion-conscious women long after her death in 1993.

The Princess was elected to the top spot by a panel

of five designers, who, for reasons known only to themselves, left out of the top-ten style icons like Gloria Vanderbilt, Princess Grace of Monaco, her daughter Princess Caroline and actress Lauren Bacall.

The clean lines of the suits, dresses and evening gowns Diana wore were reminiscent of the classic clothes worn by Jackie Kennedy Onassis, who managed only twelfth place in the *People* list. This seems an extraordinary error by the designers because Jackie invented the look Diana made her own.

Instead of looking to Europe for inspiration as most stylish women do, Diana was heavily influenced by Americans and America, and, at one point, considered living there. And it was another world-famous American beauty, a famous Hollywood blonde, whom she considered the most stylish woman of all, someone who did not rate a place on *People* magazine's list.

'Diana simply adored Sharon Stone,' says her hairstylist Natalie Symonds. 'She constantly asked me to make her look like her. She admired her short hairdo and the sexy yet classic, elegant clothes Sharon Stone wore. It's no accident that Diana began to wear a lot of cream, beige and pastel outfits just like those the star wore in *Basic Instinct*.'

Sharon Stone's clean, all-American look with a tinge of European elegance was exactly what the Princess wanted to aim for.

It reflected her own desire for a wardrobe that photographed well on her tall, rangy figure yet did not distract attention from the woman wearing it.

Sharon Stone always looks immaculate with small pieces of tasteful jewellery. At the same time, she is incredibly seductive. In Diana's eyes, she was the ultimate in powerful feminity.

In 1995, Diana turned up at the Council of Fashion

Designers Awards in New York with a hairstyle that was slicked back from her forehead exactly the way Sharon Stone had appeared at the 1994 Oscars ceremony.

'She always looks so perfect,' Diana sighed whenever she saw photographs of the film star in the press.

Whereas Diana constantly updated her image, Camilla Parker Bowles has remained stuck in the late Seventies with her flicked-out Farrah Fawcett hairdo and tea-cosy ballgowns. When she finally attempted to dress up for a big official banquet she attended on 20 June 2000 with Prince Charles, she chose a pink evening gown created by Donatella Versace under instruction, it was reported, from the Prince himself.

The resulting loosely-fitted dress did little for Camilla's rather neat figure. It was decorated with rivulets of rhinestones and resembled nothing more than a baggy, bargain-basement frock around which some Christmas fairylights had been strung.

Some of America's wealthiest *grandes dames* had flown over for the event and, to put it delicately, they were rather taken aback at Camilla's appearance. It was clear that they had seen better dressing on a salad. One guest at the party, gossip columnist Aileen Mehle, writing under the name Suzy in *W* magazine, discreetly reported, 'The pale pink dress got mixed reviews — and was pulled to bits in the press next day.' She added it was rumoured that Donatella, who has raised large sums for one of Prince Charles's charities, will design Camilla's clothes in the future. With claws not quite sheathed, the columnist observed, 'Perhaps that move should be reconsidered.'

While everyone was keen to see what Camilla was wearing, Suzy noted that 'the one who actually seemed to care less about the whole thing was Camilla, who, it is said, doesn't fixate on what bag or what shoes go with what outfit and sometimes has to be reminded of same'. In other words, Camilla will never be one of the *grande dame* sisterhood who think of nothing else but making the best dressed list.

Camilla's lack of interest in looking smart is something she shares with the Queen, who believes her clothes should be appropriate and practical rather than pretty or elegant. Some cynics believe that Her Majesty deliberately chooses expensive designer outfits which look as if they come from chain stores to avoid exciting envy among the masses. If so, she succeeds brilliantly.

Although she is always immaculately turned out, the Queen pays little attention to trends and sticks to styles that enable her to move easily on official engagements. She favours pleated and A-line skirts, and dresses with matching coats, always in vivid jewel colours that enable her to stand out in a crowd. At home, just like Camilla, she prefers tweeds, twin-sets and horsey headscarves, the ideal outfits for walking dogs and pottering in the garden.

Prince Charles grew up surrounded by women like his mother who choose clothes for comfort and durability rather than high fashion. Therefore, it should not be very surprising that he fell in love with a woman who follows the same style of dressing, someone who would rather have a new pair of jodhpurs than a Giorgio Armani suit. As Aileen Mehle so neatly sums up Camilla's look, 'Give her britches. Give her a horse. Give her the country. Give her Charles. Make her happy.'

Diana never really enjoyed horse riding, despite the lessons she had from her cavalry officer lover James Hewitt at Knightsbridge Barracks and later at Windsor. They were simply an excuse to spend time with him and, after she broke off their relationship, she never went riding again. Basically, Diana was a town girl at heart, whereas Camilla exemplifies the country mouse. She looks her best in jodhpurs, boots and a hacking jacket, all of which show off her taut, trim figure.

The Princess was 14 years younger than Prince Charles's mistress, which obviously gave her an advantage. She had a lovelier face, longer legs and a dazzling smile, but her far less attractive rival still managed to steal her man.

It's more than probable that Diana was difficult to live with. She was prone to throwing tantrums and, for most of her marriage, lacked any sense of self-worth. Her disturbed family background had left its mark. She needed someone who would love her unconditionally. Unfortunately, so did Charles. They were two needy people, both looking for something the other could not give. This was the main rock upon which the storybook marriage of the Prince and Princess of Wales foundered. And there, lurking in the shadows, was Camilla.

Now the Prince's spin doctors would like us to believe that the tide has turned in favour of Camilla. After all, they assure us that both William and Harry have given her their seal of approval. We are told that William made overtures to his father's mistress when he happened to turn up at St James's Palace while Camilla was in residence. They got on so famously, according to leaks from Charles's office, that William invited her to join the family cruise around the Greek Islands in the Summer of 1999. Not true, say other royal sources, who confide that William is extremely angry about being used.

At the time of writing, Charles's sons and his

mistress have never appeared in public together. When it does happen, it must look relaxed and informal, so that it does not appear staged as a public relations stunt.

Camilla must also not appear too close or affectionate with the young princes when they are finally seen together. This would surely bring accusations that Camilla is stepping into Diana's shoes. She has already taken over Diana's husband and her home; to be seen 'mothering' Diana's boys would set back the Camilla promotion by years.

So William and Harry will eventually be the key to Camilla's success or failure, just as they are also the last great hope for the monarchy.

14

*D*id Diana die in vain? Three years after her death, little has changed. The House of Windsor, which seemed to rock on its ancient foundations at the beginning of September 1997, is now standing secure, its guardians preserving it with the same cold efficiency as they always have done. At times, it is almost as if Diana had never existed.

The tidal wave of emotion, which deluged Britain in the days and weeks after the Paris car crash, quickly receded. The cleansing release of feeling had become embarrassing. It was so un-English. The sea of flowers and candles left in the wind outside Kensington Palace were cleared away and quickly churned into compost.

The country rather abruptly returned to a kind of normality and the Princess began to fade from the public memory. Her former home was stripped of its contents and her staff dispersed to other jobs. The canonisation was cancelled and the Diana cult disbanded.

On the first anniversary of her death, a sponsored walk through London had to be postponed indefinitely for lack of interest, and only a handful of mourners turned up to watch the Royal Family attend a memorial service at Crathie Church near Balmoral. By the third anniversary of her death, no memorial services or concerts had been arranged and Althorp, her family estate, remained the only place where people could gather to remember her. But even that shrine to the world's most famous woman opened only for 61 days each year from the beginning of July to the end of August. By the year 2000, the number of visitors to Althorp had decreased and it was revealed that Diana's former husband, the Prince of Wales, had not once visited her grave since the day of her funeral.

Newspaper columnists and TV pundits had predicted that the nation, convulsed by grief during the week between Diana's death and her funeral, had changed for ever. There was a strange assumption that the outpouring of sentiment shown, as people sobbed openly in the streets of London, would continue indefinitely. Hard hearts would soften and compassion become the new watchword.

Daily Mail columnist Richard Littlejohn noted that, 'We appear to be going through an extraordinary period of mass catharsis.' He admitted that he himself did not share or understand it, 'but it is no good complaining that the reaction to Diana's death isn't really British. It is now. We are just going to have to accept that.' Millions dipped their hands into their pockets and donated money in her memory. Everyone believed that, after Diana, the world would be a sweeter place. It seemed Britain was on the brink of a new, more kindly era. It didn't happen.

Andrew Samuels, Professor of Analytical Psychology at Essex University, observed in the *Independent on Sunday* that public indifference three years on was simply a reaction to the extreme emotion shown in 1997.

'Suddenly we have become very British again — only more so,' he explained.

Why did we forget so soon what the Princess meant to the world? What happened to the sense of empowerment people felt as they called the Royal Family to account for their treatment of Diana, in death as in life? During those seven days that shook Britain, the demand for change seemed irresistible.

Just days after the Princess's funeral, the *Times* newspaper reported that her passing had increased public pressure on the Royal Family to change radically. Britain's first family had endured a week of unrelenting criticism for its failure to show publicly that it shared the nation's sense of loss. The Royal Family was in crisis. Courtiers, summoned back from their summer holidays, were unprepared for the hostility which overnight had swamped the Queen and her relatives.

In its survey, the *Times'* Gallup poll indicated that the Windsors needed 'to reinvent themselves' and that a monarchy in the starchy style of the Queen's father George VI had outstayed its welcome.

There was strong support from roughly half of the population for the Prince of Wales to renounce the throne in favour of his elder son William. This revealed a dramatic decline in support for Charles, as until then only around a quarter had favoured skipping a generation. And more than half of those polled (53 per cent) felt that the days following Diana's death had done damage to the public standing of the Queen and her family. Significantly, only 11 per cent, little more than one in ten, thought the monarchy should be abolished.

But the poll showed a clear demand for 'a more democratic and approachable institution on Continental lines'. Gallup was not alone in coming to these conclusions. Other opinion polls reflected similar attitudes from the majority of Britons. Around the time of Charles and Diana's wedding, such questions and answers in a poll would have been unthinkable. Clearly, the Royal Family is losing its grip on the nation's affections.

There is little sign today that the warnings of 1997 have been heeded. Who can detect any radical change in the sovereign or the system which surrounds her? The Queen and her family continue to fulfil their public duties in the same rather desultory way, ignoring the message of the opinion polls that they should be more approachable.

Not one of the Royal Family has adopted Diana's touchy-feely style, as if to ape the woman they all resented would be beneath contempt. They are still locked into outdated habits and customs, unwilling or unable to adapt to a world accelerating through a new millennium.

They adhere strictly to royal protocol as if afraid that, without it, they will no longer appear royal and be seen as the rather ordinary people that they are.

Anne, the Princess Royal, is a perfect example of this obstinate attitude. In all her years of official duties, she has never once picked up or cuddled a baby, never got down on her knees to chat to a toddler or offered to spoon feed an undernourished child.

'Nobody would say that cuddling isn't important,' she explained once in an interview. 'It's just that different people work in different ways to get the message across. I don't see it as important. I think it's something you do with your own children at home, something people do privately. The very idea that all children want to be cuddled by a complete stranger, I find utterly amazing, especially in front of the press.'

These words, when she uttered them less than a year after Diana's death, sounded like a side-swipe at her late sister-in-law. It was almost as if she was declaring her defiant determination to avoid change. No spin doctor, image-maker or opinion pollster was going to change her way of working. She had also forgotten one vital fact. Cuddling a destitute tot makes a better photograph for the media covering her charity work. Without publicity, both the charity and its champion may lose public support. Anne seems to forget that she is in the PR business as well as the royal business.

The Queen's only daughter has always remained aloof from what she regards as performing for press cameras. In this, she is only demonstrating openly what all her relatives believe privately.

Her parents are both considered too elderly now to change their thinking or their *modus operandi*. After 50 years of public service, it seems only fair to allow them to do their job in their own way.

'The Duke of Edinburgh will never change, no matter what happens. He is what he is and you can like it or lump it,' a senior Court official explains. 'In fact, most people seem to find his bloody-mindedness and his occasional gaffes rather endearing. They show that he is his own man.'

While this may be true, it does not help Britain's relations with foreign powers when the Head of State's husband insults host nations. Philip rarely apologises for his blunders and even corrects those who try to explain that he did not mean what he said. He once complained that some messy electrical wiring looked as if it had been installed by Indians, thus infuriating most of Britain's immigrants from the Indian sub-continent. A well-meaning journalist asked if he had meant cowboys rather than Indians, an understandable mistake if he had been referring to unprofessional workmanship. The Duke insisted that he had not. He had said 'Indians' and that's what he meant. He would not allow anyone to let him off the hook.

The Duke of Edinburgh was born in 1921 and most people of his age have been retired for more than a decade, but he and his wife, who is five years younger, soldier on. Some members of their staff explain that, with their advancing years, the Queen and Prince Philip can no longer tolerate cameramen's flashguns in close proximity, so the number of journalists close to them has been cut down. Other royal aides say that a smaller group of pressmen is easier to accommodate in crowded hospital wards, factories and other facilities that the royal couple visit. Whatever the reason, more journalists complain about lack of access and are less keen to work with members of the Royal Family in such limited conditions. So much for a more approachable monarchy.

Newspaper editors have also discovered that the Royal Family does not boost sales the way it once did. In twenty-first-century Britain, a pop star or a football hero splashed across the front pages will increase circulation more effectively. One reason for this may be that the average age of the senior royals is now 60-plus. In an era dominated by ageism, the House of Windsor has little appeal to young people.

Those close to the Queen apparently still fail to appreciate this. They seem to lack a fundamental understanding of what is needed to be respected and popular in today's fast-moving world. No politician would dream of running for office without advisers who demonstrate formidable public relations skills. Yet the Queen gets by without anyone at a senior level with journalistic expertise.

There have been some attempts at innovation, but most appeared rather contrived and backfired. The Queen, looking rather uncomfortable, had a cup of tea in a Glasgow council flat. She also changed cars outside a McDonald's hamburger restaurant, although she didn't go inside, and she spent a day in the West End's theatre land mingling with stage stars, directors and producers. Although the Queen avoids going to the theatre whenever possible, she was even persuaded to attend a show the same evening.

She also hired a Communications Director, seconded from the business world, who appears to have made little difference to the old regime. The only visible change some claimed he has instigated has been the promotion of the Duke of York, who now has a more prominent role in the family, carrying out far more official duties than previously. On advice, Andrew has also allied himself with a high-profile charity, the National Society for the Prevention of Cruelty to Children, which could do for him what the Save the Children Fund did for his sister, the Princess Royal. But this minor change is hardly going to solve the problems now confronting the House of Windsor.

Andrew is a hard-working and decent man, but he is destined to become increasingly irrelevant as his nephews William and Harry grow up and move into the spotlight with their own families.

Another example of royal aides' lack of media savvy came at a reception held at Windsor Castle during which the Queen moved along a line of guests heading towards a girl punk with fuschia-tinted hair. As soon as they noticed what was about to happen, several senior courtiers asked for the photographers to be removed. Fortunately, a press officer with more common sense argued convincingly that the journalists should be allowed to stay. The resulting photograph of the Queen meeting the pink-haired punk made every newspaper the following day.

If the Queen and her relatives want to be more in touch with the public, they need advisers who themselves are more in touch. But there are several senior members of the family who seem to forget that to maintain a degree of popularity they depend on the media to transmit their hard work to the masses.

They must not only do good works, they must be seen to be doing good works. Yet they offer the minimum amount of co-operation to reporters and photographers.

The exception is the Prince of Wales who has slowly gained greater public esteem since dropping to the bottom of the popularity polls in late 1997. He has prospered as a result of a carefully orchestrated PR campaign masterminded by his top advisers. It has been done so skilfully that, at the same time, his mistress Camilla Parker Bowles has also gained more public acceptance when she has appeared in public at his side.

When Diana died, Charles had not spoken to any members of the media for ten years. The criticism he had received during that time had persuaded him to avoid all contact with journalists. Suddenly, all that changed when he realised that he needed to woo the

THE TRUTH

press to gain favourable publicity. Like a presidential candidate, he began a charm offensive which quickly transformed his image. Just as Bill Clinton survived one of the greatest White House scandals of the last century, the Prince of Wales managed to increase his ratings at the polls. After all, he, too, was running for office. He was campaigning to claim a throne that half the people of Britain wished would pass to his son.

There is little doubt that he did not enjoy being pleasant to the men and women who so recently had been his tormentors, but he concealed it superbly. He drew the line at throwing cocktail parties for the press, as the Queen does at the start of every tour abroad to meet the people who will accompany her. Drinks parties cost time and money which Charles must feel may be better spent. So, on a flight to South Africa, the Prince of Wales simply wandered back from his first-class cabin to chat with the hacks at the back of the plane for a few minutes. Soon, reporters and cameramen alike were laughing at his jokes and friendly relations had been resumed. How amused Diana would have been to hear about this *volte face*. The Prince, whose supporters had so often accused her of manipulating the media, was now doing exactly the same.

Occasionally, even the shiny new Prince Charming slipped up. In February 2000, he embarked on a tour of Caribbean islands which was remembered mostly for the number of exotic and ridiculous hats he donned. It became known in the press as 'The Silly Hat Tour' and, back in London, the masterminds of his gleaming new image were not pleased.

The blame for the Prince's sullied image was privately dropped at the door of Charles's press officer Sandy Henney, which most royal correspondents thought was grossly unfair. One pressman with years of experience in Downing Street notes, 'Both Tony Blair and Gordon Brown have people who check out venues where they appear looking for possibly embarrassing situations. Why doesn't the Prince of Wales have someone doing this? His over-worked press officer was too busy organising the media to alert him to the crazy headgear.'

Six months later, Ms Henney left the Prince's staff after a mix-up over official photographs of Prince William, which looked like a convenient excuse to get rid of her.

No longer eclipsed by his wife, Charles is now enjoying a resurgence. It is almost as if the clock had turned back to the 1970s, the era BD (before Diana) when he was the royal Action Man admired and respected by everyone.

For the Prince, this was a golden age when he was a carefree bachelor, considering no one but himself. There was no wife demanding his time and attention, just a long line of beauties who came and went just as rapidly. But always, when another girlfriend went the way of so many others, there was the patient Camilla, who asked for nothing but to love him.

Until Charles walked down the aisle of St Paul's, he was the oldest unmarried Prince of Wales in history. Journalists who covered the story of his rollicking love-life were convinced that he enjoyed being the world's most eligible bachelor. They were wrong. As we now know, the reason he took so much time choosing a wife was the woman he really wanted was already married.

When pressured to provide the throne with heirs, he chose a girl he believed was sweet and compliant. As she was so young and inexperienced, he undoubtedly thought he could tutor her to his satisfaction. He never expected that she might have a mind of her own and want more than just a part-time husband. So Diana was found wanting and dumped, but she refused to 'go quietly' and left the House of Windsor kicking and screaming until the whole world knew of her fury and disgust.

Other Windsor spouses have suffered, just as Diana did, from the harsh royal system, which protects blood royals and crushes those who find marrying into the family is not as wonderful as expected.

These are the silent victims who have never revealed their suffering for various understandable reasons. Royal blood does not run in their veins, therefore they are mere appendages to the monarchy, devalued and sometimes almost destroyed by private unhappiness.

When Diana refused to be one of them, she became a feminist icon, a symbol of every woman who was fighting to free herself from the tyranny of a paternalistic system. The sisterhood greeted her as the patron saint of battered and abandoned wives, the Mater Dolorosa of oppressed women everywhere and sometimes used her pain to attack all men.

Despite her troubles, Diana was never anti-men. She was first and foremost a man's woman, whose dearest wish was to find a white knight who would come galloping into her life to cherish and protect her. But once she stepped outside the high walls of the royal Court, she became prey to so many factions anxious to exploit her for their own benefit.

Foremost among these were the Republicans who cited Diana as proof that the monarchy was rotten to the core.

'She was a Republican heroine,' Christopher

Hudson wrote in the *Evening Standard*. 'Her life shows them [the Royal Family] up as cold and unfeeling.'

The overwhelming reaction to the Princess's death prompted writer Anthony Holden to ask, 'Was Britain finally escaping its imperial past, cramped by outmoded tradition and looking with fresh young eagerness to a modernised, European future?' (*Her Life and Her Legacy* by Anthony Holden, published by Random House.)

It would be a great mistake to believe that Diana was a Republican sympathiser. She did not want to abolish the monarchy, merely to modernise and humanise it. How could she wish to destroy the Establishment which her sons would one day lead? After all, she hoped her son William would be a fine king, who would make amends for all the errors committed by his royal predecessors and initiate a new, enlightened era.

William, whose face is a haunting reminder of his mother, and Harry, with his Spencer red hair and freckles, are her living legacy, but they also carry the burden of Diana's legend. In particular, William is often seen as a substitute for the lost Princess. While teenage girls want to marry him, older women want to touch a remembrance of what used to be. This is an unhappy state of affairs for William who must be allowed to become his own man and not live for ever in the shadow of his mother.

Shy and overly sensitive, just as his father was at the same age, William shows signs of having difficulty coming to terms with his destiny. He has a well-developed loathing of the media, which was evident long before his mother's death. He has been known to walk backwards to prevent cameramen catching a glimpse of his face and often hides on the floor of cars to avoid being seen.

He is moody and sometimes defiant, especially when it comes to public appearances. He used to say, 'Do I have to?' when it was suggested he should join his father at some major event. Now he simply refuses and his indulgent father never insists.

'He has lost his mother,' he reminds staff. 'Let him do what he wants.'

Some royal aides explain that William is merely going through a rebellious phase, just like any normal teenager. 'He'll grow out of it,' they say. Others worry that adjusting to the life mapped out for him is proving painful. He is a typical angry young man, but then he has a lot to feel resentful about. Unlike his friends, he cannot choose a career and make his own way in the world. His life has been programmed from the day he was born. It is a daunting prospect.

Prince Charles endured a similar testing experience in the Seventies when he often gave way to uncontrolled bursts of anger. Many of the people close to him observed the misgivings and apprehension he felt about his future role. He had left the Royal Navy for a life of official duties which appeared like a limitless void stretching ahead until the end of his days. According to Jonathan Dimbleby, author of *The Prince of Wales, A Biography*, Charles felt 'trapped in a role that had an outer form but no inner meaning, in which custom and ceremony — the rush from one engagement to another — concealed a vacuum from which he recoiled almost in despair.'

Anyone who has witnessed at close quarters the working life of the Royal Family would urge William to escape while there is still time, to run to some nice, quiet republic where he can live a more normal life. Sadly, as his mother learned to her cost, there is no normal life for such as he, either within or without the Royal Family. Jacqueline Kennedy Onassis never managed to evade the spotlight after leaving the White House, even when she was dying. Today, her only surviving child and her grandchildren are still fodder for the tabloids.

So for William, a life of soul-destroying banality lies ahead, one which has virtually destroyed his great aunt Margaret, sent his mother almost mad, given his father a life of frustration and turned him into a figure of ridicule. But should William decide to run away from his responsibilities, he would be unfairly passing on his burden to his younger brother.

Few people realise that members of the Royal Family, although vastly privileged, have little real power. In their working lives, they are puppets whose strings are pulled by the Foreign Office. They can go nowhere without clearance from Whitehall mandarins. It is especially noteworthy that the Queen and her relatives, although they may have many Jewish friends, never travel to Israel. To do so would displease the mega-rich kings of the Arab states, whose massive and regular orders for weapons keep our armaments industry ticking over.

Money talks more loudly when it comes to the Royal Family. The only notable exception to this anti-Israeli rule has been the Duke of Edinburgh who travelled to Jerusalem for the burial of his mother, a former nun who wished to be interred in the land where Christianity began.

It is a sad fact that a less intelligent young man than William would not question what his future role will require of him. Perhaps, like his father, he will slowly realise that he can make a great contribution through his position as monarch-in-waiting. He can speak out on controversial issues, while a sovereign may not. If he has inherited his mother's craving for freedom, he may rise up and recoil from a life that is a luxurious prison sentence, agreeing to carry out the bare minimum of duties. Or he may choose to seize the opportunity to become the king Diana always hoped he would be — more involved with the people and sharing their concerns the way she once did. There is a great deal a dedicated twenty-first-century sovereign could do to make Britain a better place.

Blatant discrimination still exists in the Royal Family. Younger brothers take precedence over their older sisters and any member of the family who marries a Roman Catholic drops out of the line of succession.

'These are not matters for us, but for the Government,' a Palace spokesman points out.

But a king determined to reign over a more equal society could urge Parliament to repeal the 1701 Act of Settlement, which protects the Protestant succession, and make daughters succeed according to their order of birth, rather than give way to younger brothers.

William could show his support for better public services by sending his children to state schools, by using the National Health Service for routine procedures, rather than private medicine, and giving up perks like the royal train.

He could travel occasionally on the London Underground to prove that he shares the difficulties of ordinary commuters, and he could refuse lavish gifts and expensive holidays from wealthy benefactors, which his father continues to enjoy. If this turns the House of Windsor into a so-called bicycling monarchy, does it really matter?

Time magazine once called William 'the saviour of the monarchy'. It may be difficult for him to forget, even for a short time, the expectations his family and the nation have for his future. Prince Charles may have already passed on to his son the warning of his revered great uncle Lord Mountbatten who used to say that the monarchy would last only as long as kings and queens were worthy of the job.

A cousin of the Russian tsar, Britain's king and Germany's kaiser, Uncle Dickie, as the Queen's family knew him, grew up with the twentieth century and gradually watched many of his royal relatives lose their thrones through stupidity, pride or bad luck. When he wondered why the British throne remained so stable, he concluded that it was because his English cousins were not glamorous figureheads, but hard-working and modest. He also saw those qualities embodied in his great-nephew Prince Charles.

This idea is, no doubt, still on the Prince's mind as he considers how best to advise his elder son.

The years ahead are crucial ones for the young man who will be King William V. One scandalous slip-up could wreck his present popularity and inflict terminal damage on the monarchy.

So, much is demanded of Diana and Charles's son. William must follow not just his own interests, but those of Britain and the Commonwealth. He must be smart, but never a smart alec. He must be dedicated and hard-working but never seem harassed or overwhelmed by his job. And if all this sounds as if he must be super-human, that is the very last thing he should appear.

As well as fulfilling this demanding job description, he will be expected to honour his late mother by continuing much of the work she left unfinished. Most people would like to think that would be her greatest memorial.

Sadly, most of her charities are struggling without Diana's glowing presence.

'We miss her dreadfully,' a spokesman for the English National Ballet says. 'The Princess was involved in all aspects of the company. She was very hands on and interested in everything from the welfare of the dancers to fund-raising. We don't have a patron now. She was simply irreplaceable.'

Her last campaign to eradicate landmines has clearly lost momentum without her support. The Mines Advisory Group has reportedly had to suspend its projects in Bosnia and, like all the other landmines charities, is desperately in need of major funding. As yet only just over £2 million has been handed over to 13 landmines charities by the Diana Memorial Fund, although more is promised.

If William can keep such worthy causes in the forefront of our minds and generate the cash to keep them operating, he will be a fine successor to his mother. Of course, he may discover other organisations to which he wants to lend his support, or seek out people on the margins of society who also need help. In this, he will also be following his mother's example. But, above all, by becoming a modest, dedicated and compassionate king, he will be fulfilling his mother's dream.

15

It may take many decades before we can assess the place Diana, Princess of Wales will hold in history. Was she a reformer who tried to force an unwilling House of Windsor to adapt to a new age? Or just a tiresome troublemaker who fired a few Exocet missiles at the ship of monarchy, holing it below the water-line but failing to sink it?

Most Britons now seem to believe that she was simply a seeker after truth and justice, who refused to live a lie and fled from her sham marriage. But outside it, she sadly learned she could never truly be free.

Martin Amis, writing in *Time* magazine, said she will be remembered as a 'phenomenon of pure stardom'. To some extent, that is true. She didn't act like Marilyn Monroe, make music like Jacqueline Du Pre, or create poetry like Sylvia Plath, three other famous women who also died tragically too soon. It would be unfair to pigeonhole her in the category of women famous just for being famous. Although, initially, her fame derived from a brilliant marriage, quite soon she was renowned just for being spectacularly herself.

It is doubtful that anyone will appear to equal her appeal until Prince William marries. Any young woman who agrees to marry him, aware of Diana's sad saga, will be a perfect example of hope over knowledge. A life under intense scutiny is not an inviting prospect, but at least future royal brides now know what to expect. They no longer need walk down the aisle believing in fairytales. Diana's ordeal has, at least, served one good purpose in forewarning girls who fall for handsome princes. Don't put your daughter on the throne, Mrs Worthington!

When historians do finally try to determine what Diana meant to her age, they will discover one giant obstacle in their path. The Princess's close family destroyed most of her private papers within weeks of her death. This crime against truth and honesty resembles in its misguided panic the censorship of Queen Victoria's diary by her youngest daughter, which has robbed us for ever of knowing the real woman beneath the crown.

Letters, memoranda, invoices, bills and other revealing documents were either shredded or burned in a desperate bid to protect Diana's reputation, at least that is what it seems her relatives were trying to do. These important papers should have been preserved, not just for future generations, but for her sons. Unhappily, William and Harry were not of age when their mother died and the executors of her estate had total control.

If Diana had not been divorced, her secret papers would have been held in the royal archives at Windsor Castle and released only when they could no longer do any damage to those living, to responsible scholars and historians.

Now we may never know just what Diana thought, how she really lived and what she intended.

When the last person who met Diana has died, how will future historians understand just what impact she had in person? Although she was a photographer's dream, one of the most photogenic faces of the last century, no photo ever really captured her extraordinary charm. Diana in the flesh was always more devastating than any picture.

Then there was the jokey personality that helped to set nervous people at their ease. This talent for winning friends became evident soon after her engagement at a Buckingham Palace garden party. While showing off her sapphire and diamond ring, she told an overawed group from the Provinces, 'It's so big I scratched my nose with it — the ring, I mean, not my nose!'

Diana loved to crack gags, but frequently forgot the punchlines so she had to write them all down. Her staff remember that she was always asking them, 'Got any new jokes?' She was quick-witted and often came up with a crushing one-liner for anyone who stepped over the mark. Once, when asked why she had disappointed photographers by wearing a dress they had seen many times before, she made them all laugh by declaring, 'I suppose you'd like it better if I came naked.'

Sun photographer Arthur Edwards, who regularly tackled her about something she had said or done that he didn't like, complained when she appeared with an ultra-short haircut.

'If you keep this up, you'll end up like that pop star Sinead O'Connor,' he warned.

Giving the balding cameraman a long look, Diana replied, 'At least I've got some hair, Arthur.' Then she leapt giggling into her car and told her chauffeur, 'That soon shut him up!'

They developed a game of verbal ping-pong, each trying to get a laugh out of the other whenever possible. On a wet afternoon in Norwich, the cameraman donned an old tweed cap to keep his head dry. As soon as Diana spotted him, she walked over and quipped: 'Are you wearing that hat for a bet?'

When he was hit by a bout of food poisoning in Egypt, Diana sent her doctor round to minister to the hefty photographer and, when he recovered, she joked, 'I'll tell you this. It's done wonders for your waistline!'

Occasionally, the photographers managed to even the score. On a trip to Pakistan, Diana threw a party for the press and noticed that freelance photographer Anwar Hussein, who is a Pakistani Muslim, did not have a glass in his hand.

'Oh, why haven't you got something to drink?' the Princess asked.

'They won't give me one,' Anwar fibbed, pretending that the waiters wouldn't serve him because Muslims are not supposed to drink alcohol.

'This is terrible. I'll go and get you one myself,' Diana told him. 'What would you like? Red wine?'

The cameraman then decided that the joke had gone too far. He couldn't allow the Princess of Wales to turn into a waitress just for his benefit. He explained and apologised, but Diana just laughed.

In public, she loved to giggle and gossip but at home she was far more serious. On her return from Angola, she repeatedly told f riends, 'Those children! Those poor limbless children! I can't get them out of my mind. When I go to bed at night they are all I can think about.'

She was also much more spiritual than most people might have guessed, although she rarely went to church. On the morning of Prince William's confirmation, she told her hairstylist that she was not looking forward to joining her ex-husband family's for the occasion.

'But it's a very important day in William's life,' she explained. 'One day he will be the head of the Church of England and I want him to understand fully all the responsibilities he will have. It's important for everyone to have something to believe in.'

Her affection for Mother Teresa was genuine and she desperately hoped that the saintly nun would recover from her last illness so that William and Harry could have the privilege of meeting her. When she visited Mother Teresa's convent in Calcutta, she prayed with the nuns in their chapel, and her eyes were brimming with tears, like those of everyone else present, when the sisters sang for her.

When it came to religion, Diana found her own path through a myriad of beliefs. People scoffed at her faith in astrology, spiritualism and alternative therapies, but she clearly found them comforting. They helped her to withstand the assault of powerful opponents and fight her corner.

Few women throughout the ages have played such a dramatic role in the 1,000-year history of the monarchy. Some may consider she should be recognised as a modern-day Eleanor of Aquitaine, the medieval queen who was also rejected by her husband but planned to avenge herself through her sons.

Others may compare her to Caroline of Brunswick-Wolfenbuttel, another princess who was cast aside once she had served the purpose of giving the throne an heir. The German princess bore no physical resemblance to Diana. In fact, she was so loud and coarse that her groom, George, Prince of Wales, almost fainted when he first met her.

'Harris, I am not well, pray get me a glass of brandy,' he gasped to an aide.

George had already secretly married a commoner, Mrs Maria Fitzherbert, with whom he lived happily for 12 years, but his father George III was urging him to produce an heir to the throne and he was deeply in debt. As a married man, he would receive a much larger allowance from Parliament.

By the time he married Caroline in the Chapel Royal, St James's in 1795, he had rejected Maria after becoming infatuated with an older woman — Frances Villiers, Countess of Jersey. Although George and Caroline had a few happy months when they first married, Lady Jersey was always hovering in the background.

Soon after the wedding, the new Princess of Wales announced she was expecting a child and, in January 1796, she gave birth to a daughter, Princess Charlotte. Once he had the heir he needed, George demanded a separation from his wife. He seized custody of their child, banished Caroline from Court and within a few years was regarded by the people as a heartless monster. Crowds rallied to support the Princess and many parliamentarians joined them.

In 1820, George III died and his son, the Prince Regent, became king, thus making Caroline his queen. But when his coronation was arranged, he refused to allow his wife to take part, so she drove up and banged on the locked doors of the abbey demanding to be admitted.

THE TRUTH

Caroline believed that she had the loyalty of Londoners and hoped that they would dash to her aid. In the event, there was no revolt against the new king. Tired of the royal marriage scandals, they abandoned the uncrowned queen and, totally humiliated, she had to drive away. Three weeks later, she died from a sudden illness.

Like Caroline, Diana banged on the doors of the Establishment with her *Panorama* TV interview. She forced the world to witness her frustration and anger. In doing so, she won the sympathy and the support of the British people, but it was worthless in her battle against her formidable foes. She was stripped of the title Her Royal Highness, her name was removed from the Church of England's prayers for the Royal Family, and her divorce settlement, in the region of £17 million, was derisory for someone of her status.

Newspapers complained of the way she was treated and one even started a campaign to reinstate her title, but the Royal Family totally ignored them all and soon the clamour died away. As Queen Caroline learned, the people are not easily roused.

One cynic explained that Diana was actually nothing more than the star of a long-running, real-life soap opera, and when she was written out of the script, she simply disappeared and was soon forgotten.

But in the immediate aftermath of the Paris crash, presidents, prime ministers and pop stars all vied to pay tribute to the lost Princess. Bill Clinton declared that he and Hillary had been very fond of Diana.

'I will always be glad I knew the Princess,' he said. 'I admired her work for children, AIDS victims and getting rid of the scourge of landmines.'

President Yeltsin echoed these sentiments.

'Diana was loved by the people of Russia,' he

announced. 'Many exceptional projects that touched the lives of ordinary people have been put into practice in Russia with her direct participation.'

Tony Blair coined the phrase that would be taken up by so many others when he called Diana 'the People's Princess'.

In his impromptu tribute, he said, 'She was a wonderful and a warm human being, although her own life was often sadly touched by tragedy. She touched the lives of so many others in Britain and throughout the world with joy and with comfort. We know how difficult things were for her from time to time. I am sure we can only guess that. But people everywhere, not just here in Britain, kept faith with Princess Diana.

'They liked her. They loved her, they regarded her as one of the people. She was the People's Princess and that is how she will stay, how she will remain in our hearts and our memories for ever.'

Three years later, the soap opera continues, but now the tributes to its late star have ceased and the attacks have begun. The former Conservative MP George Walden points out that Diana was far from being a social revolutionary.

'Her revolt against the old élite, of which she was a part, was confined to opposing its contraints on her personal freedom,' he writes in his book *The New Elites, Making a Career in the Masses*.

It is true that she did not divide up her goods and give them to the poor, or even leave any money to charity in her will, but her memorial fund has more than made up for that.

George Walden judges the Princess by the company she kept. He says the people she liked best were from the media, fashion and entertainment worlds, which is debatable. There is plenty of evidence that her closest companions were servants, astrologers, healers and other 'ordinary' members of society.

He vaguely criticises her personal behaviour (perhaps he has led an exemplary life himself) and asks why the public were so willing to forgive her headline-hitting indiscretions.

Mr Walden, a former Minister for Higher Education, complains that the orgy of weeping for the Princess was demeaning, because Diana, like all members of the 'New Elites', was patronising, a superb practitioner of the art of condescension. He is critical of those who worshipped at her shrine and believes that we would become a better society through her death. In other words, that Christ-like she had died to save us. The majority of those who mourned, he claims, were poorly educated people 'at the lower end of the social pile'. Who is being patronising now?

While much of his argument is specious, he seems to be missing the point. The British people no longer tug their forelocks when they meet a member of the Royal Family. In fact, one of the most remarkable aspects of the last century was the death of deference. Politicians, princes and pop stars no longer automatically inspire awe or even respect. The people who earn our admiration are the self-made men and women with special skills or those who have triumphed over some tragedy.

Ordinary citizens were delighted when Diana was nice to them, not because they liked being patronised, but because they genuinely believed she was 'one of us', rather than one of them. She was the first member of the Royal Family who had scrubbed floors and washed laundry for a living. When Prince Charles found her, she was working as a lowly assistant in a London nursery.

Diana had a rare ability to transcend barriers of class and creed. And not just in Britain. George Walden forgets that the Princess inspired the same reaction from people in countries as egalitarian as Australia and the United States, too. She was respected for what she did, not what she was.

Film star Joan Collins sums up the feelings of most when she says, 'Diana was my heroine because she stood up for herself within the Royal Household which was extremely difficult to do. And I also admired her because she was so wonderfully caring.'

Perhaps Diana's greatest role was as comforter of the afflicted. Some of the most abiding memories of her at work show her real concern. Sometimes, it was just an arm around a grieving mother in Bosnia, a handshake with an AIDS sufferer, or an embrace for a leper. By her example, she could transform attitudes as she did on a 1989 visit to AIDS babies at a children's hospital in Harlem. At the time, ignorance about the illness was widespread and, in that area of New York, the homes of AIDS sufferers had been burned to the ground.

By proving that she was not afraid of contact with its sufferers, she did more to promote understanding and compassion that any other public figure of that decade, or perhaps every decade in the last century. Sometimes she devoted her time to those who seem more privileged than the rest of us. But as she realised only too well, they suffer the same as the rest of us. Cosima Somerset, the Marquess of Londonderry's daughter, was befriended by Diana in 1996 when her marriage to the Duke of Beaufort's son, John Somerset, broke up.

She was at a very low point in her life, but Diana understood her pain and helped her to get through a very difficult time. The Princess invited her to travel to Pakistan with her and Cosima's aunt, Lady Annabel Goldsmith, to support Imran Khan's cancer hospital.

Cosima also joined the Princess on a holiday in Majorca. They spent a 'girlie' weekend at the luxury hotel La Residencia, sharing a suite, enjoying exotic beauty treatments and discussing everything from their childhoods to their children. Looking back now Cosima says, 'I miss her terribly. We shared the experience of being separated from our husbands and uncertain about what the future held. We had both broken away from large, powerful families and therefore we had lost our protection. Both of us were considered "hysterical, unbalanced, paranoid, foolish". We were cast out but we at least had each other.'

Diana didn't differentiate between rich and poor, smart or stupid, high-born or low. She had a way of making everyone feel special, a gift given to only a rare few.

The late Lord Runcie, the former Archbishop of Canterbury, touched on how hard Diana tried to live up to the adulation she received when he said, 'She had a real, tender desire to be what everybody expected her to be.'

All the time, Diana was cracking jokes and jesting with the press, her private life was utterly miserable. But for years she never let it show. Perhaps her sense of humour was her safety valve, a way of coping with the unbearable. She laughed and the world laughed with her. When she wept, she cried alone.

Diana was, above all, a woman of contradictions, at once wilful and hard-working, vulnerable and vengeful, lacking self-esteem yet secure in the knowledge that what she did was right. Early in her public life, when the world regarded her as just a pretty little ornament on her husband's arm, her late father the eighth Earl Spencer once said, 'Diana's pure steel underneath.' He never uttered a truer word. Her strength under furnace-like heat was extraordinary. Diana became a human rapier of cold steel, who skewered the Royal Family. Whether she lanced a festering boil or inflicted almost fatal wounds, it is too soon to say. The Windsors are great survivors and seem to believe that these injuries have healed. They forget that, after Diana, every prince and princess, each king and queen, will be measured against her memory.

Diana taught them all a new way to be royal.